# *living in the*
# MOMENTS

### ENJOYING THE MOMENTS OF
### LIFE, FAITH, MARRIAGE, AND MOTHERHOOD

#### 11 YEARS OF BLOGGING
#### BY ANNA SKLAR

*Living in the Moments – Enjoying the Moments of Life, Faith, Marriage, and Motherhood*

© 2018 by Anna Sklar

Books are available on Amazon and Kindle

Contact the author at:

Blog—*Living in the Moments* - annasklar.ca
Etsy Shop—*SklarInk*—etsy.com/ca/shop/SklarInk

**ISBN-13:** 978-1719531900

**ISBN-10:** 1719531900

To Every Single One of My Readers – Past, Present, and Future
(and some of you who are all three!)


Thank you so much for sharing the moments with me.
There were days, months, and sometimes years that you carried me
through the hard moments of life, faith, marriage, and motherhood.

And when you shared the easy moments with me it made them all
the more happy and bright.

I pray your moments are good, full of life, and rich with hopes and
dreams. May these carry you through to the other side of the
moments that are lonely, sad, and difficult.

Always remember – you are not alone.

We journey together.

Blessings ☺

# INTRODUCTION

This book reads like a diary.

The pages are full of blog posts I typed out for 11 years – from 2007 to 2018. Words that speak of *Living in the Moments - Enjoying the moments of Life, Faith, Marriage, and Motherhood.* Find more of my words at annasklar.ca ☺

The blog started out as a way to connect more with the *Mom's Moments* readers. I created their monthly newsletter in October 2006 and co-founded the online ministry in 2007 (which is no longer active). I edited the *Mom's Moments* newsletters until June 2009 and continued writing for them until June 2010.

I love blogging. It is a fantastic creative outlet, an easy place to share life with family and friends who live far away, and now it has become a book in itself. A record of those precious years of having children in the house. A digital growth chart full of words instead of numbers.

Today my youngest son turns 13, so it's extremely fitting I type these words as I bid farewell to the childhood years and embrace the teenage years. There are two teenage boys in my house now, and it's an amazingly-busy, exhausting, exhilarating place to be as boys become men right before my eyes.

This year the blog has become more of a library of my writings instead of an on-going transcription of my life. A gathering place for all the words that have been shared so far. Snapshots of the different kinds of moments I've lived the past 11 years – raising two boys, mothering a child who is not with me, serving in the church as a pastor's wife, figuring out domestic life, and finding my voice as a writer.

I can't tell you what the blog will be next year or the next or the next – it seems to grow along with me, and life often takes me by surprise. I do know that so far it has been a pleasure, an honour, a gift, and a blessing to blog for so many years, and share the moments with so many wonderful people.

Here's to enjoying the moments still to come…

# CONTENTS

# 2007

**April 30th, 2007**

**My First Blog Post**

*Cleaning and scrubbing can wait till tomorrow...*
*For babies grow up we've learned to our sorrow...*
*So quiet down cobwebs...*
*Dust go to sleep...*
*I'm rocking my baby and babies don't keep!*

- *Excerpt from Song for a 5th Child by Ruth Hulburt Hamilton*

I don't know how many times I've read this poem. My mom made a cross-stitch out of these words, with a picture of a woman rocking her baby. She framed it and it stills hangs in her house to this day. I still read it at least once when I visit her. These words still speak to my heart, and I know they spoke to my mother's heart, or she never would have made a cross-stitch out of them!

Now I'm a mother, and I've learned from first-hand experience that babies really don't keep! I've learned to balance housework with tickle fights (most days), and my to-do lists with story time. I've learned that tiny little people get bigger if you blink, and rocking babies becomes a treat instead of a chore.

It's only fitting that in my first blog I should thank my mother - for teaching me that I am special, for letting cobwebs grow and dust settle, for rocking me until I was too old for it, and for helping me grow into the mother I am today!

I love you Mum!

**June 8th, 2007**

### "I Can Trust the Waves for I Know the One Who Made the Ocean"

The other day I was saying to a friend that there is so much change happening in the lives of those around me! I remembered something I had written just over 3 years ago, when we first moved to Northern Ontario. I'd love to share it with you...

*Yesterday I was able to drive to the waterfront in my hometown with my son - the lake used to be a short walk away from our house when I was growing up. I used to fall asleep to the sound of the waves crashing during a storm, and some of my best tobogganing memories and stone-skipping lessons happened there. As I walked with my son, down the same path I walked as a child, and stood near the edge of the cliff (and held on tight to my son!), and watched the waves crashing, just as I did when I was a child, I realized there will always be things in life that will never change. I felt God drawing near as He spoke to my heart and showed me, once again, His unchanging nature, His steadfast love, His sturdy, stable will for each of our lives. So many waves, so many changes in us, in our lives, but He is so much bigger, and His love is so vast! Many times, I have visited that waterfront, and listened for God's voice, and He has never failed to meet me there. What a treasure to be able to share that with my son.*

I wanted to share this memory, wanted to encourage you with this reminder: some-things-don't-change. How wonderful to know this truth!

**June 22nd, 2007**

## Graduation Day

Now I'll never be able to hear the song *What a Wonderful World* without getting teary-eyed! My oldest son graduated from Senior Kindergarten yesterday, and the class had a short ceremony to celebrate.

The kids sang a couple of songs for us, one being *What a Wonderful World,* and they gave us these beautiful books they made from their year in school (complete with a page for photos - the teacher asked for a baby photo, then she added a picture taken on the first day of school, and one taken at the end of the year - WELL, I'm getting teary-eyed just writing about that!).

One family donated medals with each child's name on them! What a great gift for my son who is VERY into getting medals and trophies!

I'll share my thoughts on the day... life passes quickly - good times and bad times, though the bad times seem longer when they are happening. Kids grow and learn and hopefully they keep talking to us and sharing their lives with us! I looked around at all the young faces yesterday, and hoped and prayed they'd all turn out OK, and they'd be friends for the most part, and they'd encourage each other towards good instead of bad. This is my hope.

And from a mother's heart... that was a tough one... watching my son on stage, looking tall and handsome, knowing another year has gone, hoping that for him it was a good year, thanking God for his wonderful teacher and the MANY things she has taught him, hoping he'll have a similar teacher next year, knowing there's still so much to learn (about life and about academics!), and trusting my son is in God's hands no matter what life brings. I'll say it again, ENJOY EACH MOMENT of parenthood as best you can! I know I am.

## August 1st, 2007

For the life of me I can't find the blog post that went with this poem, or even remember if I actually got around to writing it! But I remember having this fantastic forest/creek adventure with Elijah after reading this poem my mum gave to me…

### I Took His Hand and Followed

*My dishes went unwashed today*
*I didn't make the bed,*
*I took his hand and followed*
*Where his eager footsteps led.*
*Oh yes, we went adventuring,*
*My little son and I…*
*Exploring all the great outdoors*
*Beneath the summer sky*
*We waded in a crystal stream,*
*We wandered through a wood…*
*My kitchen wasn't swept today*
*But life was gay and good.*
*We found a cool, sun-dappled glade*
*And now my small son knows*
*How Mother bunny hides her nest,*
*Where jack-in-the-pulpit grows.*
*We watched a robin feed her young,*
*We climbed a sunlit hill…*
*Saw cloud-sheep scamper through the sky,*
*We plucked a daffodil.*
*That my house was neglected,*
*That I didn't brush the stairs,*
*In twenty years, no one on earth*
*Will know, or even care.*
*But that I've helped my little boy*
*To noble manhood grow.*
*In twenty years, the whole wide world*
*May look and see and know.*

*-Author Unknown*

## August 13th, 2007

### Things Are Looking Up!

Today I finally started my vacation.

I've been away for a few days already, but today I broke free of the to-do list I've been carrying in my head, and just chilled with my sons, my niece and my very pregnant sister.

We went to the park, had a picnic lunch on the living room floor, climbed trees (yep, I still love to do it!), and watched the old, old silver birch tree dance in the wind.

We enjoyed life together.

I know it's not possible to throw away our to-do lists every day, even when on vacation, but it felt so good to throw it away today!

I continue to realize the importance of seizing the moments we're given and making the greatest memories we can from them. Sometimes those memories require no effort, like lying in the grass and watching the trees. The effort is purely mental - to block everything else out for a few tiny moments, and just live to the fullest with what's right in front of us.

I don't accomplish this great mental feat often, but when I do, it's well worth the effort!


## August 26th, 2007

### The Strength of a Woman

Today was a great day.

I watched in awe as my sister cared for her 3-day-old son, spoke kindness to her husband, lovingly roused her 2 & 1/2-yr-old daughter from an afternoon nap, welcomed guests into her home, socialized with neighbours on her front lawn, and still managed to smile for most of the day.

And all this after a c-section!

What struck me most was her strength. We all carry it inside of us. Life throws us twists and turns, but we have the ability to flourish in them, if we choose. That is how we find out how strong we really are.

Not in overcoming the moment, but in living the moment.

Today I watched my sister live in her moments - with strength and love. It was a beautiful sight!

## My Special Teachers

A few life lessons I've learned from my special teachers:

- Great memories hide in the routines of daily life.
- Hugs and kisses have magical healing powers.
- It's possible to see God in all the moments of a day.
- Adventures are waiting around every corner.
- Quality time means more than quantity time.

Who are my special teachers? My two sons, who share life with me, help me to experience it fully and challenge me to see through their eyes. I look forward to many more lessons in the future!

*- Written for the September 2007 issue of Mom's Moments*

## September 21st, 2007

## Finding Vacation in My Every-Days

I was wondering why I felt overwhelmed after just returning from vacation.

Well, now I realize it was a matter of changing routines, helping my 6-year-old adjust to a new teacher and classroom, watching my husband venture off to work every day, and being tired of the set-up of our house!

So I buckled down to my new schedules (I find writing a lot of lists and filling in EVERYTHING on the calendar helps me settle into new seasons - from weekly breakfast and lunch menus to kids' programs to what I hope to accomplish during my toddler's nap times - I'm definitely a person who needs to see things in writing in order to function properly!).

I also try my hardest to spend quality LISTENING time with my 1st-grader and help him with all the transitions he's experiencing.

For my husband I try to save at least a smidge of energy for him at the end of the day so I'm not grumpy and nagging at him. I try to talk to him about more than maintenance stuff and hope he can do the same for me. Plus Season 4 of Corner Gas just came out on DVD so I know how I'll be spending my hubby-time for the next little while! He got me hooked about 2 years ago and now I love the show!

As for my house - I couldn't sleep one night and came up with a brilliant plan to rearrange the furniture in our small living space. I presented the idea to my husband the next morning and after the initial "No way!" he started moving the couch and we were on our way. My interior surroundings experienced a needed switch-around, and now I feel refreshed and ready for the long northern winter indoors with my littlest son.

One last thing - I've learned that life is just plain busy, especially with children - there's no getting around it. So how do I get through the next 15-20 years without being constantly overwhelmed?

I'm going to look for tiny vacations in my every-days. Doing an errand or two alone, playing with my boys instead of just watching them play, watching a chic flick, going out with girlfriends once in a while, laughing with my husband, writing newsletters and blogs, and chatting with my mom and sister on the phone are all things I enjoy. I will try to remember to put them on my lists and calendars along with all the other things that fill my days!

**November 8th, 2007**

## The Irony of Needing My Children

Some days are harder than others. Daily life makes me weary sometimes. Mess, clutter, crying children, dirty diapers, unpaid bills, getting everyone where they're supposed to be (and on time!), and then what's for dinner?

There are moments when I want to scream, or run away for a few hours, or just have a minute to myself. But then...one of my sons smiles at me, or tells me a joke, or sings a song, or dances around the kitchen, or hugs me, or says he loves me, or tries out a new ninja move...and suddenly it's alright, life is good again in that instant, my sanity is restored.

Then it dawns on me that I need my children. In order to try my best to be a good mother and run the house in a way that provides stability, fun, comfort and security, I need these little people to make me laugh, to love me, to entertain me, and to distract me from worrying and stressing. Funny how life plays out - what do I need most to raise my children in a positive way?

Well, I need my children! Ironic, isn't it?

**December 10th, 2007**

## 'Tis the Season of Sickness

We are experiencing our first bout of winter illness in the Sklar household. We made our first-ever family trip to the doctor last Friday - luckily only one of us needed medicine (my oldest son has sinusitis and bronchitis! Yikes! And he's still smiling!) But I think I have to go back since my chest REALLY hurts when I cough!

So begins the time of fevers, runny noses, coughs, aches and pains. At first mention this ordeal sounds miserable, and for the most part, the days of childhood illness are exhausting for parents, and in turn we often find ourselves ill as well. But there's another side - a softer note to the season - I saw it this week as I cared for my two sons. I woke up one day with my 2&1/2-year-old beside me (daddy had

14

slept in with our oldest to watch his fever and listen for him coughing) and he opened his little eyes, put his little hands on my face, and said, "I love my mommy." I mean, honestly, does life get any better than that?

This week as my son stayed home from school, there was more sibling rivalry, more work around the house, more emotional energy and creativity needed to answer all the statements of "I'm bored". But again, there was another side - there was more time for tickle fights, cozying under the blankets to read books, making forts with the bunkbeds, baking yummy treats, talking about life, watching Christmas movies, and playing video games TOGETHER instead of me having a mountain of chores to do while one son is occupied for an hour.

As you live through another season of colds and flus, remember the flip side - though it might mean a change of routine, missing work, cancelling Christmas parties, or even illness for yourself - I encourage you to make the most of your sick days, relax and chill with your kids as much as you can, and catch a glimpse of those rare, precious moments when you KNOW you are TRULY enjoying your role as mother, despite the hardships that life inevitably brings.

# 2008

## January 16th, 2008

### You Will Find Rest

This past week my youngest son had to wear a cast on his little leg. He had a nasty fall at the park over Christmas. He fell about six feet onto a patch of ice - of course my arms were waiting to catch him - just out of reach. So he went down hard.

The doctors asked us to monitor his healing, but he was still limping 10 days later. So it was decided that he should wear a cast for a week and that would slow down our very active two-year-old enough to let his body heal properly.

Well, the first cast they put on was plaster, and he ripped through that pretty good in about four hours, so the next day we were back at the hospital for a fiberglass cast - made extra thick - and that did the trick. Getting it off yesterday was another story - took them at least 1/2 hour to saw through the bulky thing! But it's all good now and my son is hopefully well on the way to recovery.

This week I was constantly reminded of this Bible verse:

*Come to me, all you who are weary and burdened, and I will give you rest. - Matthew 11:28*

My son was definitely burdened by his cast - so much so that he could barely walk. He HAD TO REST, he had no choice. And the cast was also a burden to my husband and me. We had to carry our little guy everywhere - we were supposed to keep him off his feet as much as possible. Our backs are still aching and recovering from the near 50 pounds we hefted around all week!

But in the midst of the burden of caring for our son, and the weariness of watching him adjust to the disability he experienced, there was also great rest - reconnecting with him, falling in love with him all over again, remembering how much I love being around him, realizing he's a really great kid - despite his two-year-old-ness!

We knew the cast was the best thing for our son, we hoped he would heal, and we knew it would be over soon. I imagine this would be a great way to look at the trials in all our lives, to have certainty that things will work out for the best, to hope for healing, and to know the trial will pass in time. Give your burdens and your weariness to Christ - he asks us to - he can absolutely handle them, and He wants us to rest in Him.


## February 3rd, 2008

### Lost at the YMCA

It happened in less than a minute. The whole scene played out so fast, yet it has left a huge imprint on my heart. My youngest son and I were enjoying a snack in between his toddler classes at the YMCA. I was chatting with a friend and trying to steer my son in the direction of his next class. He was there - I turned - he was gone. I've been playing the scene over and over in my mind - what could I have done differently? I recall the feelings of panic that immediately set in. I hoped that in the next second he would come into view, as my mind frantically tried to search for a plan. I should see him by now - he wasn't that far ahead of me - how did he get away so fast? I searched the most dangerous option first - the hallway to the outside doors - NO. I searched where he SHOULD have gone, his next class - NO. The gym - NO. Oh Lord - where IS he? I started to ask people if they'd seen my son. In reality only about 20 or 30 seconds had passed. 20 or 30 seconds too long for any mother.

The plan my mind had formulated took me once again to the most dangerous place - the doorway to outside. As I turned the corner, my face a mask of panic and fear, my heart full of dread, my mind a mixture of the most frightening thoughts...there he was. My little angel in the grey sweater, walking down the hallway towards me. He was safe, I could see him, he was beautiful, I would be holding him in 2 seconds.
I said to him, "Where did you go? Mommy couldn't see you! I was so scared!"
He stepped behind a big red pole and said, "I was hiding."
Should I yell, scold, hug, cry, or laugh? That day I was able to pull

off a calm, swallow-my-heart-before-I-freak reaction - who knows what it would have been any other day!

He had never hidden from me in a public place before, so our relationship entered the You're Never Getting Even The Slightest Bit Of Distance Away From Me Again phase! The nightmares of losing him have started. I now have a greater understanding that he is, in fact, becoming very independent and wanting to do more on his own. I'm thankful that there is Someone bigger than me or my son who is watching over him, protecting him, comforting us both through the scary times of growing up. It's a great feeling to have the Maker of the Universe helping me raise my sons - He can see where I can't, and He knows every tiny detail of what's happening around us in our days. Thank God because I need all the help I can get!

## May 3rd, 2008

### They Sleep

The day was long
With play and song
So much to see
"Mommy watch me!"
Did you enjoy your day?
What does your heart say?
Dream as you sleep
Sleep long, sleep deep
New days soon dawn
And sleep is gone

## June 2nd, 2008

### Safe in the Storms

*He who dwells in the shelter of the Most High will rest in the shadow of the Almighty. I will say of the Lord, 'He is my refuge and my fortress, my God in whom I trust"... He will cover you with His feathers, and under His wings you will find refuge; His faithfulness will be your shield and your rampart. - Psalm 91:1-4* (Read the whole chapter of Psalm 91 for more comforting words!)

My son and I ventured out for a walk to the park today - a very sunny, pleasant day in Northern Ontario. We strolled along, Elijah enjoying the view from his wagon and me enjoying the sun on my face and the wind in my hair (along with a few blackflies)!

Life was good...until a few minutes after we arrived at the park and a thunderstorm hit. Luckily there was a shelter for us to snuggle under as we waited for the storm to pass.

As we sat there, huddled together, keeping each other warm in the chilly rain, two wonderful things occurred to me. I thought about how the storms of life are often unexpected and sometimes we just have to find a sheltered place to wait them out. And I thought about how my place of shelter is in the strong arms of God.

The geese on the lake beside the park squawked in protest to the blasts of rain, then they finally flew away, their time of peaceful floating so rudely interrupted! Just when it seemed the rain was letting up and we could make a run for home, another wave of heavy rainfall would cover the park. Sometimes in the storms of my life I've thought the coast was clear, that it's safe to come out from shelter, only to have to run back into the arms of my Heavenly Father.

Once in a while lightning would strike - sometimes very close to us - I was just praying we wouldn't be hit! I never felt that I wasn't safe in the shelter, it's just that lightning is so unpredictable, so focused in its attacks, it seeks out the best avenue for its electricity, the most direct path to its target - vicious when you think about it - cold and calculating!

And in the midst of the storm I also saw the most beautiful and encouraging sight. Seagulls, white and majestic, soaring through the rain, no squawks to be heard, letting the rain fall freely on their wings, unafraid of the lightning, flying high and flying free.

I watched it all from my safe and secure shelter at the park.

After a while the rain subsided, I saw a patch of blue sky and I loaded my son back into the drenched wagon for a rather brisk walk home! We enjoyed a few moments of sunshine before the next storm hit. I think that's how it is for us as well - there WILL be breaks in the storms. The rain WILL subside. There WILL be blue skies once again. Rest WILL come.

We are free to choose how we want to live in the storms of our lives. Will we squawk in protest, run, be impatient for them to end, or fear the next lightning strike?

I would love to be like the bird, riding the raindrops, confident of my path through the storm. In all honesty my first reaction is to huddle under shelter and wait until the coast is clear. I feel so safe under my Father's wings...

## June 25th, 2008

### Fill 'Er Up!

Lately I've been feeling really tired, run-down, weary, empty. I long to be filled...but how do I do that? I've forgotten! My husband had a great idea - make a list, even if it's a mental list, of the things you enjoy doing that "fill you up". Mine are watching chic flicks, going for walks or hikes (even in the rain!), reading, writing, watching my boys smile and seeing the world through their eyes, baking, hanging my laundry out to dry, and a new one is gardening. I also love the water - swimming, canoeing, paddle-boating, whatever! So my list is long, and that gives me a lot of room for flexibility and variety. I've been able to plan some of these events into my days as I refocus, clear my life of all the clutter I've put in there recently, and remember who I am and what I love to do. Life is so full, there is so much to enjoy, if I only look for it, embrace it, and live it to the fullest. As I begin to do the things that make me Anna, the empty feelings fade, and I experience the fullness of the life that is all around me. It's a wonderful thing.

## September 1st, 2008

### Building A Strong Family

We have been working on some major home renovations these past few months. The upstairs floor of our house had to be ripped apart – down to the studs on the walls. I've noticed many parallels between building a strong home and building a strong family.

It all starts with a solid frame. Before we started the renovations, we asked a trusted contractor if our home was worth fixing in the first place. He told us we have a solid frame and a firm foundation to build on. In our family I know that our faith in Jesus is what we build upon. We have a firm footing as we learn more about Him together.

There was no insulation in the walls of our old house, nothing to keep out the weather extremes of the outside world. Before I filled the walls with R12 I had this wonderful idea. I gathered many Bible verses and stapled them to the outside walls of our house. What better protection for our family than the Word of God? Then I realized that unconditional love and acceptance are what insulate a family from whatever may come from the outside.

We're at the point now where we can start to paint. I'm looking forward to watching our personalities come to life on the walls. What colours will we choose? Each member of our family is unique – each with their own hopes and dreams, likes and dislikes. I hope our house is a place where they will discover who they are meant to be.

Last will be the flooring. We'll cover over creaky floor boards with laminate soon. But I'm glad for the creaks, they remind me that our house has character and a history because of its age. Our family has its quirks, inside jokes and shared experiences that lie beneath the surface of what others may see. I'd never want to change the character of Team Sklar.

I look forward to watching our house become all that we've envisioned, and the same goes for my family as we build our home together.


## September 3rd, 2008

### First Day of School

I've been grumpy the past few days. I thought it was because I was ready to ship my oldest son back off to school, but I was wrong. As I stood in the kitchen this morning making my specialty (whole wheat chocolate chip muffins - yum!) I turned on the radio to try and lift my spirits. I was hoping to muster a smile and some cheery remarks to encourage my son before he faced another year of school.

What came over the radio waves and into my kitchen? Find Your Wings by Mark Harris. I started crying. Oh, THAT'S why I'm so moody. Not because I've had enough and want my kids to go away, but because I want them to stay. Next time the first day of school rolls around I'll be sending my youngest son off to face the world as well. It will be the end of an era for me. No more full-time-stay-at-home-mom status. This has been my role for the past seven years and it's one career I don't want to end. This is the longest I've ever held the same position!

We all piled into the van to take Josiah to school. Elijah seems to enjoy taking his big brother to school and picking him up. As I walked up the stairs I'd walked a thousand times already, I had flashbacks of the past 3&1/2 years. Carrying Elijah up in his infant car seat, then on my hip, then holding his hands as he walked up on unsteady feet, then holding one hand as he held the rail with his tiny fingers, and then being told he could do it himself and watching nervously a few steps behind.

As I walked up the stairs with Elijah today he strode up them confidently and reached for my hand. He knew he could do it alone, but he wanted me to walk with him. I think that's how it will be next year. Secure enough to know he can do it but wanting to share his experiences with me. I hope and pray it will be like that throughout his whole life as he continues to walk towards the man he was made to be - one step at a time.


**November 18th, 2008**

**Scenes From the Soul – 5 a.m.**

It's 5 o'clock in the morning. She sits under a cozy blanket, alone in her living room, listening to the sounds of her loved ones sleeping in the rooms beside her.

Everything is peaceful - except her heart. The events of the past year have been catching up to her lately - affecting her sleep, her health, and especially her heart. There is no peace in her heart just now. So many things have interfered with her peace - or is it just that she's LET them interfere?

23

She remembers quiet evenings reading her favourite magazines, watching a good movie snuggled up to her husband, innocent laughter shared with her sons, discovering the world with her youngest on afternoon walks, playing her favourite songs on the old keyboard, and card games with her boys. Where did it all go? And when was the last time she took a moment to watch the trees dancing in the wind, gaze at the stars on a clear night, or enjoy the colours of a sunset?

Her life is full - but she's let in some things that don't need to be there - filling up her days with checklists and perfectionism. She's been letting go of the important things in favour of the superficial things. Her time with God is slipping, her husband feels left out and her kids are whiny. But there is hope. There's always hope.

At 5 o'clock on a Monday morning, when the stresses and pressures of life threaten to overwhelm her once again, she sits on her couch, closes her eyes, turns her face to heaven, and listens... for the still, small voice... the gentle whisper in her heart... reminding her of a love that is beyond all understanding... and a peace that exists in ANY situation... if only she remembers to look for it...even at 5 o'clock in the morning.

## December 7th, 2008

### It's My Choice

Lately I've been reminded that I have an important decision to make every day of my life...Will I be happy or not? I am married to a man I truly love, and he truly loves me in return. I am raising two boys who hug me and kiss me at least once a day. I am well-fed, warm, and have a closet full of clothes. So why am I grumpy with my husband, frustrated with my sons and anxious about the future? The hard truth I've had to face is that I choose to be those things.

Tonight I hit a wall - I've been in the house most of the week caring for my two sick boys. I really had to step back from the activities and commitments and just focus on what's right in front of me - my family and my home. This morning I had the same choice I have every morning - will I be happy or not? Today I chose to be happy with what I have, who I am, all the wonderful things that make up my life. And you know what? It was a good day despite everything that could have made it bad - had I chosen to look at it that way.

I hope I make the same choice tomorrow and the next day and far into the future. But I will probably have to be reminded again since I seem to easily forget this key to a happy life - choosing it, finding the good every day, no matter what.


## December 30th, 2008

### Hope For Winter

Take heart - the days are already getting longer, and it will be spring before you know it! OK, maybe I'm exaggerating a little since December 21st was officially the first day of winter. But that day was also the shortest day of the year, so the days actually ARE getting longer already! This thought will keep me going on the long, cold days ahead!

The question I have to ask myself is what will I put into those days? Will it be snowball fights, skating on the outdoor rinks in town, tobogganing, and LOTS of hot chocolate? Or will it be sulking, watching TV, eating cookies, waiting for the spring to arrive before I make an effort, and LOTS of hot chocolate? *Notice the hot chocolate will be included no matter what?!*

So far I'm happy with the choices I've made, the snowball fights I've already had, the snowmen I've already built, the tobogganing I've already done, and of course the hot chocolate I've already shared with my sons (Carnation Rich Milk Chocolate is my favourite!).

Winter came early for us this year, with record snowfalls in early December, and continuing over the Christmas holidays. Such a huge change in weather in such a short period of time. I've tried to embrace it, and every time I've made the effort, I'm happy with the results. Seeing the rosy cheeks on my two boys, watching them create with snow, making snow angels, tackling them into the fluffy white stuff, storing away the beautiful images of heavy snow draping the evergreens, and feeling the warm glow in my heart that made it possible to stay out way beyond the time I felt the first chill.

I hope to make the same choices in the coming months - to savour the winter moments - even though it DOES take half an hour to get our snow gear on!

# 2009

**January 24th, 2009**

## The Mask I Wear

A while ago I noticed a difference in the way I act OUTSIDE the house vs. INSIDE the house. Sometimes the change occurs the minute I step through the door. Did I lose the caring, attentive, playful mom at the playgroup? Did I leave that Anna in the van? Where did she go? And where did this impatient, irritable, frustrated Anna come from? I don't remember bringing HER home! Which one is the real me and which one is the mask?

This was <u>not</u> a realization I wanted to come to. I <u>don't</u> want to know that sometimes I am one person to the rest of the world and another to my family - the former being the "nice" Anna.

So I'm trying to take off my mask. It takes way too much emotional energy to maintain the facade. I'm trying to be real, just be myself. And that's just too bad if I'm not a perfect mother, if my eating habits aren't stellar, and if I'm not a social butterfly.

As I remove the mask and come face-to-face with who I am vs. who I present to the world, I find there are actually a lot of similarities. I really <u>am</u> a good mother, I eat <u>pretty</u> healthy and I'm not quite as shy as I thought I was. I make lots of mistakes in front of other people now and try my best not to worry about it.

A lot of my motivation has changed. Wearing the mask always motivated me to act according to how I wanted others to see me. Taking the mask off motivates me to act according to how I want to see myself. I strive to be the same person in front of a group of people or at home with my husband and kids.

It's very freeing - being real. Sure I have to work on a few things, but the mask wasn't hiding as much as I thought it was. And when I come home, and step inside my house, I hang my coat on a hook and realize I don't need a hook for my mask anymore. I can clear out the emotional space I used to save for the mask and use it for the ones who need it most - my family.

**February 7th, 2009**

## The Song of Salvation

Can you hear the tune? It plays just for you
And for me... and for her... and for him
We're all invited to hear the song
To open our hearts and sing
There is another who wants to steal the song
He'll use every trick in the book
A big audience, nice clothes, a better voice
They're just lies from the biggest crook
God is the only audience for the beautiful song
Clothes don't matter to Him
Your voice is not what God can hear
He listens to your heart as you sing
Anyone can learn the sweet song of salvation
There are no words to rehearse
The tune keeps echoing throughout time
One single, solitary verse
The music asks us to believe in Him
And tells us there's a plan for all
Of hope, and peace, and joy, and acceptance
As we answer to the song's call
The song of salvation will never stop playing
Why would we want it to cease?
We sing along as we learn the song
Piece by heavenly piece


**February 16th, 2009**

## When Mommy Gets Sick

Do you remember when your mom used to bring you ginger ale and crackers when you had an upset stomach? Or when she used to appear at your door, magically, with cough syrup in hand in the middle of your 2am coughing fit? Or when she'd get you cozy on the couch with a box of Kleenex, cherry Halls, a warm blanket and the remote? My mom was good at pampering me when I was sick. I NEVER had to fend for myself. Thanks Mum.

29

But what about now? With two rambunctious germ-spreaders in the house and my husband and I taking shifts at being sick, who is supposed to take care of who? Usually I get sick first and try my best to care for our preschooler in between dozing on the couch, reading *Thomas the Tank Engine* books, coughing fits, watching Elijah's favourite video, and finding the Advil. Then just as I'm feeling better, my husband takes his turn at being sick, stays in bed most of the day, has long, hot showers and tries not to ask for much. Yes, there's a little double-standard there - I'm still "working" when I'm sick, and my husband isn't - but some days I get to take a nap at "work" or go out for ice cream *just because*, and he doesn't - it all balances out in the end.

So my most recent bout of sickness came the past couple of days, and I noticed a real difference this time... I DIDN'T try to keep up with our social schedule and just chilled by myself at home instead. I DIDN'T try to keep up with our household schedule and just tidied what was driving me nuts instead. And I DIDN'T make excuses or promises to my sons today as I cared for them both and my husband went off to work. I simply told them "Mommy is NOT feeling well, so please try your best to get along today." And that was that. They let me go back to bed for an hour while they watched *Treehouse*. They didn't complain about what I made for lunch. They had a bath, got dressed and brushed their teeth and hair when I asked them to. They did a great job of not fighting. They snuggled in bed with me and read *I Spy* books... it was just about as close as we can get to perfect. *Thank You God.*

Maybe part of it was their dad pulling them aside to ask them not to fight before he left this morning. Maybe part of it is that they're getting older and things might just be easier for a bit before adolescence strikes. Maybe part of it is that God heard the prayers they offered on my account this morning. Maybe part of it is that for the first time I refused to feel guilty about being sick, and just relaxed and tried to get better. Maybe it's all those things.

On the sick days I still miss my mum, but my guys are doing a pretty good job at caring for me. I'm also getting better at "sucking it up". And I wouldn't trade anything for being the one who cares for my husband and boys when they are sick. Now I get to be the mommy. That's worth a few "working sick days", isn't it?

## March 1st, 2009

### Rollin' With It

Life has been quite a roller coaster ride this week. Monday we packed for our all-inclusive trip to the Dominican Republic with our boys. A wonderful, fabulous treat for our family that we'd dreamed about for years - the finances were provided at Christmas - an amazing gift.

We arrived at the airport to find out our trip was delayed by four hours... ugh. But we rolled with it - our flight was supposed to leave at 10pm - so we drove around with the boys and they DID sleep for a while in the van, then in the airport lounge. We woke them up to board the plane at 2am, they were grumpy but excited, we were exhausted but happy, and we all crashed an hour into the flight. We arrived at our resort a little late, but in great spirits, put on our bathing suits immediately and headed for the beach, sand and sunshine - glorious!

The next day we received the very sad news that my husband's grandfather passed away. Staying for the remainder of our trip was not an option, we wanted to be with our family, NEEDED to be with our family, so again we rolled with it. We looked at all our options for flying home, the best one being to leave Friday at dinner time. This meant we still got to enjoy another two days at the resort, and we'd be home in plenty of time for the funeral.

We did enjoy the rest of our trip, soaking up the fun and sun, and making lasting memories with our boys. And we did come home early, the funeral is tomorrow morning and we are surrounded by family - it's amazing how so many people from all over the place can come together in such a short period of time.

There's been many ups and downs this week, and the ride isn't over yet. But I've learned that life is unpredictable, plans should be made but with the knowledge they could change at any minute. And that doesn't mean the plans are ruined, just different. I've learned to roll with it, take life one day at a time, find the enjoyment as much as you can, because one day it will be time for the ride to end.

I hope to look back and know that the ups and downs balanced each other out, that I held my arms up in the air to enjoy the ride as much as I could, and I wasn't afraid to go on the roller coaster that went UPSIDE DOWN! That I didn't play it safe... but rolled with it instead.


## March 23rd, 2009

### Connecting With My Best Friend

I haven't spent much time with God lately. I miss Him very much. His patience amazes me. I know He's waiting for me to open myself up to Him. I know He wants me to let go of my grip on the things in life, to give Him all that's in my heart, my head and my soul.

I might even be avoiding Him, and finding my solace in fleeting things like food, TV and finishing the home renovations. I don't know.

The longer I go without reading my Bible, or learning something new about God, or praying, or spending time with other Christians, the emptier and emptier I feel.

Even 12 years after rededicating my life to God, I still choose to ignore my best friend sometimes. But I think this is the longest I've gone without intentionally connecting with Him.

I've discovered I still need Him. Maybe even more so than when I first gave my life to Him. This puts to rest the nagging thoughts that maybe I was just going through the motions of Christianity as I diligently read my Bible, prayed and went to church. Now I know that I do those things because I want to, need to, choose to. Not because someone tells me to.

I've discovered that everything I am is wrapped up in who God is. At least, that is how I want it to be. I want to, need to reflect His love, hope and peace to a very hurting world. I want people to see Jesus when they look at me.

This morning I finally spent time with God. And you know what? He missed me too, I could feel it. It was good to connect with my best friend.


## March 30th, 2009

### Music to My Heart

We have a keyboard that sits in my bedroom, sometimes waiting for weeks for someone to play it. I am so happy when one of my boys turns it on and experiments with different sounds and lyrics. It's music to my heart. So far I haven't been able to get the oldest to realize that lessons would be a good idea (though he's very interested in learning to play the drums!), and my youngest is only 3 - still a little young for lessons.

This morning my littlest guy turned on the piano, and what followed was a masterpiece in my opinion. He sat on my lap, banged out a melody on the keys and sang, "I love my mommy and she loves me. I love my daddy and he loves me. I love my brother and he loves me, but he doesn't like it when I give him kisses." It was so beautiful! To hear my son singing his love for me, and his confidence in my love for him just made my heart soar. Better than Handel - well, to some extent!


## April 9th, 2009

### Answered Prayer

We pray with our boys as we drive our oldest to school in the mornings. This morning my husband prayed that I would see something of Jesus. Sometimes he says things like that, hopes things like that for me... and I always get a little anxious about how God will answer those prayers - what if it means stepping out of my comfort zone? It's not easy for me - an introvert, fighting off a sore throat and throbbing head, trying to get through my daily schedule of playgroups, errands, housework, all while trying not to yell at my stubborn preschooler.

Today I did see Jesus - I have hoped for a while to know my neighbours better, and today one of them stopped into our yard, with all the kids she watches in her home daycare, and I couldn't have been happier about it. My boys played with a few kids, I had some great conversation, and soaked up some precious sunshine as well. Jesus loved to stop and talk to people, people felt so free to drop in on Him, He welcomed so many into His presence just by being Himself. My boys showed me Jesus today - they were happy to welcome others, spend time with them, and just enjoy life with them.

And again I saw Jesus at dinnertime - we stopped to pick up a pizza, a man was walking along the road and suddenly went down, partially falling under a truck that was stopped for traffic. The truck driver didn't see him, I watched in horror as the man's head lay beside one of the back tires, and my husband leaned in the horn and shouted for the driver to stop. The sound of the horn roused the fallen man, and his head bolted up to safety, my husband saved his life I'm sure. My hero. Then Josh ran out of our van, helped the fallen man up and over to sit on a bench.

I joined my husband and the man, we talked with him for a minute, he was shaking and needed to get to a store down the street. Josh offered to help him along.

As they walked my husband discovered the man was dizzy from lack of food, yet he was going to spend the little money he had to buy cigarettes at the store. Heartbreaking. Josh hugged him, and I'm sure prayed for him as he left him at his destination and rejoined us in our van. My husband showed me Jesus as he saved a life, helped a stranger, walked and talked with him for a while, and showed compassion.

That's how Josh's prayer was answered today - I hope that when others looked at me today they saw something of Jesus. I hope that serving others and enjoying their presence will become such a part of my life that next time I'll think to offer the stranger some pizza, or maybe even sit on the roadside and eat with him.

## April 11th, 2009

### Scenes From the Soul – The Journey

She stands in the middle of a long, windy road. There is a long journey ahead of her. She has no idea where it will take her, what she will experience, or who she will be when it's all over. There will be many forks in the road, and she will have to do her best to pick the right route. No map is given for this journey; she will have to rely on God to navigate the directions. There will be big potholes to avoid, and places of rest to find along the way. Sometimes she will saunter down the road with no particular place to go, and other times she will run so fast that she will exhaust herself in a hurry. The scenery will amaze her; she will discover so many beautiful mountains and valleys on the journey.

Best of all, SHE WILL BE CHANGED by the journey. It's not that she hates who she is or any of the things in her life. She has bad days and certain vices just like everyone else, but she is overall very happy with her life. She just knows there's MORE.

And that's where her journey begins.

## April 16th, 2009

### Survival Days

Some days it's just about surviving. Mothering my boys sometimes brings these glorious, perfect days that I wish would never end. I connect with them - we laugh and play and talk. We're on time for everything, there are no tantrums or frustration (for any of us - including me!), and the beds were even made before school. At the end of these days all I can see in my mind is their smiles and their beautiful eyes looking at me with joy and love. What a wonderful feeling! I feel great on these days - like I can handle the job of mother no problem.

Then there's survival days. I had one yesterday. We were late out the door in the morning, I had to doze on the couch by 11am (I absolutely crashed - maybe from the antibiotics I'm on?), I continued to have zero energy, couldn't play much, my son was bored, we ate too much Easter candy and I spent too much time on the computer (maybe I was bored too with having no energy to do anything else?!). By the end of the day I saw moments of fatigue, distraction, frustration and impatience in my mind - not much connection, not many smiles.

Motherhood brings good days and bad days. That's simply life. I'll try to remember to take the good, learn from the bad, enjoy the moments as much as I can, forgive myself and my kids and move on to the next day. You never know what it will bring!


## April 29th, 2009

### Big Blue Eyes

My sons both have big blue eyes. They are so beautiful! I have to make sure to really stop and look into their eyes at least once a day. I mean REALLY look. There is so much magic in their eyes. In their eyes I see a whole other world, the world of a child, the world of innocence. There's wonder, excitement, unconditional love, honesty and sincerity in their eyes. There's a deep grace and forgiveness in their eyes. I see so much of God in their eyes. It's such a precious gift to look into their eyes each and every day. Especially when their eyes are surrounded by emerging freckles or gap-tooth grins! I pray my boys will always carry some of the magic with them, no matter how old they get or what happens in their lives.

**May 10th, 2009**

**Happy Mother's Day**

Thank you. For reading what I write, for sharing life with me, for supporting me, for encouraging me. I feel so blessed today. I know I live a full life with many good things wrapped up in it. There are so many who don't. I pray new things for them and I hope new life for them.

Mother's Day is such a reminder that my life is way more than I ever imagined. I was actually overwhelmed at breakfast, by the love my guys showed me. They spoiled me, you know? And usually it's me trying to find new ways to spoil them. I didn't expect it. Not because I don't think they can pull it off, but because I feel spoiled every day. I really do. Hugs and kisses from an adorable almost-four-year-old with freckles on his nose and a GREAT smile. Mischievous smirks and 'I love you mom' as my 7&1/2-year-old flies into his classroom on a school day (I wonder if he'll mind if I walk him into class in grade 8 - do you think I can still get away with it then?). And mid-day phone calls and holding my husband's hand as we drive out in the mornings to face the day.

I don't ever want to expect more... I always want to be happy with what my guys give to me. I don't ever want to hold them up to an ideal... I always want to be happy with who they are. Encourage them to more when needed but love them for who they are.

I hope you had an AMAZING day today - whatever it brought to your life - whether you're a mom or not. Blessings abundant on you!


**The Garden of Childhood**

When we bought our home four years ago the garden was so overgrown and neglected. We had to clear away MANY weeds to discover the beauty that was waiting underneath! Now we can see the fruits of our labour. The lilacs, lilies and roses spoil us with their fragrant blossoms.

As I watch our boys play in the yard, surrounded by our gardens, I know the task of raising them will require much hard work. I hope and pray they will never feel neglected, that I can pluck the weeds that threaten to hide their beauty and discover exactly who they are meant to be.

I can already see the fragrance and colour my little men bring to their world, nurtured by those who love them.

*- Written for the May 2008 issue of Mom's Moments*

## June 3rd, 2009

### Faith From the Mouth of a Babe

These are some really cute things my just-turned-four-year-old said recently - I jotted them down so I don't forget them!

- God is watching over us. Everybody in the world.

- I praise the Lord that God has come to save us.

- God gives us a million life in our hearts, so you can't die. (The "million life" might have been inspired from watching his older brother play video games, but still... he's connecting his concepts together, right?)

- When people die, just bodies die, not life and heart. Only one thing dies.

And when he saw me writing down what he was saying, he asked me to write down this prayer:

Dear God, thank You for watching over us and You are strong and healthy. And thank you God for Sarah (a good friend of ours). And thank You God for rest. And wrestling. And going to bed. And taking a nap. And drawing with pencil crayons and markers. And thank You God for Jesus and God. And thank You God that Jesus and God are brave and strong and invisible. Thank You God for Jesus and God that are healthy and strong. Amen.

I'm posting this to encourage you all and share something wonderful and CUTE! My littlest man has his bad days, just like all other kids, but sometimes he has these GREAT moments, and I want to remember those as I strive to live out the "bad" moments with patience and love!

Hold on to the good, take what you can from the bad, and just keep going - you really ARE impacting your kids!

## July 7th, 2009

### Seeing What the Day Brings

There's something I've been working on for a while... a long while. But I've been "getting it" more often lately, and I'm excited about it, so I thought I'd share it with you.

I am a person who loves to make plans and lists and schedules. I love to accomplish tangible tasks and take on projects and meet deadlines. All this gives me a wonderful sense of accomplishment. And don't get in my way when I'm focused on the task at hand! Watch out!

This doesn't bode well for my husband and sons sometimes and would occasionally isolate me from the rest of the world as I went about completing whatever project or task or deadline I was working on. And it created a lot of unnecessary stress for me, especially when the project or task or deadline wasn't really that important. Sometimes I would make stuff up just for that sense of accomplishment. This was good for getting me through the sometimes boring, mundane days of being a stay-at-home mom.

But I think I might have been looking at it all wrong, because lately I've realized that yes, there are very boring days in life sometimes, but there's also this whole other world that I was missing in the midst of my lists and schedules. It's what happens in the middle of checking off the lists, and in the moments in between the playgroups and grocery shopping and dealing with Laundry Mountain. It's the unexpected call from a family member or friend who makes you laugh until you cry. It's the spontaneous walk around the neighbourhood and all the discoveries of nature that can bring. It's

39

the impromptu conversations with neighbours. It's the unplanned game of hide and seek or tickle fights with little ones. And it's absolutely the unanticipated prayers and devotional times that happen when the house is quiet for a few minutes!

I still have my lists and my schedules - they keep me grounded, and sane, and help me stay calm when someone says to me "I'm bored" or "I'm hungry". But I'm learning, ever so slowly, to let go sometimes. And I'm trying to remember to keep my eyes wide open and see what the day REALLY brings, not just what I plan it to bring. I love what I'm looking at so far!


## July 29<sup>th</sup>, 2009

### Looking At What I Have

I'm having a hard time. The reality that my youngest son is starting school in about 5 weeks is sometimes overwhelming for me. I've been a full-time stay-at-home mom for 8 years now and have spent a lot of time with two very wonderful little boys. Sure, there have been days when there's more yelling than laughing, when I'm exhausted before breakfast, when I wished I was the one heading out to work in the mornings instead of my husband, and when the monotony of routine caused the days to blur for months at a time. But there is a whole other side to raising kids that I'm going to miss while they're busy at school, and the many other things that will continue to fill their days as they grow up.

It's the unexpected, the awe, the surprise, the wonder, the spontaneity, the FUN. There's still a huge part of me that actually WANTS to change diapers still and wade through more sleepless nights - because that means I would also get more first words, first steps, and first smiles. There would be more rocking babies to sleep, and peek-a-boo, and walks with the stroller. It's safe to say I'm in a bit of a difficult stage of letting go.

So I'm trying hard to look at WHAT I HAVE instead of what I DON'T HAVE. I don't have any more babies in the house, but I do have two wonderful boys with whom I still share an abundance of time. I'm sure I will learn more and more games and activities as they continue to grow up, and there will be lots of fun with those! I have a constant source of imaginary battle scenes (and sometimes I get to be the princess and just let my heroes take out all the bad guys!), I have interesting talks about God, I have bike rides, I have more time in the camper, I have more chances to volunteer in the community and at the school, and I have some much-anticipated time to myself to think and write and do "Anna" stuff. I still have lots of time for tickle fights and neighbourhood walks, and I still have the summers with my boys (until they start going to camp - but let's not go there right now!).

So I'm trying to see past the mourning of a phase in my life that I REALLY enjoyed. And I know it's not over, my boys aren't heading off to university just yet, but I MISS them already. I'm learning to let that spur me on to grab hold of the next phase of raising these boys of mine - to squeeze all I can out of the days that are coming, to live in the present instead of the past. Hard though.

And I've already told friends and family that Auntie Anna would be more than happy to babysit any future babies that are coming. So make sure you take me up on that ladies!

Enjoy the days you get to spend with whatever young ones are in your life...


**One Day...**

You'll have to reach down to give ME a hug
You'll read stories to yourself
Even your big boy bed will be too small
Your shoes will be much bigger than mine
It will cost at least double to feed you
Your razor will sit right beside your daddy's
Someone else will snuggle with you
I'll miss these precious days with you
And enjoy you in such different ways
One day...

*- Published in the Summer 2009 issue of Mom's Moments*

## Scenes From the Soul – Summer Sky

She stands in the middle of a field. It's night time. The blackness is broken by the faint outlines of tall, old, magnificent trees. The sky is lit with the distant fire of at least a billion stars.

She has a crystal-clear realization of the extreme enormity of God. The God. Her God. The One who holds the universe in the palm of His hand. The One who breathes each star into existence. The One who set time into motion and knew EXACTLY when she would be standing in that moment, in that field, on that night.

With heart wide open and hands stretched to heaven, she utters a faint "Thank You." There are no real words. Her heart wants to touch, her body wants to embrace, her soul wants to fly to the God who made it all. It is pure, absolute, true Love that created her world and the world beyond. The world she can't touch, can only glimpse, as she stares into the night sky.

*One day. Soon enough. Not yet. Much more to do. Look for Love wherever you are, whomever you're with, whatever you're doing. You'll find Me. I'm in it all. You just have to look. I made it all. My fingerprints are everywhere. Not just in the stars. I'll give you eyes to see Me. You only need to ask. Look for me in the love of your husband and in the eyes of your children. Hear me in the laughter of your friends and the rustling of the leaves. Feel me in each hug and kiss, in the wind in your hair and the sunshine on your face. Know Me. Share life with Me. I made it all for you.*

She closes her eyes, at peace, holding heaven in her heart, full of a Love that is even bigger than the night sky, taking it with her, everywhere, always, forever.

- *Written at Family Camp in August 2009*

**September 9<sup>th</sup>, 2009**

## My Last First Day of School

If you follow my blog, you'll know that I've been really sappy and emotional about my youngest son's first day of school. I know to some this is ridiculous, I know all the reasons I shouldn't be sappy, I know I should be happy that my boys are growing up to be wonderful human beings (despite the incessant body parts and functions talk) - but all these sensible things haven't helped me in the least these past few weeks. I'm not trying to be unreasonable, I'm simply handling this phase of my life as only I can. And apparently that's to be very sappy and emotional. Two things I am usually NOT!

My son was very excited as he ran into the schoolyard, just like his older brother did 4 years ago. At least this son stopped to give me a hug and kiss before he walked into his class. I am trying to take all these things as positive testimonies to the fact that I'm raising two confident, secure, out-going, friendly little men. But it's hard to face the reality that the hugs and kisses will get fewer and farther between, that the days will lack their presence more and more, and that I have ALOT of letting go to do.

I don't regret for a moment the past eight years of being a stay-at-home mom. I know it's not for everyone, and at first I didn't think it was for me, but it's amazing how things can change. I've had my hobbies, my small home-business of making wedding veils, my online ministry to moms, and my playgroup at church. I've been to the YMCA more times in the past 6 years than I'll probably ever be again. I've met so many great people, I've seen so many great sights - most of which were behind the camera as my sons were encountering another milestone.

I'm thankful for all the memories these past eight years have brought, little treasures for my mom-chest. And I have to keep remembering something a friend of mine recently said, "Anna, you know it's not OVER." She's so right. It's just different, and less, and things have to change. And when you really like the way something is going in your life, it's hard to change, isn't it?

I have the chance right now to re-group. My husband has encouraged me to take a break, to listen for what's next, and to not jump into anything else right away. I'll try, I'll really try. Plus I still have my youngest son at home part-time :)

Life continues, life changes, life moves, life passes... but not without some sappy, emotional times!

Happy first day of school, little man.

**September 13th, 2009**

**Canoeing to Church**

I attended a Ladies Retreat this weekend at Camp Norland in Northern Ontario. And this morning I did just what the title says I did... I canoed to church! I don't think the retreat could have gotten any better than that moment for me. There were many highlights of the weekend - being surrounded by godly women, hearing encouraging insight and teaching from an inspiring woman, eating great food, bunking in with two good friends & strengthening those bonds even more, and organizing the camp bookstore (I LOVE organizing, and right now my house needs a top-to-bottom organizing after more than a year of renovations, so it was nice to start with a small camp bookstore this weekend!).

But this morning... ah this morning... in a canoe with a wonderful woman who I got to know even more the past two days (and now I know she's even more wonderful than originally thought), the waves were just enough to make paddling a challenge, the paddle dipping into the water, letting droplets fall off its back before sinking into the water again, the rocks and water reeds and cliff faces blending together to create beautiful scenery, the church stood in the distance, across the lake, beckoning us to enjoy the fellowship that waited there.

The simplicity of the situation captured us both... the pioneer-ness of the morning, flashbacks to yesteryear, to 1893 when the church originated, and attendees probably had no choice but to paddle the waters in search of fellowship. We loved that we found our bearings back to camp by rock formations and the appearance of the shoreline instead of maps and road signs (we DID get lost for a few minutes but seen as there was no stopping to ask for directions on the water, we were left to our own devices and relied on the land that surrounded us!).

As we pulled up to a flat rock face that protruded from the water near the church on the lake that holds such a dear place in my heart and parked our ride for the duration of the service, we marveled at the morning, the opportunity to canoe to church... and how pure and simple life can sometimes be... and just enjoyed every second of it.

Thank you Kipling Church, for the impact you've made on me, and so many others, bless you as you continue on into the future God has for you on Deer Lake in Northern Ontario.

## September 16th, 2009

### I Think My Plants Are Screaming

I was doing a little "gardening" today in my front yard, and for a second I imagined what it must be like from a plant's point of view. Not just any plants - MY plants. Every time I come out to visit them, they have four choices - small gardening spade, pruning scissors, saw or shovel. I don't think they mind the spade or the scissors, but they must scream at the sight of the saw or the shovel. Poor things.

When we bought our house 5 years ago, it had been rented out for the 12 years prior to that. Unkempt, mistreated, crowded and unloved - my garden needed a total overhaul - but first I had to get to it through all the weeds. Some plants didn't make it - the crab-apple trees with the huge thorns had to go, along with a good chunk of the raspberries that had taken over half the lawn. The fuchsia rose bush stayed, the pink phlox, the orange lilies and the solitary purple amaryllis.

And the lilac trees - I think we finally have an understanding. They've seen me come out with a saw, and use it, and they've thrived from the "pruning" (can you call it pruning when you use a saw?). I've left some of those glorious plants to grow into tall trees and some will have to make do as small bushes.

The rose bush constantly sees my scissors, yet it still thinks it can get the upper hand - rebellious, stubborn bush that it is.

The poor amaryllis was quite content to grow its solitary flower this year, basking in the knowledge that it's my husband's favourite flower, but sadly it wasn't my scissors, shovel, saw or spade that caused the pretty flower to meet its fate - instead it was a frisbee, thrown in good fun by my oldest son, that made that particular plant scream. We tried to save the precious flower by putting it in water, but its early end was inevitable.

Today I came out with the shovel. And I used it on my pink phlox. They were smack-dab in the middle of the lawn, and people were always tripping over them as they tried to play around the growing mass of pink. So I moved them beside the rose bush - hopefully the pink hues will blend together nicely, and harmony will reside in my garden.

I hope that's it for the shovel and the saw. I hope my plants don't have to scream anymore. I hope to just enjoy my garden, add a few more treasures this year and next, and give my plants a safe place to call home. They really have given me some wonderful sights and smells these past 5 years!


## October 7th, 2009

### How Am I Doing?

People have been asking me a lot about how I'm doing with my youngest son just starting school...

Well, I don't know how I'm doing most days. I am beginning a new phase in life - one in which I don't have a little boy hanging around with me 24/7. Now I get some hours to myself... but I'm still not sure how I feel about that.

Today was long. During the first few days without the boys I kept myself very busy with things around the house and the garden. But the weather turned nasty quick, and the jobs around our not-quite-finished-the-renovations house are still a little overwhelming. Most days I just look around and give up. But today I started a list of the still-to-do's, and I can work my way through it during the winter months. Can't believe how much there STILL is to do - but that's the nature of a total house-gut and rebuild - inside and out - what WERE we thinking?!

I really do have to say that it's beautiful, though, and becoming more and more everything we dreamed and visioned. On Sunday we had about 20 people in our house for a dessert party - and there was enough room for everyone (though I still need a few more places to sit!). Just what we hoped - a place where us and many others would feel loved, safe, happy and warm.

So that's good - the house is coming along, and it looks like that will be my part-time job this coming year - instead of paying huge amounts to ask other people to do all the jobs that still need doing. I enjoy the fixing up (who knew?), and hopefully it turns out nice through my efforts!

Back to the boys - I MISS THEM. Today I forgot their backpacks - discovered this when we arrived at school. Proceeded to drive home, pick up said backpacks and drive back to the school - totally worth it because my oldest son (just turned eight) actually gave me a kiss when I stopped in his class - right in front of everyone! Wow, that floored me, and it also made the drive back seem like a treat instead of a hassle. This morning my youngest son crawled into bed with me as he woke up, grabbed my face in his little hands, and said "You are so gorgeous." I mean honestly, it doesn't get any better than that! Sure there are crazy hard days when it seems like they just argue with me, cry, and fight with each other - but then I get mornings like today.... and I forget about the other stuff (for a little while at least!).

So that's how I'm doing. Accepting of the changes in life, continuing to treasure the precious moments with my boys, starting to enjoy the times to myself, looking towards what I can do instead of what I can't do, and taking it one day at a time.

And today was good.

**November 14th, 2009**

## I Was Amazed on a Recent Field Trip

This was my first field trip without my youngest son tagging along (which I never minded). I had a chance to hang out with my 8-year-old's Grade 3/4 class, spend time with his friends, and just check out the whole "scene" as we ventured off to a Remembrance Day Ceremony at the local arena. I was a little worried before I went - I didn't know if Josiah really wanted me to go. I'm nervous about overstepping my bounds as he gets older. He's my first, and he's absolutely teaching me everything I know about mothering boys. Poor guy! So I double-checked that he still wanted me to go, and he reassured me all was well, so I went!

I'm so glad I did... it started with me entering his classroom and him shouting, "Mommy!" The kids snickered a little, but it was all good. I smiled at them and joined the group. Then I didn't have a chair to sit on, and my little gentleman went across the room and got one for me. I find great hope in the chivalry that he showed me - one day I WILL have a daughter-in-law - and she will be AWESOME! Here's where I try not to start gushing about finally doing some girly things and playing with grandbabies (I'm way too young to think this way - good grief!).

The field trip just got better and better. Josiah saved me a seat on the bus - I was way behind him in line to get on the bus, and I came up the steps to the sound of him yelling, "Seat saved!" FOR ME! My heart came up my throat. We chatted on the way to the arena, we talked with some of his fellow classmates, and then the ultimate thing... the icing on the cake... he held my hand as we walked into the arena. Life does not get any better. I was more self-conscious than he was - wondering what the other kids were thinking, would they make fun of him later, hoping there weren't any bullies watching. Silly mommy.

I realized something great that day - Josiah is still my little boy. He's growing up more and more, he's almost as tall as me, he hates it when I try to pamper him, he's becoming more independent by the second, but he still does and always will love me. And sometimes he'll hold my hand on a field trip and proclaim to the world that he's happy that I'm with him, that I'm special enough to warrant getting a chair for me to sit on, and saving me a seat on the bus, and shouting, "Mommy!" with such joy at the sight of me.

Some days will be completely different, and I'll wonder where the field trip son went, but I'll know he's in there somewhere.

I catch these glimpses sometimes of the man he's becoming, and those glimpses are such a treat. On the field trip I caught a glimpse of how he'll treat the most special woman in his life. And one day that won't be me. I'll enjoy it while it's still my turn, but I'm also really, really, really happy that one day my little boy will make a woman feel so loved, cherished, and respected - like the way I felt on Wednesday.

Can't wait for the next field trip!


## December 1st, 2009

### Crispy Crunch for Santa

It started out as a quick trip to Sears to pick up a parcel. Then as I went to park in the usual area of the shopping mall lot, I just had to turn around and park in the lot I NEVER even think to park in. But it was pleasantly quiet, and I was glad for the change.

There were kiddie rides in the mall entrance and Elijah had to stop and try them all out, and what the hey, I even tried one out too!

Then at the Sears entrance, we saw him - Santa Claus (or a reasonable facsimile). He looked jolly enough and the only other child in sight was too busy proclaiming her disinterest in sitting on Santa's lap, so I gave Elijah the option of visiting with the man in red and white.

They had a lovely chat - Santa and Elijah. I watched them and smiled from a distance. Elijah informed Santa that he didn't like the candy canes Santa was giving out, and they went on to have an elaborate conversation about the best kind of candies and their favourite kinds of chocolate. From my eavesdropping I learned that

Elijah really wants Space Police Lego for Christmas (duly noted - already picked some out for him while in the Sears store) and that this particular Santa's favourite chocolate bar was Crispy Crunch.

An idea formed in my head and I presented it to Elijah - we agreed that it would be great to buy a Crispy Crunch for Santa and give it to him on our way back out of the mall.

Then I found out I'd gone to the wrong Sears store. HHHMmmmmmm.... what are you up to God? That happened to be the only reason I'd come to the mall (I avoid malls as much as possible, especially around Christmas). The only thing I could think of was that there was a Santa Claus in a shopping mall somewhere who happened to need a little boy to give HIM something for Christmas, so that maybe that would help him be a jolly old soul to all the kids who would visit him in the mall this Christmas season.

We found our Crispy Crunch at the other end of the mall, Elijah told the cashier who it was for, big smile on her face and "Say hi to Santa for me!" - first person blessed.

We retraced our steps to Santa, rehearsing what Elijah would say, my heart ecstatic at the idea - what fun! Then my little man went up and sat down beside Santa again, Crispy Crunch hidden behind his back. At just the right moment, he pulled it out and said "Here, this is your favourite. Merry Christmas." It's a good thing he'd chosen to wear his sunglasses to the mall that day, because his smile was bright enough to light up the whole place, along with everyone else's smiles at that moment. Second, third, and fourth persons blessed - Santa, Mrs. Claus and the photographer.

Mrs. Claus approaches Elijah and says, "You have such a wonderful spirit and a great big heart." Fifth person blessed - my Elijah.

We walked away, hand in hand, my son and I - sixth person blessed - me.

Sometimes I'm so in the moment that I can see it all, from every angle, and not miss a thing. Today I had one of those moments. There are times when life is so busy and distracting that I must miss a million moments, but today I didn't.

50

Thank You God for sending Elijah and I on a wonderful detour to the North Pole to give a little back and bless a lot of people - including You.


## December 14th, 2009

### The Brooch

Yesterday I was looking for something to spruce up my outfit a little. It was the annual Carols and Communion service at church, and I wanted to look somewhat nicer than usual.

I was rooting around in my jewelry box and came across a white brooch. Instantly I was back in time, to an era when my British grandmother used to twirl my 7-year-old hair gently into ringlets with wet rags before bedtime. In the morning I would wake up and untwirl the fabric, feeling like a princess. She wasn't able to visit often, her home was a farmhouse in the English countryside, and my home was in the suburbs of Toronto. But we had a connection, her and I, that spanned countries and generations.

I remember her letters, I remember her smile, I remember her soul. And I remember the brooch. I have two of them. Another she gave me just before she got on a plane bound for her homeland. I told her that her brooch was pretty and sparkly, then she pulled it off her coat, bent down to my level and placed the treasure in my little-girl hand.

This Christmas season I remember my Grandmother. Her name was Edith. She raised two boys in a centuries-old farmhouse called Denby Hill Farm in Oakworth, West Yorkshire. She washed her clothes by hand and did her dishes under a window that saw the cows walk by twice a day for milking. Her life was not easy, but her faith in God was strong.

I can imagine her looking out over the moors, the wind in her white curls, finding strength for the days ahead. Maybe that particular day was a Sunday. Maybe she'd found something extra-special to wear to church when she looked in her jewelry box that morning.

And maybe, just maybe, it was a white brooch.

51

# 2010

**January 6th, 2010**

**First Hello for 2010**

I'm not the most consistent blogger out there, nor the most organized. But I love to write these posts and connect with whoever reads them! So this is my first hello for 2010.

I was dusting my house (NOT my favourite thing to do!) and as the dust disappeared, so did the fogginess from my head. I feel like I've been in a daze since just before Christmas. We were able to see many of our family members this Christmas season, and I'm so grateful for that. It also meant putting about 3000 kms on the van! And after almost a week of being back in our house, getting back into a routine, and settling the boys back into school and activities, I feel pretty close to normal again.

What were the highlights of the holidays for me? Memories. Lots of them, with lots of different people, each one such a blessing. I loved watching the boys with grandparents, aunts, uncles, and cousins. I loved being in the homes of people I love, hearing their laughter, talking with them about life. I loved giving presents (and getting them is never a bad thing either! This year was the year of socks for me, but I love socks, and I got some funky ones!) and seeing the delight on the faces of those receiving the presents. I loved the snow falling, cozy rides in the van, sharing a room with my sons and hearing their sleepy breathing. I loved the unexpected moments like seeing my aunt, uncle and cousin at a birthday party for three of us with December birthdays, and playing piano with my 2-year-old nephew, and braiding my niece's hair, and tea with my sister-in-law in a cool cafe. I loved experiencing new traditions like the *Jesse Tree* and the *Jotham's Journey* book. I loved all the Christmas movies, I loved each cup of tea my mum made for me and served to me as I sat for a minute in her recliner and gathered strength, patience and enthusiasm for my two rambunctious boys. I loved the winter hike with my sons and my dad and discovering the frozen beaver dam across the river in their backyard. I loved spending time with my brother and my sister - she can make me laugh like no one else can!

I loved dinner out with my brother and sister-in-law and catching up on life with them. I loved HGTV for 2 hours on my birthday morning. I loved wrapping until 2 am so that I could just relax for the rest of the holidays.

I loved all of it, tired though I was by the end. And the icing on the cake was stopping to see the Dead Sea Scrolls at the Royal Ontario Museum on the way back home. What a wonderful conclusion to a wonderful season. I can't explain what the greatest thing was about seeing the pieces of parchment under the dim lights behind a black curtain that kept the ever-so-fragile words intact for all to see. I loved being able to show them to my sons, though the 4-year-old may not remember, I'll tell him of the time when... and the 8-year-old will always remember the magic of the moments in that room. The awe, the mystery, the sacredness of the exhibit. I have a picture stored away for my memories of the beautiful penmanship on the parchment, and my son peeking into the thick glass, stepping back in time for a brief while, seeing them writing the "Words that changed the world". And that blesses me to overflowing.

I hope your Christmas season was full of good memories too, though I know sometimes they are hard to see...

Looking forward to another year of connecting with you...


## January 12th, 2010

### The End of Another Day

They sleep, and soon I will sleep. Those loud, crazy, rambunctious boys of mine are quiet, peaceful, at rest.

Every night I put them to bed, and I hope that the memories they have from the day are good ones, encouraging ones, ones that build them up instead of tear them down, ones that grow them more and more into the men they were meant to be. And I hope that I played a part in those good memories somehow.

Every night I process the day, I relive the moments, I take away all I can from them - learning, changing, and planning what I would do if THAT moment comes up again, glad that I survived living it out the first time! (Even if my response was less than stellar) Or I laugh, enjoy and store away gems in my treasure box of motherhood, knowing THAT moment went really well, couldn't have gone any better.

I may not share all the bad when I write about being a mom. Not because I'm covering it up, or putting on a front, but because I just want to let it go, start afresh, tomorrow is another day, move on, hoping for good. I want to be real and transparent and honest, but I also want to leave the not-so-good behind. There are MANY hard times, bad times, frustration, anger, discouragement, doubt, confusion, you name it. But there are also MORE than many good times, and those are the ones I want to store away at the end of the day.

Tonight as I venture off to sleep, I look forward to the morning, to another day, to all that it will bring - hopefully good, but more than likely some bad too. The thing is... how will tomorrow end? That's up to me - letting go of the bad, holding on to the good - loving, learning, living the only life I've been given, as only I can.


**January 25th, 2010**

**Married to An Extrovert**

My husband recently took a test that scored him a 95% on the scale of **extro**vertedness. He loves to be the center of attention, he loves to be around people, and he loves to speak his mind. He absolutely loves an audience.

Then there's me. I would most likely score a 95% on the scale of **intro**vertedness if I were to take the same test. I long for time alone, love the quiet, need a few lessons in conflict resolution, and avoid attention at all costs.

There are two ways I could look at our situation - an extreme introvert living with an extreme extrovert. I could try to change him and be miserable with trying to keep up with his social schedule, or I could appreciate the differences in us and seek a balance that works for our social needs.

I tried the ideas mentioned first, but to no avail. Josh was quite happy with himself (as he should be), and I was exhausted from all the mingling.

After 10 years of marriage we've learned more and more about loving each other for who we are and trying to meet each other where we're at. I am free to stay home if I'm mingled-out, and he's free to sing in the grocery store. I remember when we first married, he would grab my hand as we did a few groceries, start belting out a big-band tune and twirl me around the aisle. It was more than I could handle most days, but he learned to tone it down, and I learned to live in the moment, red cheeks and all.

Today we had reason to visit a medical clinic (no worries, nothing major!), and as soon as we walked into the small waiting room, I could feel the inspiration building in Josh. A little girl was trying to keep herself amused in a very boring atmosphere, and she was singing a song and dancing around. He immediately started singing and dancing along. He had the whole waiting room laughing. And I stood beside him and smiled. It took me back to when I first met him - I was a receptionist at a chiropractor's office and he was a patient. Every time he came in for an appointment he would have everyone laughing within minutes. I remember sitting behind my desk, pulling up his file on the computer, and checking to see if he was my age.

One of the reasons I love that man is for his freedom. And I no longer want to change him to make life "easier" and less "embarrassing" for me. I just want to love him, as best I can, with all I've got. Do I look forward to dancing in the grocery aisles? Some days... I'm getting there...

*P.S. As soon as my husband read this post, he had a great idea - I should write a blog solely about him. Ever the extrovert. I replied, "So you can have an even bigger audience!" And we had a good chuckle about it.*

Josh wrote an article to give you a look at the flip side:

**Living With An Introvert...**

Having been married to my beautiful wife Anna for over ten years, I have come to realize the truth of the expression, "Opposites attract."

In a course I completed a few years ago, we both did a battery of tests and profiles. One showed our personality trait in the area of extrovert vs introvert. The person who went over the materials with me shared that he had never seen a couple so far apart on the scale as the two of us.

Thinking that her shyness was something to be fixed, I tried to introduce her to the outgoing life in a few ways. To start with, I just dragged her along on my hectic and relational schedule and figured that she would pick it up as we went along. All she did was get tired.

I went back to the drawing board and tried to slowly turn the temperature up a degree at a time with the same results. At the end of the day when everyone had gone home, and I was chomping at the bit and ready for more, she was cocooned in a blanket in a catatonic state on the couch.

And then one day it hit me (no, Anna didn't hit me, I was too quick).

I realized that all the energy that I was pouring into others relationally could be better spent if I poured some of it just into her. And as I took the time to sit with her and watch the sunset, stroll along the boardwalk at the lake, or read in bed before turning out the lights, I saw a wonder and beauty that I had sometimes missed.

Yes, I saw the beauty of the setting sun and the cool evening breeze off the lake, but most of all, the beauty inside Anna that I fell in love with. A strong and peaceful spirit that tries to live in each moment and helped me to do the same.

Yes, I am comfortable in the spotlight. Yes, I am energized by being with others and laughing, talking, and playing. Yes, there are roles that I must fulfill that require me to do these things. But more than that, I have come to realize that I am most at home when I am with Anna and fulfilling the most important roles in my life - husband and father.

## February 3rd, 2010

## Living in the Moments

My little men sleep. But oh, how annoyed they'd be with those words! So I'll subtly change that first sentence to read *My **young** men sleep.* For there is nothing little about my two sons. They have big personalities, big voices, big imaginations, big ideas and most important of all - big hearts. Thank God I get to be loved by these two young men.

This blog of mine is called *Living In The Moments*. Yet I find that lately I've been living those moments once the boys are asleep, once all is quiet, once I can reflect and process and play out the day just one more time. I wish for, hope for, long for a change in me that allows me to live in the moments while there's still daylight!

To **really** look into my son's eyes and see the ultimate beauty of innocence, purity and child-like wonder. To **really** hear their laughter that fills my house with sounds sweeter than any music I've ever heard. To **really** play with them, no inhibitions, no to-do lists, no chores or schedules looming in the back of my mind. To absolutely live in the moment. Oh God, I ask for so much more of this in my days. That it won't all just blur together into a haze of fatigue and mundane. To be able to see the depth in their eyes, hear the joy in their laughter, live in their world as we play.

Tonight as I peek at them sleeping soundly in their beds, may I remember the day with such clarity and peace and joy because I lived in today with my boys. And not have a sense of missed opportunities or drudgery from the day. Please let it be so tonight, and tomorrow night, and the next night and the next - on into forever. Living in as many moments as I can cram into a day, even if we never leave the house for a second.

It's all about enjoying them and the gifts they are to me. Hoping to be a gift to them. Thank You God, for the wonder of motherhood, and all the unexpected treasures it's given me these past 8 years.

**February 7th, 2010**

**Laryngitis Wasn't the Answer I Was Looking For**

Have you read my last post about wanting to really live in the moments with my boys? I expressed my heart-felt cry to really hear their laughter in my days, look deep into their wonderful eyes, and play like I had nothing else to do.

Laryngitis wasn't the answer I was looking for, but it's the answer I got. I'm not saying I was stricken with illness to teach me a lesson, but in the illness I find the lesson learned. It started Thursday with the beginnings of aches and fatigue and a sore throat. Friday my voice came and went as it willed, and I was forced to listen instead of speak. What a gift! I know that sounds crazy, but that was the day I **really** heard their laughter! In **my** silence, I heard **them**.

Saturday my voice was completely lost. I was forced to communicate with whispers, facial expressions and wild hand gestures. In the lack of words, I spoke in part with my eyes, and that was the day I **really** looked into theirs.

Today I stayed home from church and a playdate with another family. I was really upset about missing out on what I knew would be a day full of play. In their absence, I spent time with them the only way I could, and I used my day to finally(!) get the photo albums in order. I flipped the pages, filled in the blanks with memories on film, and was forced to looks at years past. I came to realize there have been many times these last 8 years that I have **really** played with my boys. What a treat to realize that truth! To look back on the years and know that they hold such grand adventures and discoveries and milestones and lots and lots of smiles for all.

I know the illness is leaving me, and I'm so glad for that. I think today was the day I made the switch from sick to better. As life returns to normal, will I take the lesson learned with me into the days that come? Will I listen? Will I look? Will I play? Well... I hope.

**February 21st, 2010**

**Scenes From the Soul – I See You**

She sits at her computer, focused on the work at hand. When she started her work it had been a dreary winter day. Nothing but gray sky and snowy ground had greeted her when she looked out her office window. It was hardly worth opening the blind. But the scene outside had changed as the minutes counted down her busy day. She was almost done her work, it was almost time to leave, and she suddenly felt a warmth through the window that spread to her soul, beckoning her to stop, to look, to listen. She turned her face to the sun and heard His voice. The voice that was unmistakable, unshakable, unimaginable. So clear, so beautiful, so real.

*I see you child. I see you working. I see your ideas, your plans, your dreams. Don't be afraid of them, don't let go of them, don't detour from them. I put them there and I will use them for My glory. My purposes are more than you can fathom. Just trust me. Leave it with me. Don't carry it all on your shoulders. You were never meant to.*

*I see you child. When you think you are not enough for the task ahead, remember that I am enough. Every word is from me. Hear them in your soul and share them with others. I will take those words where I want them to go. I will use your efforts, your obedience and your trust for such wonderful things. One day I'll share with you all we've accomplished - together.*

*I see you child. I see the woman you are today. I saw the woman you were yesterday. I see the woman you will one day be. She is absolutely breathtaking because her heart has been mine for many, many years. Truly mine. I'll give you glimpses of her once in a while, but you are not ready to be that woman yet. You need to grow into her shoes. Always remember how beautiful you are today, simply because I see you through My eyes of love, and you are My perfect child. Made holy by My Son. Redeemed, pure, **mine**.*

*Never forget that I see you child, I love you child, and you are **good**.*

**February 27th, 2010**

**New Version of Old Poem**

My mum had a poem hung on her wall that I memorized early on in life. She cross-stitched the letters into words that made a real impact on me, and I remember them even now. My first blog post ever was about those words. Here they are again, along with an updated version of my own that I've thrown in. (Note: I realize it's truly ironic that I'm writing this in my blog, using my computer!)

| Mum's Poem | My Updated Version |
|---|---|
| Cleaning and scrubbing | Emailing and blogging |
| can wait till tomorrow... | are for another day… |
| for babies grow up | for my boys will grow up |
| we've learned to our sorrow... | and stop wanting to play... |
| so quiet down cobwebs.... | so close down the inbox... |
| dust go to sleep... | turn off computer's hum... |
| I'm rocking my baby | Boys want new adventures |
| and babies don't keep! | And mommy wants to come! |

-excerpt from *Song for a Fifth Child* by Ruth Hulburt Hamilton

**March 7th, 2010**

**Got His Motor Runnin'**

My husband has wanted a motorcycle forever. But I was always just way too afraid of the whole thing. Something changed in me last year - I didn't want to be the reason for unrealized dreams in our marriage. And yes, I'm still afraid!

So last summer my husband scoped out the best price and best kind of motorcycle he could find. He purchased a 1982 Honda Nighthawk in excellent condition and aced a motorcycle driver's course. But he couldn't get the motorcycle started for the life of him once it was sitting cozy in our shed. Patiently he tinkered with it, got advice, purchased a few small parts and finally took it for a spin at the end of last summer.

It's still winter here in Northern Ontario, but it's uncharacteristically warm, and the sunshine was calling all three of my men today. They've been out for hours. And my husband pulled the bike out of storage for its first glimpse of sunny weather this season. BUT he couldn't get it started. I came out for some chit-chat and as soon as I walked past the bike, it caught and roared to life. I just know it's beckoning me. But I'm not in the least bit ready to sit on that Nighthawk. Maybe one day. Maybe one day I'll take a motorcycle course and buy my own bike. Maybe one day we'll drive them clear across the country. But not today.

Enjoy your first summer of motorcycle riding Joshua - you've waited a long time for this! But as you head out on the highway, remember the adventure waits at home, and MIGHT join you one day... MIGHT.


## March 16th, 2010

### Laughter in the Turbulence

There's a bit too much in my heart to write about all in one post, but I wanted to start to process it all, and this is the only way I know how.

My son was sick - just a run-of-the-mill flu that gave him some shakes, fever and fatigue. After a few days he got better. Then he got worse. High fever and vomiting sent us straight to the hospital. But his symptoms were still hiding - an ultrasound showed it wasn't appendix, further tests showed it wasn't meningitis. Then his eye started to swell, and we suddenly knew. He had developed sinusitis and it had spread to his eye. But how bad was the situation? A CT scan showed the spreading was only into the front of his eye - the skin around his eye, and not to the back which would have been oh so much worse because that's where the Central Nervous System and the Brain hang out.

IV started because of severe dehydration, pain meds started for his increasing pain, antibiotics started to fight the infection, prayer started to stop any further spreading of the attack on his body. Arrangements were made to air-lift him to a more equipped children's hospital hundreds of kilometers away. Daddy went with him, mommy caught the next plane which left 6am the following morning. Friends rallied, younger brother put into care of wonderful friends, prayer cover increased around the globe.

I sit on the plane which would take me to join my husband and son, and I cry, and I pray, and I plead with God to make it all OK. And then I hear laughter. A little girl's laughter. Across the aisle from me. There was some turbulence, and while all the adults were scared and clutching their armrests, she was laughing with utter delight. And I thought if only I could be so trusting, so sure, so confident that even though we never know the outcome of turbulence, the main thing is to enjoy the ride.

I'll never forget the sound of her laughter, God's gift to me during one of the darkest days of my life. And I'll learn from that laughter for the rest of my days.

Today I can breathe again, my son sleeps soundly in his room, the eye swelling is decreasing, the pain is decreasing, the nausea is gone, his spirits are high, and once again I hear his laughter during my days. And his laughter makes me laugh, and I continue to ride out the turbulence.


**April 26th, 2010**

**Service With a Smile**

My oldest son had an idea the other day. He came to Josh and I with a request to make the bedtime snack, to make something a little special for his brother. Please understand - the way these two boys fight sometimes, I almost broke down in tears just from the words "I want to make a surprise for Elijah". They really do love each other - yes they do! Hallelujah!

Josiah laid out the plan - starting with a piece of toast (he's gotten very good with the toaster oven), then a layer of jam, then some fruit for eyes, nose and mouth. We would keep Elijah out of the scene until the surprise was completed, then TA-DA!

There was apprehension - would his little brother like the surprise? When Elijah discovered there would be a surprise, his mind immediately went to the toy he'd like most that day. So would he like the gift if it came from the heart (and the kitchen), and not from the toy store? I reassured him his brother would LOVE it, because he LOVES Josiah.

The surprise went according to plan - I let Josiah make the whole thing, I was only there if he needed me, oh, and I did cut the apple slice for the mouth and halve the grape for the eyes, and I did wash the strawberry nose. Then came the presentation - the perfect plate and the perfect spot. It was all ready.

A shout up the stairs brought our youngest son down to his surprise.... and... he LOVED it! They were both grinning from ear to ear - the blessed and the blesser. It was absolutely amazing for my mommy-heart to see that, and to have that memory for my treasure box of motherhood.

I'm TRYING to hear my boys - REALLY hear them, to let them work out their own personalities, to mess up my schedules and plans sometimes, and to just be in the moment.

This little plate of love, toast, fruit and jam was a beautiful act of service - with a smile. Smiles all around. A wonderful thing to all who had a part in making and devouring it.


**May 10th, 2010**

**Scenes From the Soul – Jesus in the Every-Days**

She went about her day, just like any other day full of errands, household chores, and caring for her family. They had just come back from vacation and things were a little muddled. She began by taking her oldest son to a non-existent dentist appointment, then proceeded with the grocery shopping, the oil change for the van, and the hunt for tulle to make a veil for an up-coming wedding. It was all very mundane. But as she drove home, most of her tasks completed, the grayness of the mundane dispersed and she saw what had really happened that day. She'd really spent the day with her Saviour, letting Him lead a little, following Him as He went about His purposes for her day.

*Did you see me at the fabric store? Did you see My grace in you as you talked with the clerk who was adamant that they'd never carried the tulle you needed, though I know you'd bought it there many times before? All she needed was a simple smile and thank you, instead of a fight with a stubborn customer. Thank you for letting me be there with you.*

*Did you see me at Walmart? Did you see My encouragement in you as you started a conversation with the woman who tends that beautiful garden down the street? You've always admired that garden, you've seen it at least twice a day for the past 6 years, driving in and out of your neighbourhood. I set up the perfect "coincidence" for you today - to run into the garden lady. I know it was hard for you to start the conversation, I know how shy you are at times, and I heard you as you prayed "If I see her one more time I'll say something" It only took three of those prayers today! Then I knew you could not deny the inevitable and I gave you the perfect words to encourage the garden lady and put a smile on her face today and let her know someone appreciates the beauty in her hard work. Don't worry, it gets easier the more you do it, and maybe next time you'll only pray one of those "If" prayers! Ha ha and thank you for making Me smile.*

*Did you see me at the grocery store? Did you see my compassion in you as you stopped, just for a moment, and noticed the care that man took to clean up those carts? It was important to him, and you listened as he told you, and you helped him clean up the last few carts. Did you hear him say thank you?*

She returns to her house and her chores, and the mundane-ness stays away for the rest of the day... and maybe the next day and the next too? And she realizes that with Jesus, there is no mundane.

## May 24th, 2010

### Remembering Caleb

When May 19 - 23 rolls around every year, it is never an easy time for Josh and I. These few days mark the anniversary of the time between the discovery of the stillbirth of our middle son, Caleb, and laying him to rest in the cemetery. That was in 2003.

May 19 was the day when the doctors couldn't find his heartbeat, May 21 was the day he was delivered, and May 23 was his funeral and burial. This year the remembering began on a Wednesday.

Wednesday brought a bittersweet time as I helped a friend pack up her baby clothes to get ready for an upcoming move. I found a few precious items in the piles that I had passed along to her - clothes my boys have worn over the years, and the memories of them as I held those clothes again reminded me that God has given me two sons to raise, and one was His to raise. Caleb will never wear that Christmas outfit I remember buying 8 years ago for his older brother, instead he'll be forever clothed with the beauty of heaven.

Friday was Caleb's birthday and we launch a helium balloon into the sky every year. We go to a park with our sons, we pray, we all hold the string and kiss the balloon, we sing Happy Birthday and we let it go together. We see who can keep it in sight the longest - Josh always wins. This year wasn't as sad as other years. This year Josiah had the idea to include jelly beans for Caleb, and Elijah wanted to include a verse. He picked one that we had read that morning. So we attached the candy and verse to the balloon string and we marveled at how our boys are making this celebration their own. Elijah shouted out "Here comes your present Caleb! Don't forget to get your present!" And I laugh and take joy in what I have, because that's the best thing I can do to honour my Caleb, and I blow a kiss to the heavens, and I watch my boys play at the park.

Sunday is the last day to of the intense remembering. The day of Caleb's funeral and burial. This year we were at church and *Teen Challenge* was visiting. A wonderful ministry that helps men overcome their addictions and sets them free to experience God's love and new life. They share their stories and they sing. I love it when they visit. As the service comes to an end, Josh spontaneously asks the men to sing one more song. They are caught by surprise, but they pick a song - or should I say God picks a song and whispers it to them and they begin to sing... *I Can Only Imagine*. This was the song that spoke to our hearts the most during May 19 - 23 of 2003. This was the song that we played at Caleb's funeral. This was the song that inspired the words on Caleb's gravestone - *Surrounded By Glory*. And as they sing God's gift to us that morning, I look at the men singing, and I picture them standing beside Caleb one day and I see the look in their eyes when they realize how God used them the morning of May 23, 2010 at All Nations Church. I am reminded of how much God loves us, and how seamlessly He weaves everything together. We just have to trust. We have to trust because there is nothing else to do.

And so our intense time of remembering Caleb comes to an end for 2010. It's been 7 years. It doesn't get easier, and I guess I hope it never does. But it does get better, fuller, more of joy than sadness, more of looking forward to meeting him than constantly missing him.

We will always remember Caleb, he is part of our family, he is part of our days, he is part of our hope, and he is part of our future. And that's always a wonderful thing to remember.

Love you angel boy - big kisses from Mommy!


## May 26th, 2010

### Ouch

I got a blister from gardening last week. It's right on the joint of my finger, so it's taking a while to heal, it got infected and it hurts!

Yesterday it occurred to me that I'm putting a lot of focus on my little boo-boo. In the midst of the slight pain I feel from it, I totally forget about all the things that are going right with my body. I'm overall in very good health and no complaints to speak of! I take my good health for granted all the time.

I think it's like that in all areas of my life. My first tendency is to notice what's not working right, what's not efficient, what's hurting me or others I love. The Gratitude Community I joined is helping me focus on the positive and learning to let go of my perfectionism (at least in some areas!), it helps me relax and enjoy the wonderful things in my life a little more.

It gets easier to see the good in my days, which far outweigh the bad. With God there is always good, because He is good.

My boo-boo is healing and so am I - from my pessimism and perfectionism. More smiles, more laughter, more peace - a win-win situation. Yes, I still hurt, still feel pain and still need to heal, but in the midst of that I can find ALOT of good.

What are the good things in your life? Start to make a list and see how it changes you from the inside out!

## July 15th, 2010

### Glimpses of Heaven

A week ago I was swimming in a Northern Ontario Lake at sunset. My husband and my sons joined me for the swim. Just us. It felt like we had the whole lake to ourselves. We laughed together, played together and cooled off together. We stopped for a "cloud moment" and gazed at the many types of clouds God had laid across the horizon just for us to see. Or so it felt like that night.

Sometimes I get these glimpses of heaven, of what life will be like one day in eternity. No sadness, anger, sin, frustration. Just pure joy. No hurt, murder, fighting, evil. Just indescribable love. No earthquakes, tsunamis, hurricanes or floods. Just complete rest.

But then I realize it will be way, way better than anything I can imagine, and I shake my head with incredulity, and I carry on in the moments I've been given, taking that gift with me. That gift of a glimpse of what will be. And I thank God that just for a split second I got to live it out here.

## July 16th, 2010

### You Beckon Me

Suddenly I feel Your presence
As You beckon me from across the green field
Trees, flowers, water, peace, quiet await
You want to share it with me
You want to talk with me
You want me to come to You
As You beckon me
I walk across the green, green grass
The trees speak Your name
In the rustling of their leaves
The birds sing Your praise
In their melodies from on high
The sun shines Your light
In the radiance from above
And I feel You
Your warmth
Your comfort
Your peace
Your love
For me
For all I see
For everyone
I'm so glad I heard Your voice today
May I hear it every day
As You beckon me

**August 14<sup>th</sup>, 2010**

## Blueberry Fields Forever

*Therefore I tell you, do not worry about your life, what you will eat or drink; or about your body, what you will wear. Is not life more important than food, and the body more important than clothes? Look at the birds of the air; they do not sow or reap or store away in barns, and yet your heavenly Father feeds them. Are you not much more valuable than they? Who of you by worrying can add a single hour to his life?*

*And why do you worry about clothes? See how the lilies of the field grow. They do not labor or spin. Yet I tell you that not even Solomon in all his splendor was dressed like one of these. If that is how God clothes the grass of the field, which is here today, and tomorrow is thrown into the fire, will he not much more clothe you, O you of little faith? So do not worry, saying, 'What shall we eat?' or 'What shall we drink?' or 'What shall we wear?' For the pagans run after all these things, and your heavenly Father knows that you need them. But seek first his kingdom and his righteousness, and all these things will be given to you as well. Therefore do not worry about tomorrow, for tomorrow will worry about itself. Each day has enough trouble of its own. - Matthew 6:25-34*

I stand in the middle of the blueberry bushes and I look around at all the tiny blue bundles of delicious goodness, and I am in total awe of God's generosity. Miles upon miles of blueberry bushes - each one full to the brim, there for the taking by whatever animal or human comes to feast.

No matter how many berries I pick, no matter how many birds or bears enjoy them as their next meal, there will always be more. There is no need to worry about not having enough, no need to fight over who gets what, there is more than plenty for all. Such is the generosity of God.

If only we could see it. If only we stopped worrying about His provision. If only we trusted Him just a little more.

May I be like a lily in the field - in the blueberry field - and know that tomorrow is taken care of before I even open my eyes. Any worrying that I do is unnecessary and fruitless.

For I am loved by a mighty, generous God.

-   *Written while camping at Halfway Lake in Northern Ontario*

## August 16<sup>th</sup>, 2010

### The Simple Things

There is at least a little pioneer in me. My grandparents were farmers on the hills of England, my dad helped to tend the farm for many years of his life. My mother is an avid gardener and can grow just about anything. I come from two people who love to work the land, who love to care for nature, who see the possibilities in the earth around them.

I often find it hard to keep up with the world around me. I seek out renewal and refreshment in playing with my sons, cooking a delicious meal from scratch, reading a good book, or being in the great outdoors. The simple things.

At the moment I'm writing this I sit in our tent-trailer, parked at a camp in Northern Ontario. The wind is so strong I may be lifted off the ground as I put my pencil to paper, the clouds are moving fast across the sky, and the trees are laughing as they dance a jig on the air rushing ever so quickly through their leaves. The simple things.

These are things that money can't buy, things God bestows on His children, in abundance, on a daily basis. Love, family, friends, laughter, conversation, nature, words. The simple things.

Such a delicate balance exists between just enough and too much. I clean the clutter from my house at least 2 times a year - a complete overhaul. I restore balance for a short while until the clutter starts to creep in again. There is this longing in me sometimes for more, newer, cleaner, faster or easier things in life. But I've come to learn that it's the simple things that bring me peace and balance. And when I forget this truth, as I know I will, it's a wonderful feeling to rest in the simple things when I finally remember to look for them. Feels like home. The simple things.

## August 18th, 2010

### Nothing Too Good For My Family

I love my husband and my sons with all my heart. I want the best for them. I feel like nothing is too good for them. Then I realize that often times I don't meet my own expectations.

For a long time, at the end of each day, I would replay the events, conversations and general happenings of the hours gone by. I would constantly try to figure out better ways of fulfilling my roles - from caring for my sons, to cooking and cleaning, to my relationship with my husband. I relentlessly heaped the pressure on myself, always thinking that I needed to be more and do more for my family. I never met my own expectations. I was never good enough. It was exhausting.

I finally had a lightbulb moment. My job was to be the best I could be, not try to be someone else. My job was to listen to what God was asking ME to do, not what He was asking others to do. My job was to love my family for WHO THEY ARE, not try to change them into people they are not.

Such freedom came the moment I first realized I was free to be me, Josh was free to be Josh, and Josiah and Elijah were free to be Josiah and Elijah! Such joy came as I realized that my job was to enjoy these men (both young and not-so-young) that God has given me to share my life with.

I still experience relapses in my perfectionism, but they occur less and less. The burden I put on myself is becoming lighter and lighter. I am good enough, Josh is good enough, Josiah and Elijah are good enough. More than good enough.

God put our personalities together to form a family - Team Sklar - and I'm excited to discover more of who we are in the years to come!

## August 21st, 2010

### Calming the Storm

*Then he got into the boat and his disciples followed him. Without warning, a furious storm came up on the lake, so that the waves swept over the boat. But Jesus was sleeping. The disciples went and woke him, saying, "Lord, save us! We're going to drown!"*

*He replied, "You of little faith, why are you so afraid?" Then he got up and rebuked the winds and the waves, and it was completely calm. - Matthew 8: 23-26*

I had tucked my children in to peaceful slumber in the camper on a mild August evening. We were all tuckered out from a day of fun in the sun with good friends at Family Camp. Not much time could have passed before I awoke with a start.

The camper was lighting up with trails of lightning scurrying across the night sky. Thunder boomed and roared as it chased the lightning across the dark clouds. This game of tag between the elements roused me from sleep with instant terror. My heart was beating fast, my eyes were wide open, there was no slipping back into restful unconsciousness.

Then I glanced at my children - still peaceful, still slumbering, not a hint of terror on their cherub faces. I was instantly reminded of the story of Jesus calming the storm. I was just like one of the panicked disciples, fearing the worst. Then I looked at my children again and realized they were just like Jesus, they showed no concern for the imminent dangers of the camper being hit by lightning, flooded by rain or picked up and swept away by the wind! They... just... slept.

I prayed that God would calm the storm, just as Jesus did, but the celestial game of tag carried on through the night, oblivious to the curfews of the camp. I couldn't tell who was "it", the thunder and lightning were giddy with the fun of it all - constantly catching each other, it seemed there was no end to their antics.

Then I prayed for peace, that I'd be able to sleep through the storm, just like my boys, just like Jesus. There I found the lesson learned, there I found the peace, and as I drifted into slumber once again, I heard this saying playing in my mind:

*Sometimes God calms the storm... sometimes He lets the storm rage and calms His child.*

And I learn yet another wonderful lesson from my children and I thank God for them once again.


## August 23rd, 2010

### Sing to Me Mommy

My boys listen to worship music as they fall asleep each night. Our current CD of choice is *Arriving* by Chris Tomlin.

When my boys were younger I would sing them to sleep. It started one night when Josiah was 1 and became a habit after a while. After Elijah arrived on the scene almost 4 years later than Josiah, my oldest son had an instant roomie. They shared a room until Josiah was 6 and shared a double bed for a while when neither one wanted to sleep alone.

I would crawl in between them, lie down to read them a Bible story, and then start singing. I have a repertoire that's developed through the years. My first two songs are *Lord Prepare Me* and *Create In Me A Clean Heart*. It's been a while since I sang to them. They have their own rooms now and my husband and I alternate which one we tuck in at night.

At Family Camp this year we sang a familiar tune in chapel - *Lord Prepare Me*. As soon as the words popped up on the screen, my youngest (who is just starting to read) said, "Mommy, you know this song. You sang it to me when I was a baby going to sleep." The biggest smile appeared on my face and spread to my heart. He remembered. We exchanged a precious smile and we went on to sing the song.

When *Create In Me A Clean Heart* showed up on the screen another day, and my son remembered that one as well, I thanked God for the wonderful gift He was giving to me on the cusp on my older son's 9th birthday. Only God knows how I love my boys, how I've cherished the moments as best I could, how I look forward to a lifetime of more moments and how sometimes it's not easy to watch them grow, but it is the biggest blessing in my life.

And so the gifts kept coming that week. The night before my son's 9th birthday he couldn't sleep at all. After about an hour I remembered the songs, the ones that used to put him to sleep when he was younger. I asked if he wanted me to sing. He said, "Yes please" and he was out in an instant.

Another night the power was out as we lay in the tiny cabin that was home for the night at a camp we were visiting. My oldest son asked, "Can you sing to us? Your beautiful voice always puts us to sleep." And so I sang once more, and the peaceful sounds of slumber soon came over Bunkie #3.

Just now, as I was writing this down to share with you, I was given yet another gift. I asked my youngest son to give me a few minutes of quiet, so I could think, I asked him to go see his daddy. I heard him speak to Josh for a minute and offer to sing him back to sleep. And so I hear the words to *Lord Prepare Me* once more, this time from the mouth of my little-more-than-a-babe, and my heart is full to the brim.

They do listen, they do learn, they do take what we have to give them, and they grow in it.

And I continue to share life with my boys, no matter how old they get, knowing they'll always need something of me and I'll always need something of them.

**August 27th, 2010**

**Leap of Faith**

My older son and my husband have so much fun on the rope swing

at Family Camp every year. For the past 3 summers I have watched as they grab onto the thick rope, jump off the platform and skim gracefully over the surface of the water, before letting go of the rope and plunging joyfully into the lake below.

This year I knew it was my turn. I was tired of sitting on the sidelines while they had all the fun. So I watched carefully at the different techniques used, planned out a strategy, and on the third day of camp I got up the nerve to jump, or at least stand on the platform and "see how it goes."

I waited until it was quiet - my husband had told everyone I was going to jump, so I knew there was a possibility of an audience, which was NOT cool with me. Apparently no woman had jumped for at least a few years, so the excitement was building in the rope swing community at camp.

My boys were in disbelief. "Are you really going to jump Mom?" I responded with a weak "I want to try it. We'll see what happens when I get on the platform."

I slowly walked over to the stairs, taking each one carefully so as not to slip. I made it up to the platform and told the lifeguard of my aspirations for jumping that day. The polite young man smiled at me under his fluorescent pink hat. I let a couple of boys go ahead of me, then I took my place on the edge of the platform. I grabbed the rope and... froze. Fear and lots of it kept me prisoner on that ledge for a few long moments. My boys cheered me on from the dock below. My husband had joined the tiny crowd that had gathered at the foot of the swing. I looked at the lifeguard and asked, "Does everyone take this long to jump the first time?" The polite, smiling young man reassured me that others take up to 10 minutes.

I still had time.

I looked at the water far below, I looked at the ledge I was perched on, I looked at the rope that kept both my son's and my husband's lives intact each time they flew out over the water, I looked at my two boys on the dock, and.... I... JUMPED!

It's all a blur from there, there was nothing graceful about the jump, no skimming across the surface of the water, no smile from ear to ear, just a look of pure terror that I'm sure was there until the KERPLUNK of my water-landing wiped it clean off my face. I remember lots of water up my nose, scrambling to reach the surface of the water, and then... cheers, applause, smiles (on my face too!) and a sense of wonder that a moment ago I'd been perched precariously on the ledge above.

This may sound ridiculous, but the jump changed me. It was really, truly awesome to take that leap. I jumped many times after that, and only one of them actually worked so that I skimmed across the water. The point is that I jumped - ALOT. I failed a lot too. But the one time it worked was well worth all the other failed attempts.

I think life is like that. There are so many chances to jump, to take leaps of faith, so many opportunities to grow and change and just have fun! Sometimes fear holds us back, or time of life, or a whole host of reasons. No matter if we jump and kerplunk, or leap and fall, the only tragedy would be in never getting up on that platform, looking out over the expanse, feeling the gaze of loved ones, jumping into the unknown, and hoping to soar.


## September 23rd, 2010

### Being Jesus At School

I never thought I'd be a lunch room supervisor. I giggle every time I say it. It seems so foreign to what I thought I'd be doing in my life at 36!

That was before I became a mom. Before we started raising two boys. Before we decided to send them to public school. Before I started hearing the stories of their days. Before I learned of the brokenness that exists even at the youngest of ages.

Before the desire grew and grew and grew to reach out however I could to children of the younger generation.

It started in September 2005 when I dropped off my older son for his first day of school.

I watched and listened and learned about Josiah's school, his teachers, and his classmates. We started praying on the drive to school, praying for individual classmates at bedtimes, and praying through the halls whenever we could. I volunteered whenever possible in the midst of caring for our younger son who was born 3 months before Josiah started school.

In September 2009 it was time to drop Elijah off for his first day of school.

This past year the desire to reach out grew stronger still, so I knew it was time to take action.

I volunteered to be a Sunday school teacher at church, and that continues to be very rewarding for me, but it didn't satisfy my desire to reach out beyond church walls; to be a light in the darkness instead of waiting for the darkness to come to the light.

I repeatedly noticed the need for library volunteers and lunch room supervisors in the school newsletters. I started volunteering in the library but came to realize I really wanted to be interacting with the children.

It would have to be the lunch room supervisor position for me.

So here I am. It's September 2010. It's only been a few days since classes started, but already I am very glad for my role at the school.

Already I can see why God has me where I am.

Already I am praying for specific students.

I hope that Jesus' light will shine through me to these children, that they can catch a glimpse of His love for them. I hope I am a good representative of His grace and mercy.

I hope that after a while people will notice something different, something changed about the class and they'll know somehow that Christ is a part of the good that has come.

I'm also back to volunteer in the school library a little, which is a bonus because I just love books. I hope to be a part of putting great resources into the hands of the children in the school.

The children that have come to hold such a deep place in my heart.


**November 5th, 2010**

**The Words That Remain**

The words are there, just when I need them, always. They remain, they are a constant, some going back decades, others new to me. Words of the Bible. Words of God. It's like riding a bike - you never forget how to peddle and balance. Like learning to play the piano –

seven years of lessons that allow me to play a tune whenever I feel like it. I just KNOW those things. They are part of me, ingrained, remaining with me though the years pass along sometimes at an alarming rate.

The verses come, whenever I need them. Sometimes I can't remember where to find them in the Book, sometimes I skip words and the poetry of the verse is lost as I speak, but the truth, the wisdom, the peace, and the love are never lost.

I've been speaking them more into my life lately - the Words That Remain. Reading them every morning, and never getting enough. Hearing them in my heart and trying so hard to listen. Sharing them with my sons and hoping they hear The Writer in His words.

I don't have a plan right now, I don't know how to get more of them into my life, except to keep reading, keep learning, keep growing in the Words That Remain.

## November 6th, 2010

### I Always Wanted to Be a Teacher

Do you remember what you wanted to be when you were younger? I remember one of the things I wanted most to be was a teacher. I dreamed of standing in front of a group of children and helping them learn all the basics of education.

A little while ago I realized I am living out my dream. There is still much of that little girl in me, and once in a while I meet up with her, catch a glimpse of her in the woman I am today. Sometimes she smiles and thanks me for making her dreams come true, and other times there is disappointment in her face - but I'll leave those

thoughts for another day. And there are times when the little girl inside me shows me something about myself - something so beautiful and rare and precious.

Sometimes she shows me that God's plans reign supreme, and no matter how many mistakes I made or how much others have hurt me, no matter how bruised and battered I feel some days, God has always been working out His plans for me, whether I saw that truth or not.

And so even though I don't get a teacher's salary or stand in front of a classroom full of children every weekday, I am still living out my dream of being a teacher. The four walls of my home are my classroom, the two little faces most dear to my heart are the students that look to me for direction and wisdom. My teaching aids are my Bible, my life and my heart. My curriculum consists of the most ancient words on earth and how to live out those words in our lives today.

Teachers rarely just "wing it". They learn the material before they teach it to their students. They plan and prepare and have lesson plans and attend training workshops and rely on support from other teachers. They are guided by the principal of the school. They pour out more than 30 hours a week with the children in their classrooms.

And so I must make sure I am learning my material well, developing the faith in my own life that I hope to pass along to my sons. I must plan and prepare for my role. I must find resources and ideas and have an idea of what I want to teach my children that day or that week. I must gather around me others who are filling the same role, so we can support each other in that role. And I must take my guidance from God, let Him help me with issues that may arise, trust Him to carry me through whatever comes.

I send my sons to school to learn the basics of education - math, English, science, art, music, geography, history, etc. They will go to school 30 hours a week, for about 40 weeks a year, for at least 14 years of their lives - that's almost 17,000 hours of school before they graduate high school. They should be able to learn all the basics they need to know in that time frame.

But what about the most important lessons? The ones that teach them about God's love for them, about Jesus' sacrifice on the cross, about the hope and wonder and freedom that comes from following Christ? If I left it up to the Sunday school teachers and youth pastors at church, they would have about one hour a week, about 50 weeks a year, for about 15 years (let's say ages 3-18) - that's about 750 hours.

I have read over and over in books and magazines and articles and studies that parents are the greatest influencers in a child's life. Good and bad, Josh and I are shaping our sons into the men they will become. This really scares me most of the time - the responsibility of it all - but instead of hiding under the covers and leaving all the shaping for someone else to do, I am peering out of my safe cocoon of procrastination and low confidence, and I'm realizing that God made me the mother of these boys - ME! And that is one job I am so thankful for, it is the best job I could ever hope for, it is my best dream come true.

And with that job comes another dream come true - I get to be a teacher. I am slowly but surely getting more and more excited about my role in sharing faith with the boys, growing with them, learning with them, all of us becoming more of who we were meant to be with each Bible story, each conversation about God, each fun activity that teaches a truth, each task we take on to bless another.

I always feel like I am only just beginning on this journey of teaching my boys about the One who loves them more than I ever could. I think it's because every time I learn something new about God, that one thing shows me ten more things, and I realize there will never be enough time in this life to learn all there is to learn. So I will take what I can, show the boys what I can, never stop learning, never stop growing, and look forward to the day when I will see God face to face.

Watching all the Veggie Tales videos wasn't enough, reading all the stories in the Toddler Bible wasn't enough, taking them to church on Sundays isn't enough - it's not that I'm being self-defeating - quite the opposite - what I'm realizing is that it will never be the end. I will never get to a place where I think, *There, I've taught them all they need to know about God, the Bible, Jesus and the basics of Christian living.* I will never get to that place because it doesn't exist. Neither

can I sit back in my own life and think, *I've finally arrived. I finally know all I need to know about my faith. Now I can move on to something else...*

More and more I come back to a place of anticipation, of excitement, of pure joy at the thought of the very special role I have in my son's lives to teach them about God. I feel this growing sense of euphoria because it means something wonderful for my own life - it means I must learn and grow too. Teach them what I've already learned - yes - but also teach them what I'm learning today, tomorrow, five years from now. My faith will increase as I strive to show them how their faith can increase. It is inevitable, and it is awesome.

So I sit and type and put all these thoughts together into one most magnificent realization - that little girl inside me is smiling so big, so bright, so full of joy. She will be a teacher, and she will teach about the best thing in life - her Saviour. And she will teach it to the students who hold the dearest place in her heart - her two sons.

*Lord, please help the teacher in me to teach only what you want me to teach, when you want me to teach it. Show me how to go about this wonderfully huge and important role you've given me. Let my boys learn from me and grow with me as we always seek to know You more.*

## November 24th, 2010

### Two Coins

One summer Sunday morning I was driving my boys to church and my oldest son asked if we could turn around. When I asked why he answered, "I want to get my allowance and give it all to God."

I WAS SHOCKED! My son was saving his allowance, doing extra jobs for money and building things to sell at our yard sale (as well as managing a refreshment stand)! He was intent on getting a new video game system and game he really wanted.

A couple of weeks earlier his uncle had offered him the system and game for free. Then as he saved for another toy, that one was given to him for free as well by another relative.

Well, I did turn around that morning, but I also wanted to get a better idea of my son's motives before he gave up all his savings.

"How much allowance do you want to give?" I asked.

"All of it!" he replied calmly.

"Why?" I asked.

"Because I got the things I wanted already, and I keep thinking about the story of that woman with the two coins and I always thought that was something I'd like to do. Plus I'll just get more."

My brain scrambled to think of an answer.

"Wow," was all I could say, "I'm so proud of you."

The faith of my son blew me away. His young heart was content with what he already had, and he knew it was good to give. He trusted that there would be enough for whatever he wanted next, or that he was OK to wait a while for it.

Sometimes I learn these great life lessons from my children. I hope to take this lesson of faith, trust, generosity and contentment with me far into the future.

## December 1st, 2010

### A Special Christmas List

The boys have been making a mental Christmas list for a while now. Everyone's been asking what they want, giving them options, showing them pictures... all in good fun and the generosity of the holidays. Their lists are not long, and they've made some fun choices for gifts. We'll see what Santa brings them!

A few days after their lists were made, we sat down at the table together, my sons and I, and we made a special Christmas list. We put on our thinking caps and focused on people we might know who could use something for Christmas, and how could we bless them with that item.

At first the list was pretty run-of-the-mill, with the boys thinking of presents that friends or family members would like. They did a great job of remembering what others had seemed interested in and how much fun they could have with the items.

Then I nudged them a little deeper. I reminded them that *Christmas is Jesus' birthday and what would He like for his birthday?* Blank stares... Elijah thought we should make sure our gift was one that could easily be transported to heaven (what an absolute cutie my little boy is), so what was easily transportable? Josiah was quiet... he was wrapping his heart, his mind and his soul around the possibilities.

A little more nudging... I share with them about how Jesus asks us to take care of the widows, the orphans and the poor. I ask them if that might be the greatest gift we could give Him, if we bless others as He asks.

The ideas started flowing... *Let's start with the widows. Who do we know who is a widow and what would they like for Christmas?* The named off a couple of people and suggested cards, baking, a meal out with us - our treat.

*Now... what about the orphans?* HHHmmmm.... no orphanages around here. No one we know who lacks both parents. *What about World Vision? What about picking something from their Christmas catalogue? Yes, mom, what about a goat or a chicken*? Smiles all around.

We move on down the list.... *how can we bless the poor this Christmas*? The favourite idea there was sending a shoe box through Operation Christmas Child. We headed upstairs to cross that item off our list immediately. We went online and filled a shoebox over the internet - all shoeboxes filled this way will go towards Haiti this year, and Haiti seems to hold a real special place in our hearts.

We choose a box for a boy aged 5-9. The boys take turns typing out a personal message to the boy who will receive our box. I upload a family photo and we pay for the box. Off it goes! We can picture the possibilities for our box and the boys who will one day soon hold it in his hands.

The special Christmas list is hanging on the fridge. There are still a few items to cross off, a few more blessings to spread around, a few more imaginary bows to put on the imaginary presents for Jesus this year.

Hopefully our gifts bring a smile to the baby in the manger.

### December 2nd, 2010

### A Walk in the Woods

I was visiting my family recently while Josh was away for another round of Master's courses at Wheaton College.

I always enjoy my time with family - special memories always wait for us there. Watching the cousins grow up together warms my heart and I wish the distance between both sides of our family was a little shorter and we could see Josh's wonderful relatives more often than we do.

At times it has been extremely hard and lonely living in the north. Despite the beauty of this place we call home and the opportunities we have been blessed with here, I long for Sunday dinners and holidays with family and sharing traditions of those we love.

Then I am reminded of our life here, and all that means, and I know there is a lot of good here and we live a life that most people in this world can never imagine, and the longing stops, and I live in what I have, the best I can live it, every day I am given.

Recently we enjoyed a walk in the woods with my sister, her daughter and her son. We have a new tradition forming and hike the same path each time we visit. I am excited to see this trail in all the seasons and snap pictures of our adventures there. It is a truly beautiful place!


### December 14th, 2010

### All Kinds of Tired

It's been a long fall season. A long time of putting things to rest, of allowing things to sleep in me, of giving the things of life over to God, again and again, for Him to cover with His pure-white blanket of love for me. Letting His snow come and cover me, flake by flake, until nothing but His pure-white blanket of love remains.

And I am all kinds of tired. Tired of money issues that left us scrambling for a time:

- $4000 stolen just like that out of our bank account. Its return is promised, but not yet complete.

- A van that cost more than it should have two years ago, was supposed to last at least another 3 years while we saved up cash for the next vehicle - suddenly falling apart - transmission, brakes, doors, steering - all within a month. We hoped to get a few thousand from its sale in a few years; instead we get $450 and owe $300 to the transmission shop.

- The finishing touches on the home renovations - flooring, doors, trim - cost double the labour it was originally quoted because nothing in this old house of ours is level and nothing is a quick job and when you start a project, ten more unfold.

And I know I just have to let go.

And I'm tired of the confusion - what do I do with myself now that both my boys are in school full-time? Society tells me I should be out working a full-time job and earning money for vacations and cottages and RRSPs and more, more, more. Meanwhile as I take on a part-time lunch room supervisor job at my boys' school I realize how little I have left for home at the day's end. And I feel in my soul that it's not working out.

And I know I just have to let go.

I'm tired of rejection letters from publishers for my book about pregnancy loss - after only one I was tired, two leaves me wearier, yet I will keep going. The words I wrote out two years ago have helped so many already, and God's plan for the words is coming to fruition even if I never get published.

And I know I just have to let go.

And I'm tired of sickness in our family - tomorrow morning at 4:45 I will wake up and then wake our younger son and I will get him ready for the hospital and dental surgery. It's not such a big deal except that I've been to the hospital one too many times this year and the last visit with one of my boys ended with air-lifting to another city and days and days of holding-my-breath illness before he turned a corner for the better.

And I know I just have to let go.

In this season of putting things to rest, of allowing things to sleep in me, of giving the things of life over to God, again and again - it has been my prayer, my heart's cry to see the good. I know it's there because I know God is there and I know He is good, no matter what, He is good. So I look for Him, for the good, and He opens my eyes, and I see Him, always, no matter what. Even when I don't want to.

Flake by flake, prayer by prayer, one sighting of Him at a time, His pure-white blanket of love covers all I see, all the things in my life that would drag me down so effortlessly if I let them. I fight - to hold onto Him, to hold onto the good - because it is all I can do to get through the long season of fall and enter into a season of rest and pure-white goodness and being covered by His love.

One of the ways I hold on to the good is by counting the blessings with an online Gratitude Community (I started counting a while back):

121. Snow, snow, snow down on me!

122. Hosting a neighbourhood Christmas Party and it went really well!

123. Husband who works hard in his role as a pastor and God honours that hard work always.

124. Delivering a senior's Christmas basket today with Josh and the boys to a wonderful lady in a nursing home - her tears of happiness and her hugs and her smile were SO amazing!

125. Dreams of tobogganing - SOON!

126. Snow day yesterday - the boys chose to go to school and had so much fun with the few kids that were there - so glad they just had FUN at school, trying not to be offended that they didn't want to stay home with mommy!

127. Early birthday gift from Josh - an exercise bike (I actually WANTED this, so no getting mad at my hubby) - I put it together (I'm so handy now from all the home renos, I tell ya), lifted it up two

flights of stairs on my own (I'm also buff now too) and proceeded to try it out as I looked out my bedroom window at the amazing view I love.

128. Finally getting Elijah in for his dental surgery tomorrow to remove the tooth with the abscess - we've been waiting for three months!

129. My boys - quite simply - they bless me to no end - really and truly.

130. Blogging to get it all out.


## December 21st, 2010

### The Tooth Fairy Makes a Special Visit

Elijah had some dental surgery done last week - poor guy. He was a real trooper - he had to go to the hospital and have the sleeping gas and everything. I prepared him as best I could.... *I told him I wouldn't be able to go into the sleeping room with him or be there right when he woke up, but I'd been praying for the nicest and best nurses and doctors to help him with sleeping and waking up and fixing his teeth. I told him as soon as he was awake enough, the nurse would come get me, and I'd run in and say, "There's my Elijah!" And give him a big hug.*

That usually made him laugh. And he did really well and he's my hero. The anesthetic threw him for a loop and he was pukey for 24 hours. He came out of it slowly but surely and was running around by the night following the surgery.

Elijah had to have two teeth pulled out (and 7 more needed at least a little work done!), and he was excited to put them under his pillow for the Tooth Fairy.

Here he is the next day when he finally remembered to check under his pillow. I told him I guess the Tooth Fairy brings more money for teeth the you had to go the hospital to have taken out! So he got a toonie for each one. He was pretty happy about that!

**December 21st, 2010**

**Scenes From the Soul – Breakdown at the Mall**

She stands in the store at Christmas time. She feels so tiny and alone in this big store with its loud music, its bright lights, its stockings and its Santas. Red, white, green, gold, silver - the colours of the season are everywhere. The shelves are such a mess from shoppers picking through to find just the right item. There is hardly room for the shopping carts to get down each aisle because of the crowds. She is packed in tight - physically, emotionally and spiritually.

The anxiety begins. There is not much time between its beginning and its climax. She hasn't felt this way in a long time. Her heart starts racing, her mind goes blank, her body starts to ache and almost immediately she needs to flee this place. She needs to regroup, get a handle on her emotions, pray.

She manages to purchase the two items in her cart. That's as far as she'd gotten. Two items into the list and she runs.

She feels so defeated and she starts to pray as soon as she steps out of the store.

*That's it? That's all I can get done today? My list was HUGE, and I need to get through it! I can't put anything else on my husband who is maxed out at this time of year. God help me. I can't do Christmas like this anymore. I can't do this busyness, this consumerism, this craziness that has become Your Son's birthday. Show me your peace, show me your grace, show me YOU. I need YOU to be in my Christmas. I need my sons to know YOU more this week. How do I do this? Show me what YOU want Christmas to be in our family and help me to let go of what it's always been before. Please help me get through this Christmas - honouring YOU as best I can with what I've learned and the ideas I have for this year. Take me closer and closer to what You have for us at Christmas. Help me to get through this list. Come shopping with me today. Be with me today. Show me more of Yourself today. I don't see you anywhere in the stores. I miss you in all this craziness.*

She turns on the radio to the local Christian station. They play nothing but Christmas songs at this time of year. She hopes for something that will help her get through the many tasks ahead.

She hears Joseph's Lullaby and the tears come, right there in the parking lot, and her heart breaks for the vast difference that exists between that first Christmas and the Christmas of 2010. She knows the baby didn't come for this. But the people He came for surround her still and she thanks God for reaching down through time and space to touch her tiny heart and show her He even cares about Christmas lists and shopping, because He cares about the people who are making the lists and doing the shopping. He reassures her that He will go with her today, that He will show her more of Him - always, whenever she asks, without hesitation, for that is the true reason for Christmas in the first place.

Though there are not much left of nativities and baby Jesus in the stores she visits, God shows Himself to her in the most unlikely places.

A conversation with a stranger in the washroom - a lady is drinking cup after cup of water and asks if she's ever had an ultrasound and she answers *Yes, a few actually.* And the lady wonders how much water she has to drink and how she'll get through the exam. She tells her it's not too bad, and she realizes babies are born every second in this world, and hope lies in each one, just as the Hope of the World was born over two thousand years ago.

Kindness from a stranger as they try and wrestle apart the last three carts available in the store, and the stranger tells her more carts are found, and we are back in business. And she knows that God even cares about helping her get through the list that was meant to bless

and not to spoil, and she thinks of the gifts of the Magi and the original intentions of Saint Nicholas and how gifts do have a place in Christmas.

Not many Christmas carols play in the store, but instead she hears one of her old favourites from years gone by, and she feels without a doubt that God played that one just for her, and that He is found in the most unlikely places, not just in the "Christian", and the baby was born in the most unlikely place - a stable.

She leaves the store victorious - God is still everywhere, He still shows Himself to her whenever she takes the time to ask and look, and He is definitely alive and well in this Christmas season, just as in every other season.

So Merry Christmas to you all in this year of our Lord 2010!

# 2011

## January 5th, 2011

## Word For This Year

This is a new idea for me...

A couple of blogs I follow shared their "word" for 2011 - a theme that will run throughout their year, something they want to make a priority, a special focus of the year ahead, what they think this year will bring, etc.

I've thought about it for a few days now, and prayed over many words, but I think I've come to it. My word for 2011.

Last year seemed to be a time of waiting, of faithfulness in the waiting, of uncertainty and often confusion.

The song While I'm Waiting by John Waller meant a lot to me in 2010. I listened to it ALOT.

And I heard that same song yesterday while I made dinner, and the word for 2011 was right there in the song lyrics, it had been one of the possibilities on my list, and then suddenly I knew.

It excites me.

It scares me.

It makes me smile.

It's two words that go hand in hand - not just one.... two words.

BOLD. CONFIDENT.

My friend Amy pierced right into my soul when she casually mentioned to me at our church's annual Ladies Retreat last May, "I don't know why you're not more confident Anna."

Little did she know she would set me on a journey while I waited in 2010. A journey of the soul.

*Why AREN'T I more confident?*

I don't have all the answers (who does?). But God has shown me that confidence cannot come from Anna. It has to come from God. When I look to myself to find the confidence I lack, that's exactly what I see - lack.

But when I look to God for the confidence only He can give - that's where I hit the motherload. Confidence to the brim, the ability to be bold - these are things I've never had before.

I can be confident in who God is, in His love for me, in what He did for me in Jesus. I can be bold to act on that confidence, living out the life He intended for me when he knit me together.

I don't know where bold will lead, where confidence will take me.

I shake as I type the words.

All for His glory, never for my own.

Do with me what You will.

PS - Bold is also one of the meanings of the name Caleb. My middle son Caleb was stillborn in May 2003. I wrote a small book about the experience. I wait to see what will become of the book - so many options for publication, already reached so many as we pass it on to whoever needs it... Bold... is this your year angel boy? I hope...


## January 10th, 2011

### Life's Dirt

So I just finished cleaning the bathrooms. You need to understand something about me - I despise cleaning bathrooms. I put it off until I cannot take the dirt anymore and then I still put it off, and then I finally take the plunge.

The first few cleanings after the home renovations seemed monumental and extra hard and exhausting. The first time I cleaned the main floor bathroom it took me three hours of scrubbing and shop-vac-ing and washing walls, and I know I still haven't got it all, that there is still sawdust and other construction remnants hiding in the cracks. But I let go and I move on, doing the best I can with what I have on that particular day.

I have noticed that the third, fourth, fifth time I went to clean the same bathrooms the task became easier and took much less time and I despised it less and less.

I've worked the cleaning of the bathrooms into a household schedule and as long as I stick to that schedule as much as I can while still leaving room for "life", it's much smoother sailing around here.

Now, we've only touched on a household chore, a "surface" discipline I am incorporating into my life.

What about the down-deep dirt? What about the icky stuff that not many others see except those closest to me? What about the cleaning required to keep the dirt at bay in those areas of my life? What about the discipline needed to get the cleaning done? What about my schedule for that kind of cleaning?

Well, that's what I'm working out, every day cleaning some of the dirt. It's amazing how it can build up if left unattended. I've also put off that kind of cleaning until I can't take the dirt anymore.

The deep-down cleaning is a bit harder. It's humiliating at times and requires repentance and leaning on God and admitting that this kind of cleaning can never be done by myself. But I am always glad when the chore is done, when my focus is reset, when my head and my heart are clear of all that hinders. I enjoy the fresh scent, clutter-free surroundings and sparkling cleanliness that follows.

Maintenance is required, items need to be added to the schedule. Reading the Word, praying, asking for forgiveness, seeking God in all areas of my life. No small task, but well worth the effort.

I move about the house much easier when it's clean. Stress comes from the clutter that inevitably builds up. It's a constant effort to rid my house, my life, my heart, my soul of the dirt that so easily starts to layer itself in life.

One of the ways to rid the dirt is to count the blessings, keep the negativity at bay, focus on the good:

131. Clean bathrooms.

132. Reading through psalms and loving it.

133. Bible reflections with the boys at breakfast.

134. Dreaming big dreams and leaving them with God.

135. Ideas for making the dreams come true.

136. Having enough margin in life to help a friend this weekend.

137. Images of hope.

138. My Joshua who makes me laugh and watches movies with me and fills me up and holds me tight.

139. Seeing my own inadequacies in my sons but knowing there is endless hope for something different for them.

140. Schedules that get the jobs done in my house and in my heart.


**January 15ᵗʰ, 2011**

**Marriage: What Is Your Vision?**

Where there is no vision, the people perish: but he that keepeth the law, happy is he. - Proverbs 29:18 (KJV)

When Josh and I hit the ten-year mark last year I was feeling a little lost. I knew I was happy to be married to Josh, that we were doing our best to raise our two sons according to God's will, and we were in church ministry.

These are all great things to be doing right?

Yes, but I had no idea **why** we were doing these things. I felt like I was withering away, running around aimlessly, scrambling to keep my head above water, exhausted.

In short - I was perishing.

I remembered Proverbs 29:18 and came to realize why I was perishing.

I was totally lacking in vision.

That realization set me on a course to map out vision in all areas of my life, so that I had a sense of purpose. I was able to set goals for fulfilling the vision(s) and begin to watch them unfold as the days, months, years passed.

It had to start with our marriage. I knew we were married because we love each other, because we have fun together and we go really good together. I believe God brought us together to serve Him, to honour Him, and to bring Him praise. But how was all this working itself out in our marriage? **Was** it working itself out?

Josh patiently mapped out the vision with me that I desperately needed for our marriage and for raising our boys. As we talked about vision for our marriage, I was encouraged that we were already on the same page in many areas, and the rest just needed a little talking out to come together in my head and my heart.

Vision is a new thing for me. I thought it might be limiting to different areas of my life, but it is actually extremely freeing. I am so free to live out the life I **want**, the life I'm called to as a wife and mother, and to be the person God made me to be.

I am still working on visions for the other areas of my life like writing, running the household and self-care.

Most days now I feel confident instead of withered. I look to our future with hope and excitement for all that is coming. I am so grateful for the vision that Josh and I share.

## January 21st, 2011

### Memorizing Scripture

I never really made scripture memorization a part of my life. People would tell me about its importance and give me examples of verses to memorize, but my eyes would always gloss over and my mind would always wander.

As I write this, I'm starting to get it. I'm not very good at following through with things just because someone tells me to do them. Usually there has to be a reason for me, I have to understand why and make it real.

I already know of a couple of good reasons to memorize scripture. I know it is "a light to my path" (Psalm 119:105) and that it helps "that I might not sin against You" (Psalm 119:11).

I also realize I inadvertently have many verses tucked away in my head just from years of church attendance, personal devotions, small groups, Bible studies, and growing up in Sunday school.

As I researched more Bible verses with "word" in them I came across SO MANY reasons to memorize scripture and hide it in my heart and the young hearts of my boys. There is one major reason that sums it all up in such a simple and fascinating way, and it is revealed in the scripture I hope to start memorizing.

John 1:1 says "In the beginning was the Word, and the Word was with God, and the Word was God."

And then Revelation 19:13 says "And He [was] clothed in a vesture dipped in blood: and His name is called the Word of God."

Jesus is the living and active (Hebrews 4:12) Word of God. He is the Bible made into human form. It's pure magic.

The more we know scripture, the more we know Jesus. Memorizing it and hiding it in our hearts means having more of Jesus in our lives. And THAT gives me more than enough reason to memorize God's words to grow in my own faith and help my sons to grow in theirs.


## January 24th, 2011

### Dream Big

Dreams... I've always had dreams. Some started as small thoughts, turned into do-able ideas, then over time became full-blown dreams. They are solid, a part of my soul, they never leave. I keep giving them back to God, praying for patience to endure the waiting, for peace if I need to let them go. There is no shortage of other dreams to take place of the ones that leave. There is no shame in letting them go, no failure in their absence. There is just more, different, new dreams.

There have been patches of my life that were left dream-less. Times of loss and sorrow that bore too greatly on me to dream my dreams. Days when I couldn't see past the minute I was enduring. Darkness that kept out the light. But the dreams were still there, sleeping, waiting for a tiny beam of light to break through so I could see them once again. They only need a beam, one beam of light to let you know they are there.

Dreams never die. Not really. They might change, they might grow, they might shrink, they might hide. But they never die.

They do need you to dream them, though. They need your hope, your creativity, your unique je-ne-sais-quois.

Often times dreams will bring rejection. Don't be discouraged - this only points you clearer in the true direction they should take.

Dreams will morph. Don't stifle them - this only gives you a clearer picture of exactly what they are.

Dreams will quiet. Don't let them go - this only means the time is not right, and dreams can only happen when the time is right.

Dreams will spread. Don't try to keep them to yourself - this only means the dreams are actually bigger than you could ever imagine on your own.

Dreams will often become reality. Don't be afraid of them - this only means you achieved success and sometimes success is harder than failure.

Mountain tops and valleys... dreams bring you to both places. They take you on roller coaster rides. They leave you excited and down-in-the-dumps - sometimes even on the same day! They are not tame, they are not safe, they will change your life.

The only regret would be in never dreaming them at all.

I finished a book recently called *The Dream Giver* by Bruce Wilkinson. One line really struck me. *"The size of the Need would become the size of our Dream."*

Dreams are sometimes just for us - like the dream I have of cycling across Canada one day.

But there are other dreams - like my husband's dream of building a medical clinic called Caleb's Hope (named after our middle son who was stillborn) that meet a need - a big need. How does that change the dream? I can only imagine it might include a lot more than just one clinic.

**So let those dreams loose, and while you're at it, DREAM BIG.**

**January 25th, 2011**

## Living in the Moments

I have been very impacted by the seasons lately. Not the weather seasons, but the seasons of life and the seasons of love.

My sons are growing up. There are no more preschoolers in the house. I have conversations with my oldest son that leave me with more questions, more to discover, more to figure out. My younger son doesn't need much help with daily tasks and plays very well on his own. I even get about an hour of quiet time in the mornings to read my Bible, pray and jot down a few thoughts. It's a whole new season in life. Bittersweet. Often I miss having young ones in the house. It is a constant choice to hold onto the good memories from the last season and let them carry me into anticipation for this new season of motherhood.

Josh and I have been married more than a decade. I remember vividly the man who waited for me, wearing a kilt, his long curly hair in a ponytail, as I walked down the aisle to him on our wedding day. That man has changed, grown, learned and matured. He has seasoned. And so have I. I am not the same woman I was then. But sometimes when we laugh or share a glance, I know those two newlyweds still exist, they always will. Our love has changed, grown, learned and matured. Our love has seasoned.

Seasons mean change, and they can't be stopped. As surely as winter comes, so spring will follow, then summer, then fall, then before you know it another winter. This might encourage you if you are living through a hard season. Knowing that this season won't last forever may be a great comfort to you. Or this might bring sorrow. You might be living in the best season of your life. Knowing that this season won't last forever may bring you anxiety or concern.

No matter what the season, whether hard or easy, happy or sad, grab hold of all you can from this time, knowing another season is on its way.

Be encouraged as YOU season.

**February 7<sup>th</sup>, 2011**

## But What's the Point?

Ever since I can remember, I've put pen to paper and felt alive.

I have a binder full of poems, stories, journal entries, articles, newsletters and blog entries that started small when I was a little girl. It has grown quite big over the years, in fact there are MANY binders now. All a testament to the fact that I just can't help it.

Written words are my voice. I once wrote in an email to a friend, "When I speak I have no idea who's talking. When I write I hear my voice."

I live the moments of my days, weeks, months, years, decades as life carries me through time. But when I write about those moments, they become solid, a part of my soul.

When I don't write, things get blurry and confused. My heart and my soul fill up with all these experiences, reflections and revelations. When I don't write them down I feel like I lost them somewhere along the way. Like a part of me is missing.

So I write. To process life it seems I need to put it to words.

Make no mistake, there are so many other things in life that fill me to the brim. I am so grateful for these things:

141. My husband playing the guitar
142. Looking into my little boy's bluest-of-blue eyes
143. When my bigger son laughs his deep-down joy-filled laugh
144. Walking outside in any weather
145. The trees in the wind
146. The sound of my sister's voice on the phone
147. Texts from my mum
148. Emails from my dad
149. Packing friends into my house
and of course, always...
150. More of my Saviour

And when I put those things to words, I am fuller still.

But what's the point? Where's the purpose in me putting my fingers on this keyboard, erasing the wrong words, searching for the right words, praying that God will use all this... somehow.

The point is to glorify Him. To encourage you. To share my journey. To make the good solid in me. To process the bad and let it go. To REALLY live in the moments. To let the words cement them in my soul.

If I don't write about the moments, they get lost in me. I don't want them to get lost.

The discipline I need to learn is to leave the words when their purpose is done. Not to get lost in other people's words. Never compare my words to other's words. To make sure I am writing my own words, not living someone else's words. Nor coveting their words.

**That is the point - to write my own words and live in them.**

God wrote my story just for me, now to keep to the business of living it out. Writing is part of that for me. There is no running from it.

I trust Him with the words He gives me, the story He's written for me.

*Take the words where You want them, Lord, my story begins and ends with You.*


**February 9th, 2011**

**His Needs Before Mine?**

I was mulling something over a while ago, and I'd love to share it today... it's an idea I've heard many times before, but I hope it will really stick with me this time.

The idea of putting your spouse's needs before your own, of serving them instead of being served.

Hhhhmmm... well, I cook most of the meals, I do most of the housework and our boys are usually happy and healthy. That's the gist of the idea, right?

I'm starting to wonder if there's a lot more to it.

The things I do might fall into a category marked "roles" - those are my "jobs" around the house and within our family. Those are givens.

I think putting Josh's needs before my own and serving him might mean something else.

I think it might look more like encouraging him as he works towards his Master's degree, even though it means he'll be away a few weeks of the year and busy with papers and studying beyond that. Encouraging him instead of worrying about the finances of it or the time commitment (and then letting him know repeatedly about my worries!).

I think it might mean telling him how great a father he is instead of nit-picking when he does things differently than I would.

And what if it means getting him a cup of tea at the end of the day when I'm bone-tired, instead of expecting him to get me a cup.

There are little, seemingly insignificant ways to show selflessness and big, huge ways to show service.

I think it starts with not begrudging my roles, freeing up Josh to become the man God created him to be, and going the extra mile (or inch) with a smile instead of a frown.

It means encouraging Josh to fulfill his roles, letting him know what I need to do to work towards my goals and dreams, and thanking him when he goes the extra mile (or inch) for me.

I think I might be on to something here....


**February 19th, 2011**

**Becoming a Praying Family**

*Do not be anxious about anything, but in every situation, by prayer and petition, with thanksgiving, present your requests to God. And the peace of God, which transcends all understanding, will guard your hearts and your minds in Christ Jesus. - Philippians 4:6-7*

These verses hold many great truths - we don't have to be anxious about our kids, we are invited to pray about everything, we can petition God, thank Him and make requests to Him about anything.

And when we do, we are promised that peace will be ours. Even if the answers are years down the road, or life is truly overwhelming - we are free to have peace now. All it takes is a good chat with God. That same peace is available to our children now and as they grow up.

Prayer really is just talking to God. And it's never too early to start talking to God. We can talk to Him about whatever we want, whenever we want, wherever we want, and however we want.

From peaceful thank-you's to screaming and ranting - He wants it all. And He wants the same thing from our children. Their prayers are just as powerful as ours, and all are music to the ears of the One who loves us most.

It's all about relationship, and it's not much of a relationship if you're not on speaking terms, or if you're not honest and real with one another.

The best way to encourage the prayer life of our kids is to model it for them. I've started praying at different times - on the way to school, before play dates, as an ambulance races by, as we drive by the mission, when a beautiful rainbow appears, when we see an answer to prayer, when we hear someone is sick, or when my boys share a problem with me. The trick for me is to remember to pray out loud, so they can hear the example I'm trying to give them.

The more I put this concept of continuous praying into action, the more it takes root in me. The benefits go beyond my children, to my own relationship with God.

It's wonderful how that works. My kids help me grow in God as I help them grow in God. And slowly but surely we become a praying family.

# February 22nd, 2011

## 7 Minutes to Count

I have 7 minutes to count... 7 minutes before it's time to put the cookies in the oven and clean up the kitchen a little before delivering the freshly-baked cookies to my two sons when I pick them up from school and ask if they'd like to go tobogganing and hope they say "YES!"

The oven beeps that it's ready... ready to bake the cookies and help make some memories and encourage me to live in the moments.

Five minutes now... don't want to be late...

But I want so bad to go deep for these few minutes, to reach into the recesses where thankfulness truly lives.... do I have enough time Lord?

151. A saviour who forgives, cares, loves, redeems
152. Sunshine that invites play on cold days when play is MUCH needed
153. A husband who never stops loving me, even when I'm at my grumpiest, he still smiles at me and tells me he loves me
154. Sons who fill my heart with one look at their face - they are growing into such wonderful young men, and I, ME, ANNA, I get to be their mother? Thank You God.
155. Friends who will always be friends, no matter the distance, the hurt, the time between visits
156. Glimpses of opportunities to live out the gospel exactly where I am, with exactly who I am

I'm out of time... maybe I can squeeze in one more minute? The oven keeps clicking its readiness...

157. Women who encourage one another, support each other, work together for the chance at something awesome

158. Feeling God's love in such a strong way at the cemetery last week... I almost SEE You walking with me there, putting Your hand on my shoulder, leading me on into the future without my precious boy (for now, always remember it's just for now), consoling me constantly that HE IS WELL, more than well, happy, healthy, whole, loved beyond measure, that You know what You're doing and the only thing You need me to do is trust

Five minutes into overtime now.... make these ones quick....

159. My home
160. My family

And now for cookies...


## February 23rd, 2011

### Scenes From the Soul – Tick Tock

The room is quiet. She hears the clock - tick tock - counting down the seconds of her life. So fast. Too fast. The seconds move along so quickly. She hears her life passing by one tick, one tock at a time.

Time... what will she do with the time she's given today, tomorrow, this week, this year, this decade, this lifetime?

The day ahead is full of seconds, her seconds, the seconds God has given her today. What will she do with her seconds today?

She thinks about the looming tasks to complete, the errands to run, and the meals to prepare.

Can she make those things count today? She knows she can smile at a few strangers, pray for people in the stores she visits, or drop a few coins in the charity boxes.

Can she find joy in the cooking and cleaning that's required for her household? She knows she is cooking dinner for friends she loves, cleaning keeps her home allergy-tolerable and she moves better through the house when the dust disappears.

The seconds of this day will also bring times of anticipated fun and laughter. She can count those seconds valuable with ease. The seconds she spends at her son's school - being in the classrooms and the library, stepping into their world for an afternoon, and glimpsing life through their eyes for a time each week.

A few seconds of her day will be full of kisses and hugs from her husband and sons, and those precious people will tell her they love her, maybe even more than once.

After school there is time to waste - together. She doesn't yet know what will fill those seconds. She is excited about the possibilities for that time in her day. Maybe she'll leave that up to the boys, let them decide what will go into those seconds.

The seconds have tick-tocked enough to fill 30 minutes of her time as she sat and reflected on the sound of the clock.

Time must move ahead just as she must move on to the next task.

But there is one more important thing to do before she goes...

She gives the day to her Lord...

*As the tick tock counts down the seconds of my life, make the seconds of my life count for you. Amen.*


## February 24th, 2011

### Making Peace

I lost my temper - **again**. He's just a little boy, he's just pushing my buttons, he's just testing the waters of independence. Why did I have to yell? Why did I have to slam the door? Why did I have to stomp away, knowing he could hear my footsteps taking me away from him, leaving him alone in his room?

He didn't mean to make the mess. What is the matter with me? I know he's in his room, feeling confused and afraid. I know he's crying. The tiny cherub face that I love so much is probably covered in tears. And he'll need a Kleenex soon.

I take my moment of solitude and I use it to calm down, to pray, to regroup, to take my focus off the stresses of my day. There is so much going on! So much to bog me down, discourage me and make me lose sight of the important things in my life. I need to let go of my plans, my expectations, my perfectionism. For his sake and for my sake, I need to release the stranglehold of control I so desperately crave. I need to trust God with all I am and have, not just with bits and pieces of my life.

I know my little boy doesn't deserve the reaction he got from me. I know he doesn't understand my emotions. I know he needs his mommy right now.

I curl up my knees on the couch, lay my head on my hands and try to be still. I try to pray. How do I give it all over? How do I let it all go? I have to choose it. One issue at a time, one moment at time, one day at a time. I sing quietly to myself - a song that speaks of God's majesty and power and love. One by one I give Him everything that comes to mind. One by one I feel Him take them. I want to grab them back from Him, I am so used to carrying the burden myself. I keep singing and releasing and breathing. I feel Him draw near to me and envelope me in an invisible embrace that can carry me through whatever life brings. I am safe. I am loved. I am a child of God.

The petty annoyances fall away, the selfishness melts, the self-pity scurries. I make peace - with my God and with myself. I give all my worries to the One who wants to carry them. I ask Him to forgive me and help me be the mother He wants me to be to this precious boy He's given me to love and raise up.

Now I must make peace with my son. His cries have quieted. God must have touched His heart as He was touching mine. I open the door to his sky-blue room, and my gaze meets his big bright eyes. He knows me so well, this flesh of my flesh. He knows I'm done being mad, that I want to make peace. He knows his mommy is OK, she's safe, she loves him.

I sit on his big-boy bed and hold my arms open wide. He walks into them and I wrap him in my love, just as I am wrapped in God's love. I lay my cheek on his soft, golden hair and I say what I mean with my whole heart.

"I'm sorry I got mad. I love you."

"It's okay Mommy. I love you too."

Just like that all is right in the world again. My son knows his mommy loves him, and I know I am loved by my Heavenly Father. Peace reigns supreme. We walk out of his room, hand in hand, on our way to clean up the mess in our hearts and our home - together.

*Lord, may I always be a living example of Your grace, love and peace in my son's life. May he look at me and see You. May I never make him doubt he is a son of God.*

- Adapted from an article I wrote for *The Link & Visitor*, a publication of *The Baptist Women of Ontario and Quebec*.


## March 2nd, 2011

### The Gift Of Time – Part 1

I sit down at my computer to type and the words get all jumbled and I can't seem to make sense of the stirrings of my heart.

I'm trying to rush through the thoughts and get the message across quickly, but this is a post about time. The gift of time. How can I rush these words that tell of slowing, embracing, savouring the gift of time?

So I choose to do something I haven't done for a long time. Something I love. Something that makes me feel alive.

I take my fingers off the keyboard, push my chair back from the computer, grab a pen and find a blank page in a notebook. I walk up the stairs and into our bedroom. A brilliant shaft of sunlight stretched out across our bed and beckoned me just a few moments ago, but I walked determinedly past as I hurried to type out a blog post.

Now I return to the sunlight, taking the gift of time spent in its warmth. I stretch out across the bed and look out the huge window I love. I take a moment to watch the tall trees swaying in the wind, take in the blue of the sky, close my eyes for a moment and ask God for the words.

They spill out so fast I can hardly keep up. I know I'll forget some of them, some will get lost as the thoughts come together. The paper fills up with the stirrings of my heart.

Time is such a gift. Grabbing hold of it, squeezing all I can from it and fully living in it seems so impossible some days. I get lost in all the possibilities, paralyzed by all I could do with the time I'm given.

This new phase of life - having my boys in school - leaves me with much quiet time in my days.

Some days seem too quiet and I latch on to whatever noise I can find - soul noise, that is. On those days the gift of time is lost.

Other days I use the quiet time I'm given to learn, grow, create, bless others, praise God. On those days the gift is well-received.

The shaft of sunlight shifts and the air chills in its absence. I'm glad I caught the warmth and inspiration of these few moments in the sun.

Time will move along, moment by moment. In a few weeks or months my time may be full of moments that look completely different than they do now. I may long for just a little quiet time in my days.

For now, I open my hands and my heart to this gift. I receive the time I'm given today, tomorrow, every day. I thank God for His gift of time. He created it just for us, you know. The Maker of the Universe doesn't exist in time and doesn't need it, but it is His gift to us.

*May I begin, end and live out all my days asking You what You have for me and what I can offer to You in the time You've gifted to me.*

... Back to the keyboard to type out these words to you... no longer jumbled but made clear in the Light of His gift and His time.


**March 4th, 2011**

**Turning Corners**

I'm turning many corners these days. Seeing new sights just around the bend. Not quite there but getting closer, always closer to what's around the bend.

The Bible Reading Plan 2011 is going well so far, and every time I open my Bible I learn something new about my faith, about God, about the history of His people.

Health is climbing its way to the top of my priority list. Exercise and eating right are back in the game after a time of neglect.

Extensive home renovations have come to a halt. I turned that corner with no looking back!

I was a full-time stay-at-home mom for about 9 years, and now both boys are in school full-time. I stand staring at the turn in that bend, not sure what to do with it just yet, doing my best to leave it all with God and follow Him around this corner.

Opportunities to step out of my comfort zone are presenting themselves. Though it will be hard to step out, I don't want to miss the experiences anymore.

I find contentment in my grasp. It's always been there, waiting for me to recognize it for what it really is, but I missed the boat constantly. Contentment really is found everywhere, but actually seeing it and choosing to live in it are another story. I keep making a gratitude list and look forward to reading One Thousand Gifts by Ann Voskamp in the near future.

For a time it seemed I was following the same road, and the scenery never changed. Maybe I was wrong, maybe it was me that never changed, never wanted to change, afraid to turn the corners and change the scenery.

I realized there were a few corners to turn within. I saw that the scenery was always changing but I was blind to it.

It starts with one. Me. You.

Then it spreads to more. Us. We.

Turning corners means leaving the familiar, not able to look back around the bend, letting it go, seeing what is ahead. Sometimes scary, but always worth it.

## March 7<sup>th</sup>, 2011

### My Son's Gratitude List For Today

My youngest son is home sick from school today with bronchitis and an ear infection! Pray for him if you will. I thought I'd recruit him to help me with my gratitude list today. I asked him what he wants to thank God for. This is what Elijah said...

161. Captain Underpants books
162. Best friends
163. You
164. Him
165. His Son
166. That He created the earth

That's all for today...


## March 10<sup>th</sup>, 2011

### The Gift Of Time – Part 2

I wake up realizing this - **just as God freely offers me His gift of time, so I must freely offer this time to others as He asks**.

I line up the medicine bottles and I get ready to dole out the antibiotics:

- One pill, three times a day for Elijah's bronchitis and ear infection. Started Monday morning after waking up Josh to take him to the clinic for 7am. Continue for 10 days.

- One pill, three times a day for Josiah's strep throat. Started Tuesday morning after waking up Josh to take him to the clinic for 7am. Continue for 10 days.

- One pill, once a day for Josh's sinusitis. Started after he spent the afternoon at the clinic on Friday, his day off. Continue for 10 days. Nasonex and Advil Cold and Sinus to also ease his suffering. Ibuprofen to numb the pain of his broken thumb. Cast on for 10 days. Removed yesterday after waiting at the hospital for 3 hours. Still sore but much better. *How did he break his thumb? That's a whole other post but let's just say there was a toboggan involved. One of Josh's mottos: Go hard or go home.*

My men all medicated and one step closer to renewed health, I put the pill bottles away until the time comes for the next dose.

Elijah is home from school 3 days. Josiah is home from school 2 days. Josh continues to work as much as he can and keeps up well at the church and at home, as usual. He is amazing that way. He continues his building me up, his helping around the house, his weekend cooking, his loving the boys, his hospital visits, his putting together a team of people for a missions trip to Dominican Republic at the end of April. (I think I'm going this year - my very first missions trip!)

Josh is great with the gift of time. The gift is well-received by Josh. He rests in it, easily slows down to share it with others, makes sure he shares a good dollop of it with us, his family, and he speeds up in it when there is much to do for the kingdom. He knows what time is all about and how to use the gift wisely.

**I'm never very sure how to handle the gift of time. I don't always receive it well and I don't always give it well.** I learn from my husband and my sons.

My boys' time is spent in play, in discovering, in learning, in rest, in so much activity I can hardly keep up most days. They love to spend their time with family and friends. They ask for more time with us - more undivided time, more quality time.

**I long to know at the end of each day that I gave them the gift of undivided time, quality time, just me and them and time.**

**I take on too much to fill up time instead of letting time fill up me.**

**My perfectionism requires more time than I need to give to some areas of my life.**

But I am grateful, once again, so grateful to have God's gift of time. Time that allows me to care for these three men of mine when they're all down for the count at the same time.

These precious days they're home, stepping in the days that fill my world, I let them change what my time looks like. The computer sits lonely for long periods of time. The kitchen is disastrous for the time in between required cooking or baking. The TV is allowed more time when sick boys are around, but I make sure to share at least a little of that time with them, laughing at their shows with them and wrapping up in blankets with them. Books share time with us - I read to my younger son for !even an hour at a time! and we exchange amused glances and giggle over the story we hold in front of us.

There were days spent with just one young man, or both, this past week of sickness time. The days looked so different, depending on who was in the house.

My youngest man required more alone time, more quiet play time, more "chill" time. We read together, watched TV together, sorted Lego, discussed school, blogged and wrote an email to Grandma together.

The older younger man required much attention, conversation and activity. We shot Nerf darts at paper airplanes, discussed Christianity, listened to music and made banana cake with green icing together. (Josh later took the cake to his young adults group after we enjoyed a yummy piece.) We grew together, rested together, played together and served together.

I tried to enjoy, no, I DID enjoy the time with my young men this week. Truly this was a gift, despite the sickness that forced it. They are back to school today and I wish them both health and happiness as they live in the time they have today.

Later we'll pick up the boys from school and drive a few hours to Grandma's house to share the gift of time with her.

This week was a time of letting go, leaving my agendas and schedules and busyness for another time, learning more of the "good" time-fillers and recognizing more of the "bad" time-fillers. I'd like to stay away from those and my tendencies to latch onto those when I see an empty span of time ahead of me.

*May I receive the gift of time You give me and be a good steward of this gift in my life. May I share Your gift of time as You ask me to and let go of my ideas for filling the time. Fill Your gift with more of You and less of me. Share Your gift with others, through me, every day.*

## March 18th, 2011

## Marriage: Dealing With Crisis

Crisis is a part of life, and a part of marriage. Sadness, strife, or stress can enter our days and leave us winded for a long time. Unexpected and unwelcome events can occur and leave us scrambling to survive minute by minute. I'm sure we can all relate somehow to crisis in our lives and in our marriages.

Josh and I experienced out fair share of crisis in our years together, but we also know others who experienced much more than we have. No one life and no one marriage will look exactly like another. We are all unique and our marriages are unique.

We lived through job loss, stillbirth, serious illness in our children, many moves, deaths in the family and much confusion. Your crisis situations may look similar to ours, but you will have your own unique experiences.

Only the two of you have your unique set of circumstances. No other marriage can have the same set. You know each other's loss, hardship, grief, sadness and stress in a special way because you share experiences, because you share a life, because you are one.

Pull together through the hard times instead of drifting apart. Find your strength in each other instead of carrying the weight alone. Communicate with the person who may just know you better than you know yourself. Seek counselling if you need it.

During our times of crisis, Josh and I handled our situations differently. Sometimes I needed to be alone, but I made sure to reconnect after that time, even if it meant lots of tears as we got the hurt out. Josh is great at making me laugh and sometimes I needed that laughter during the hard times. Sometimes it was a hug or a prayer.

Expressing our needs to one another and accepting each other for who we are is key in dealing with crisis. Even though we don't always understand each other's emotions, we try to validate them.

Though we may never understand the reasons behind the crisis in our lives, we can trust God to be with us through the crisis. He waits for you to turn to Him, and He can handle yelling as well as praise. Lean on Him the most - as individuals and as a couple - as you deal with crisis in your life and in your marriage.

## March 21st, 2011

### Choosing The Light

Do you ever have one of those dark days of the soul? When nothing in the world seems right, including you?

The dark glasses are on, the ones that don't see anything light, don't see anything right.

Time to take those glasses off and look at the light head-on. Stare it in the eye and say, "Bring it on" and start to count.

Wrestle your will to the ground like Jacob wrestled with God and say, "Bless me!"

Then realize you are already so blessed you can't possibly fit another blessing in.

Not until you count the ones you have.

Not until you say *Thank You*.

Not until you point your face to the light and stand there soaking it in until you feel the heat of His love for you.

Feel the light until you need to turn away from over-exposure to His goodness and grace.

I choose the light...

167. Blogs that help me get it all out... just a few minutes is all I need some days...
168. So many things to do in my days
169. Lists

170. Food on our plates whenever we want, food in the cupboards, food in the grocery stores

171. Chocolate's hold on me is weakening with His help

172. A husband who always does his best to serve his God with everything he's got

173. Attending a most special wedding on the weekend and praying God's grace for them

174. Seeing family on the March break

175. Bingeman's and KidZone fun - the boys' laughter and antics while they played

176. Driving a friend back home with us to Northern Ontario and watching her heal during the few days she was with us

177. Others in our lives who love our boys with all they have

178. Getting ever-closer to finishing Elijah's woven blanket

179. Songs and hugs and kisses from freckle-kissed Elijah

180. Josiah growing always more into the man God intended Him to be - *Let me always be an encouragement, a tool to get him there, never a hindrance, he is Your son first and foremost, I just get to be his mommy*

181. Sleeping in peace

182. Snow still falling out my window, let the white, let the light keep coming...

183. Walks on frozen lakes

184. Sharing my life with boys who constantly show me the wonder in the world and ask me to slow down and REALLY see it

185. Letting go - it's truly freeing

186. Grabbing hold of what comes in each second

187. My first missions trip in 5 weeks

188. The music that fills our house, if only we let it

189. The laughter that fills our house, if only we let it

190. The love that fills our house, if only we let it

## April 10th, 2011

## Just Listening

*Lord, Give me the words...*

It's been quiet here.

Not in the house - two wonderfully rambunctious boys make this house their playground on a daily basis and I am GLAD for that. Not in our lives - ministry and volunteer activities and boy's judo and swimming all make life very noisy sometimes.

The quiet comes within. Wanting to type posts, thinking of sitting down at the computer, then... quiet. The words flutter around in my head, here one moment, gone the next, and I give it to God. Any words I put together to make a post for this blog need to come from Him. Or else why do I do this?

It's been like this in so many ways this Lent season. Taking an inventory of my life. Everything is weighed in the light of eternity. Does this stay in my life, or does this go? Is this still necessary? Is this pouring into our family?

The most important question to ask... Does this come from God? Is this a good thing or a God thing?

Life is so full - wonderfully full.

I want to empty it of all that hinders, all that comes from me and not Him. I want to make room for the things that are from Him. I want to keep my life in balance with what He's doing.

I dream up so many ways to keep myself busy with good things. I want the dreams to stop unless they come from Him. I want to be busy with His things.

I test everything these days, not just activities. I test attitudes, thought patterns, eating habits, exercise habits, faith-at-home ideas, home improvement projects - everything. How do they measure up? Does this meet all the criteria in our already very-busy lives? Can this stay or does this go?

I ask God. He is helping me put to death a lot of things in life, a lot of things in me.

For a time the words were gone as well, and I wondered if they would come back or if they were just another thing to keep me busy.

Just as Christ's journey leads Him ever-closer to the cross, as He lets go of all that hinders to seek after His Father's will, hardest though it was... I know I would lay down the words if He asks. If they truly come from Him, He can do what He wants with them. He can give them back to me or He can free me of them.

Christ's journey didn't end at the cross, it was never meant to. Life follows death. Not just life, but resurrected life. Grave-busting life that comes after the most broken death.

And the quiet lifts. I feel the words return. I am thankful.

*May the words I type, the words I string together be pleasing to You always, Lord. Do what you will with them. Use the words to bring new life - to me, to others. May the words honour You alone and fulfill Your purposes. In Jesus' name, Amen.*


**April 23rd, 2011**

**What's So Good About Good Friday?**

It is finished. Thank God it is done.

Friday is over, and Sunday is coming. On this day, this Saturday in between the death and the resurrection - we wait.

So much time to think about what happened just yesterday. Good Friday. What was so good about Good Friday?

Truly, truthfully, the horror of yesterday, of Jesus on the cross, it sits in my soul, in my heart, in my mind. Why? Why would someone do that for me? Why did it have to be so horrible? I know what they did to Him, yet I keep myself from thinking about it. I know they beat Him so badly, I know they scorned Him so brutally, I know they left Him feeling so alone and forsaken. I keep my thoughts on other things because I can't stand to know.

I ask myself, I cry out to God - What was so good about Good Friday? Why do they have to call that day - GOOD?

He answers me in the stillness, in the silence, in the horror of the cross...

*Take a closer look. Let your eyes wander over the WHOLE scene. What do you see Anna?*

I see a man on a cross, so hurt, so alone, so much pain.

*You need to look at the others, Anna. There you will see the reason for the man on the cross.*

I close my eyes to the man on the cross, not because I want to forget, but because my human eyes can only see pain. I need to look with my soul eyes.

A tiny flicker of a smile plays at the corner of my lips. It spreads, heart fills, eyes water.

I see.

Hope.

Love.

People saved from sin and death.

There are so many in the scene at the cross. So much hope. So much love. So much salvation.

Two men on two other crosses. One on either side of Jesus.
The three crosses themselves tell us the gospel story. Jesus hung between them. They had a choice, just as we have a choice. One man chose to rebuke Jesus, the other chose to believe in Him. Jesus promised fellowship with Him in paradise to the latter. (Luke 23:39-43)

A sign hung above Jesus' head. The Roman ruler had them place it there. It spoke of the priest's charge against Jesus. JESUS OF NAZARETH, THE KING OF THE JEWS is what it said. The priests wanted Pilate to change the sign to say that Jesus CLAIMED to be the King of the Jews. Pilate would not change it. (John 19:19-22) The gospel is for everyone, for the whole world, and can get into the soul of ANY man, woman or child.

A soldier stood at the foot of the cross at the moment of Jesus' death. He heard Jesus' cry as He breathed His last. This was not a normal death on a cross. On a cross people died with agony, exhaustion as they slipped into unconsciousness. Jesus died with a loud cry. This cry caused the soldier to believe. "Surely this man was the Son of God" is what the soldier said. (Mark 15:37-39) Even as Jesus took His last breath He was showing hope to others.

I close my eyes again, focused on the scene around Jesus on the cross. I close my eyes because I see Mary, His mother. I play it in my mind - over and over - a mother watching Her son die. This scene is too close to home. I close my eyes to see with my soul. And what I see is beautiful.

"When Jesus saw His mother there, and the disciple whom He loved standing nearby, He said to His mother, 'Dear woman, here is your son,' and to the disciple, 'Here is your mother.' From that time on, this disciple took her into his home." (John 19:26-27)

The love of a son for His mother. Even as He hangs dying, He cares for her. Such beauty there.

And I see the good on the Friday. The way Jesus reached out to anyone, anytime, anywhere. EVEN ON THE CROSS.

I see that even in the direst circumstances, Jesus offered salvation and the hope of eternity and freedom from sin. He offered love.

He never stopped being who He said He was. He never faltered. Any day was good when He was around.

Now Saturday has come. Souls are silent, anticipating, hoping, longing - is it really true? Will He really rise again? Did He mean what He said?

Are we really free?

I know the answer. My soul sings it in the stillness. Hope rises within.

I know what day comes after this day.

Sunday. It's coming.

**April 30th, 2011**

## The Story Of The Nerf Gun

Over the years the boys have gathered together quite a collection of Nerf guns. The collection started with a single-shot Nerf gun and has developed into an armory of a few Nerf guns for each boy (from birthdays, Christmases, and allowance contributions).

The latest purchase was a Nerf Stampede and there is a cool story to share behind that purchase.

Elijah made a little cash at the Medical School over the Christmas holidays. Medical students ask a few children to come in and practice running through an appointment with them. Elijah loves to do this every year and makes about $80 for a morning's worth of "work"!

This year he said he wanted to buy something for his big brother with the money he made. He said he wanted to buy him a Nerf Stampede. Josiah has wanted one of these for a while.

So we agreed that this was a good way to use the money, if he was sure about the purchase. He said he was sure.

We took him to the store and discovered the Stampede was on sale that week - on for $40 down from $60. AND it came with 100 extra darts - SCORE! The purchase was made.

Josiah said thank you and wasn't sure how to handle such generosity from his little brother at first. After Josiah opened up the Stampede and Elijah saw how cool it was, he promptly asked if he could have a turn. This continued for the rest of the day, and Josiah suggested that maybe Elijah should buy his own Stampede, or Josiah could give Elijah the money back that he spent on the Stampede.

The situation was escalating over the prized possession until finally we came up with a solution that would keep the lesson of generosity intact and allow both boys to experience the feeling of being on the giving and receiving side of said generosity.

Our idea was this - Josiah now purchase a Stampede for Elijah, but only if he was sure in his heart that he wanted to do this. After mulling it over for a while, Josiah agreed that was a good idea and would solve a lot of the issues the boys were facing.

So a couple of days later we were off to the store again.

I just smiled in amazement when we came to the Nerf aisle and saw that the Stampede was now on for $20. This is an amazing price for a big Nerf gun! From previous experience, I remembered that this store honours sale prices on items recently purchased, so we would get back $20 of the $40 Elijah had just spent on the Stampede.

My heart was happy. I knew this would be an awesome lesson for the boys in how God honours our generosity and how more often than not, the giver is blessed just as much, if not more, than the receiver. I whispered a "Thank You God" and we proceeded to the checkout.

Later on as we gathered as a family, I shared with the boys about how I saw God in all this business of Stampede giving and receiving the past few days. I shared with them that Elijah's desire to bless his big brother was wonderful, that Josiah's desire to honour his brother's gift even when it was causing issues was noble, that giving on top of giving (Josiah buying a Stampede for his brother) was the best response, that I could see God at work in all of it, and that once again I was amazed that God can use anything to speak to us and show us something of himself - even Nerf guns.


## May 2nd, 2011

### A Giving Heart

Our youngest son has been learning a lot about giving. He has a very generous heart. It must be one of his love languages, and I'm so glad he's developing his Giving Heart.

A few times recently Elijah has put some of his food aside. I know this isn't just a ploy to get out of finishing his meals, because he puts foods aside that he loves as well.

Today Elijah brought me an almost-empty bowl of popcorn and said, "This is for the poor people."

*Lord, grow my son's giving heart to overflowing and provide resources, ideas and opportunities for him to live out the generosity You wove into his being.*


## May 3rd , 2011

### Seeing Young Boys' Adventures In My Laundry

Forget the laundry detergent, I truly believe my boys think that rocks, sticks, acorns, and Lego pieces are what makes their clothes clean.

Why else would they leave these things in their laundry?


## May 6th, 2011

### Connecting With The Kids When You're Out Of Town

Josh and I were away recently on a church missions trip. This was my first missions trip and I found it SO HARD to leave the boys for a week, even though they were in very capable hands.

I needed to make sure there was a consistent connection with them every day while we were away, just in case phone lines went down.

I love to write notes to loved ones and tell them what I love about them. This idea grew to leave notes for the boys for each day we were away, highlighting one thing I loved about them, or one thing that was awesome about them.

I included a picture to go along with the note.

I taped a note to the back of each picture.

The notes and photos were slipped into pockets of a shoe organizer from the dollar store.

Eight notes for each boy.

I hope this keeps a strong connection going while we're away and encourages them in our absence.

## June 22nd, 2011

### Seeing You Across The Street

There was no traffic on the usually busy street
So he jogged across four lanes before the cars returned
To their hurried this way and that
He was thin - *Too thin* I thought
Food was not a regular luxury for him
His beard was dark and thick
His hair was long and framed his face
I could see his eyes clear across the street
He caught my gaze as he moved
My eyes were fixed on him
He wore red Crocs, a blue hoodie and jeans
He carried a bag that seemed almost empty
Flung over his shoulder nonchalantly
I perched on the bench on the concrete veranda
Outside the Christian radio station
The Christian bookstore was next door
They were hosting a sidewalk sale and free BBQ
And I sat enjoying a hot dog with my sons
Chatting with friends and meeting new people
When my eyes were drawn to his
*I still have time* I thought
As he started his jog across the street
*I can still grab a hot dog and offer it to him*
*I'll chat for one more minute*
*And then I'll go*
But I chatted too long
I reached the hot dog table as he was passing the station
I stood and stared at opportunity walking by
I caught his eye and he caught mine
A moment frozen - I smiled
I watched him continue his hurried stroll down the street
I know I couldn't catch him now
Or I wouldn't catch him now?
I saw You on the street today
In Your red Crocs and Your bushy beard
I'm sorry I didn't give You something to eat

When You were most likely very hungry
My heart lives the moment over and over
Each time the ending has changed
I don't linger too long
I meet you on the sidewalk
I hand you a hot dog and a bottle of water
You say *Thank you*
We share the same smile of the frozen moment
But this time it's a *Job well done my good and faithful servant* smile
Instead of an *I love you anyways* smile
You continue down the street with food in hand
And I continue through my day with blessing in heart
And this story has a much different ending
These words tell a very different story
That will have to wait for another day
Another chance
Another moment
Frozen - with You


## June 30th , 2011

### I Love You

Elijah loves to draw. He has been working through a set of How-To-Draw papers that show him how to draw his favourite cartoon or chapter-book characters.

On this particular day he was drawing the universe. He had been looking through a book at school about planets and was trying to remember them all.

Elijah also loves to encourage people, especially when they seem upset. I'm not sure what I was upset about, but he wrote out "I Love You Mom" on his hand and showed it to me. He kept showing it to me through the rest of the night and into the next day until the ink washed completely off.

I wrote "I Love You Elijah" on my hand and I'd show it to him when he showed me his hand.

I love these sweet moments with him. They are such precious gems for my treasure box of motherhood.

Believe me, there are many moments (even days!) that I wish I could erase from all our memories, but I try to focus on the good, learn from the bad, leave everything in the past and live in the moments.


## July 6ᵗʰ, 2011

### One More Time

The van stops in the school parking lot. It is the last day of school and the teachers have planned a fun day for my boys and they know they just have this one last day to go before summer vacation.
I made my last lunches for the year, nicely tucked them in their lunch bags and put them in backpacks - ONE MORE TIME.

The old school is closing its doors this summer and a new school has been built a few blocks over to accommodate all these children who need to learn and grow and play and laugh. We gather our things from the van and walk towards the old school - ONE MORE TIME. Josiah leaps out of the van and races ahead, he's always racing ahead, eager for the next thing. He's such a carpe diem kind of guy and I've always loved that about him. I'm forever trying to keep up with him and I hope he never stops giving me reason to try. Josh takes goodies he baked in to the teachers and blesses them with his thoughtfulness - he does that a lot for people, mostly his family - Thank God for that.

As Elijah goes to jump down out of the van, I grab him in a bear hug instead. I hold him close to me, his ear hovering near my lips. I want to joke with him and keep the day light-hearted - I know he will be sad as the day ends and he'll miss his friends and teachers and super-cool classroom. His whole school experience so far, his whole 2 years was spent in the same classroom with the same teacher. He gained another teacher and new friends this year when they began the Early Learning Program in our district. Next year means a new school, new classroom, new teacher and new friends. That's a lot for anyone to handle, not to mention a 6-year-old boy. But I know he can do it, I believe in him, I believe God's got wonderful things planned for my sons and this is just a part of the big picture.

I whisper in Elijah's ear so close to my face *I don't want to take you in. This is my last day of being a mom to a kindergartener and I don't want it to end. So how about I just take you home and you don't go to your class - ONE MORE TIME?*

We laugh, he puts up with me, I tell him I love him and put him on the ground. Elijah is more of a saunter-er and takes his time at life. His pace is much easier to keep up with on the tired days, though he loves to try to keep up with Josiah just as much as I do.

As Elijah and I start along the sidewalk - ONE MORE TIME - and get closer and closer to those big blue doors that stand at the entranceway to the school, I catch a glimpse. A glimpse of Elijah all grown up, awesome, the man God made him to be. The glimpse is not an actual picture in my head, but more a feeling in my heart, a reassurance in my soul. God is working everything out for my sons to get them where He wants them, when He wants them and how He wants them. One step at a time. Closer to growing strong men of faith and noble character. This school was one of those steps.

I am utterly encouraged. I can utterly trust. God speaks gently to my mother's heart. He knows my boys are growing up way too fast - always too fast. He knows I've been opening my treasure box of motherhood and looking through the contents. Rocking and nursing tiny baby boys. Feeling their fingers around mine as they fall asleep. Them playing with my hair as they fall asleep peacefully in my arms. Their baby-gazes up into my eyes as I nurse them. Their toothless smiles, their baby laughs, always new discoveries and me getting to share it with them. Crawling, walking, running, climbing, jumping, SOARING out of my reach. Once I got used to letting go I loved to watch them in all their boy-ness. Then the words came, they spoke, they understood, and life's discoveries were shared all over again, in different ways. We no longer communicated with just with eyes or expressions, but now with words too.

So many treasures to cherish from motherhood. So many gems I've kept (I learned, slowly but surely, to find some good in the bad, put that good in my treasure box and chuck the rest as far away as I could). My box is full to the brim. Then God makes it bigger, somehow, as only He can, and whispers to my heart that there is so much more coming. He says I won't want to miss it. And if I stare too long at the treasures I already have, I might forget to add the gems that are coming next. He doesn't want me to miss a thing. He wants to give me so many gems for my treasure box of motherhood. But I have to keep accepting them as I find them. To find them, I have to keep looking.

I see it later that day as I watch Josiah get awarded for Academic Achievement and Track and Field and Battle of the Books and see the young man he is becoming. Later still as the brothers give flowers and cards to their teachers. And I think back to Elijah this morning and how I didn't want him to walk through those big blue doors. But I'm so glad I got to hold his hand and walk through the doors with him - ONE MORE TIME.

May I get to walk beside both my boys as the doors open and close in their lives. One day soon they will stand taller than me, and instead of baby-gazes up into my eyes, it will be mother-gazes up into their eyes. Both so full of wonder and love.

*Thank you God for making me a mother.*


**July 7th, 2011**

**He Knows... He Always Knows**

It's a busy time. Most days are jam-packed tight.

I ask Josh to take the boys to soccer, so I can make my to-do lists and my to-get lists for the days that are coming.

He leaves with our sons, the house grows quiet except for the Christian radio station, and my head clears. I concentrate hard because I know time is limited.

Then I hear it. The song I love so much these days. You know, the ones that just grab you and you don't really know why, and sometimes you eventually figure it out, but sometimes you don't?

I can't resist - He calls to me - *Spend time with me, Anna, just a few moments. I know there is much to do and I'm so glad you're doing it, and you're doing it well, but come and dance around the kitchen with me, sing with me, enjoy my music with me and live in these few moments with me. Then you can go back to the work I've given you to do.*

I smile, I giggle, I drop my lists and I can't get to the kitchen fast enough to turn up the radio. My windows are all open, so I don't sing quite as loud as usual, and no spins with arms open wide just now, but I sit on the kitchen floor, feel the sunlight pouring through the windows, and we sing together, me and God.

Matt Maher - *Hold Us Together*

The song ends, I smile again, I thank God for the moments with Him, I go back to my chair to pick up my lists one more time.

Then I hear it again - the call to come to Him. He plays the other song that's really speaking to me right now - one after the other He plays them, calls me to Him, and this time I laugh right out loud and I let the lists lie on the floor where I dropped them a few moments ago, and I run back to the kitchen. I can almost see Him with arms wide open, wanting to circle the kitchen dance floor with me. ME! *One more spin, Anna? I enjoyed the last few moments with you so much, and I don't want them to end, can I fill your dance card for one more song?*

I am mush in His hands. The windows are still open, so I sit back down on the kitchen floor and I sing this one with Him, my soul soars in His presence.

Tenth Avenue North - *You Are More*

Sometimes I glimpse it - how big He is and how much He loves me. It humbles me to no end. It makes me drop everything and run into my kitchen to turn a volume dial on my radio. It makes me melt down to my floor and sing with my whole heart. It makes me know I am loved beyond belief - that He would play my favourite songs, back to back, just when I have a few moments of quiet. He weaves time together and makes it so that on July 6, 2011 the radio show picks two songs to play at a specific time. Those two songs bless me so completely just when I need them. Most of all it's that He would do that for me. The Creator of the Universe, playing songs on a radio for me.

Do you glimpse it? How much He loves you? How big His love is for YOU? What small, yet wonderfully big things has He done for you lately? Did you notice them? Did you share them with Him? That's why He does them... to share them with YOU.

Humbles me right down to the core.


## July 8th, 2011

### Looking Forward To The Summer

I really look forward to my summers with the boys. I don't dread them in the least. I really love having my sons around. Truly. If anything, I worry I won't be enough company for them or be able to keep up with them. For the most part we have it worked out. We visit a lot of parks and beaches and camps and we have a lot of fun along the way.

Inevitably there are rainy days or slow days when we don't leave the house. I know they will go a little stir-crazy on those days and try not to overreact when they find ways to get the boyish energy out inside.

Ball fights are always a "hit" in our house (and don't forget Nerf wars!). One day in particular I decided to sit back and enjoy the scene in front of me - their laughter, having healthy and energetic boys in the house, and their camaraderie with one another.

What a treat these boys really are to me... God help me to always remember to see them that way... through Your eyes.

**July 19th, 2011**

**Growing Boys**

I kneel beside his bed
He is 6 years old
Just turned 6 years old
I kiss his cheek
A few times
I can't stop
Kissing these cherub cheeks
I know they will fade
He will grow
And I'll see such a different face
When I kneel beside his bed
A young man's face
Will one day lie here
And I will love him more
Than I do now
If that's even possible
I ask God
How do I teach him
More about you?
What do you want me to do?
*It's not what I want you to do*
*But who I want you to be*
Who do you want me to be?
*I want you to be Jesus*
*To the little boy in this bed*
How can I possibly do that?
*Know Him more*
*Grow in Him more*
*Love Him more*
*That's what I want you to do*
*Simply know*
*Simply grow*
*Simply love*
What about my plans?
The devotions
The prayers

The service
The worship?
*Yes, but do them because*
*You know Him*
*You love Him*
*You are growing in Him*
*Not because they are your plans*
I kneel beside another bed
He is 9 years old
Almost 10 years old
He has seen me through
So many joys
So many failures
He grows so fast
I can hardly keep up
And I know what He needs
Most from me
Is a mother who is growing faster
In Him
Tomorrow is a new day
Of knowing
Of growing
Of loving
Lord, may it be the best day yet
Amen


## September 7th, 2011

### It's OK

*But blessed is the [woman] who trusts in the Lord, whose confidence is in Him. - Jeremiah 17:7 (NIV)*

It's a new chapter for me, in my faith, in believing. I'm still afraid, but not like I used to be. I'm still shy, but not like I once was. I'm still quiet, but I seem to know more now when I have something to say, and it's OK for me to say it, it's OK for others to hear, it's OK to share, it's OK to make mistakes, it's OK to be me.

It's OK. I find myself saying it over and over during the day - to myself, to my husband, to my sons. It's OK. It really is.

I trust Him. I find my confidence in Him. Not me anymore, not my flimsy and self-conscious person. Not me. Him. And I am utterly, truly blessed by this.

Confidence in myself can take me nowhere near where confidence in Him can take me. Confidence in myself can never accomplish what confidence in Him can accomplish. Confidence in myself can love, see, taste, feel, care, and encourage in such miniscule ways compared to living out life with confidence in Him.

Such beauty, such joy, such kingdom-building abounds in trusting Him, being confident in Him.

Don't you see - no matter how much I mess it up, how tired I get, how much I fail - I can find absolute peace that He's got me, He's got all of us, He's got the whole world - IN HIS HANDS. Nowhere to run, nowhere to hide - thank God - He's always working out His plans for good, for hope, for our future.

We simply have to seek Him, ask Him, leave it all with Him, let go, let God, trust, be confident.

He knows what He is about.

Let Him in, let Him loose, let Him love us that much.

Then take that love with us everywhere we go... home, work, school, church, across the street, across the world. And then let Him in there too, let Him loose wherever we are, let Him love others through us. Be His hands and feet.

Sometimes it sounds so impossible, but I'm realizing it's really so simple.

This morning I kiss my boys and send them off to class - with his love. I book appointments for sore hubby that should ease his pain - with His love. I speak with a stranger about the kids in the Dominican Republic and she gets it and sees the need - with His love. I clean my home and think about how to feed this small brood of mine, so they grow healthy and strong - with His love. I type and type and type - with His love.

*I trust You. I put my confidence in You. And I feel such sweet release. Really? Is it true? Can I leave it all in Your hands? Haven't I already put so much there for You to fix, restore, mold, shape?*

My child, It will never be enough, I'll always want more of you, I will pursue you forever, I can't help it, I love you that much. Give me the good and the bad, trust me, let me bless you, be confident in my love for you.

## September 9th, 2011

### What Makes You Come Alive?

I read this quote the other day, jotted it down on a scrap piece of paper, and can't get it out of my head... I'm really mulling this one over. Wanted to share it with you...

***Don't ask yourself what the world needs. Ask yourself what makes you come alive, and then go do that. Because what the world needs is people who have come alive.***

*-* Howard Thurman

God made us all such unique individuals, and He made us so unique to fill such unique calls in life and accomplish His purposes, simply by being ourselves. Not what we think we should be, what others think we should be, what the world says it needs, what will make us look good, what is fashionable, etc., etc.

So underneath it all, getting right down to the heart of it... what makes you come alive?

## September 20th, 2011

### Back-To-School Reflections

School started two weeks ago. Whenever school starts I start. Reflecting, that is. It's inevitable. The house is suddenly quiet for extended periods of time, and I think, and think, and think. Even while I'm out grocery shopping, volunteering at the school, taking a walk - everywhere. I think it's because my boys aren't with me. I think it's because when I am with them, I am completely, fully with them. Or at least I try to be. So when they return to school in the fall, I have this space in my life.

In the past I filled the space with missing them. Don't get me wrong, I still miss them, but it's a much healthier kind of missing them. It's the kind of missing that enjoys the time apart and looks forward to the time together. It's the kind of missing that makes sure the time apart is used to getting things done so that the time together is used for *being* together.

*Being*. Simply *being*. This could mean anything. This could even mean grocery shopping (which we all despise). It's the moments that count, not what we're actually doing. There's *being* to do at the grocery store just as much as there's *being* to do at the beautiful park by the lake. *Being* is everywhere. Living. In the Moments. Always. Everywhere. Fully in the moments. Living.

It has taken me so much practice to get to this point, so many mistakes that I will continue to make. But at least I get it more now than yesterday, and all the yesterdays before that.

My boys are growing. And I am so glad. One day closer to being all God intends for them to be. And I get to share this day with them. No matter what fills it. I get to share a lot of the days coming with them. I have already shared almost 4000 days with my older son who just turned ten this summer.

What has filled those days? Lots of pain, hurt, sadness and regret. That's what. But oh no, let's not stop there. Let's learn from the bad, leave it in the past and realize that laughter, love and life is what filled most of those 4000 days. I may not have another 4000 with him before he leaves my home, or before he ventures off more and more into his pieces of the world God has given him to minister to in His name. I may not hold his hand through much of the next few thousand, and he may not need me to carry him like I used to. But he'll still need me to carry him. In a totally different way. In my heart, in my prayers, in faith.

The future looks different, awesome, exciting, full of wonder. Full of *being*. Living. In the moments. With those God gives me to love for however long He has me love them.

As I cleaned out closets this summer, I found boxes of cards I kept from the first few days of my son's lives. When being and surviving where entwined in a blur of feeding, changing and sleeping. Days tucked safely inside my treasure box of motherhood. I kept the cards because I love the words - some of the first words given to my boys. Words of blessing for their lives, for our life together as a family.

I was finally ready to let go of the cards and tuck away the words of blessing in my treasure box. I want to record a few of the words given - words about boys and what it means to be a boy - because my boys surely live up to the words.

Let's have a chuckle together shall we?

*Baby boys are well known for their love of good times, their talent for drama, their heart-stopping climbs, their bold statements, their drive to explore, their creative approach to what crayons are for... so whatever adventures you have with your son, you'll be thrilled and amused by (almost) everyone!*

*If he can come into the world and show you that he's a little angel from the start, if he can fuss and kick and lose his halo, then turn around and smile and win your heart... If he delights you though at times he's naughty, and makes you laugh at him instead of scold, if at one moment he can try your temper and then the very next be good as gold... if he can fill each day with high adventure and fill your life with happiness and joy, then he'll be everything you've always wanted - he'll be a happy, healthy little boy! Have a lifetime of fun with him...*

*Baby boys are wonderful, they're playful and they're fun - they know just how to make you smile, no matter what they've done... so just enjoy your little boy and watch him learn and grow - and in return he'll give to you the greatest joys you'll know!*

*Baby boys come in all shapes and sizes, shy and adventurous, full of surprises, with misshapen halos and mischievous grins, small, grubby faces and sweet, sticky chins. They'll keep you so busy, and yet all the while, nothing can brighten the world like their smile!*

*To make a little boy, star dust was sprinkled; it settled in a twinkle in his eye. The music of the waves became his laughter. His lips were curved to hold the question: Why? Sinew was used to knit his frame together, so his strength could give and take the stresses of life. The storms of time would bend but never break him - he'd grow up strong and unafraid to live. He was given a smile like sunrise to welcome each day with eager joy. This child was made strong and beautiful, so all could see that he was indeed a special gift.*

And these cards were just really nice!

*There's a wonder in so many things, in all the joys and gifts life brings, and yet the greatest wonder lies within a newborn's trusting eyes. Each time you look into your newborn's eyes, may you see all the wonder of today and all the promise of tomorrow.*

*A baby is... someone precious from the start, bringing joy to every heart, full of wonder, full of fun - giving smiles to everyone. Huggable when wide awake, ready to play patty-cake, lovable when sound asleep, counting tiny baby sheep. Growing taller every day, learning darling things to say. Aren't you lucky, happy too, having someone sweet and new?*

*It's said God made children to bring the world joy, through the giggles and laughter of each girl and boy... It's said God made children to bring the world sharing, pure understanding, kindness, and caring... And specially to show us His peace from above, for it's said God made children to bring the world love.*


## September 22nd, 2011

### How Is Your Heart?

I wear a heart monitor for two days. The past few months I feel flutters sometimes, skipped beats sometimes, strange things sometimes. I go see my doctor and she says it's actually quite normal for hearts to "restart" now and then.

*When do you notice it?* she asks.

*Mostly when it's quiet, when I'm sitting or lying down, when life is still.* I answer.

Maybe it's been a long time since life was still, or quiet, since I let my heart sit or lie and **rest**.

Maybe when I do, I realize there is something wrong with my heart.

Maybe not my earthly heart, but my soul heart.

Maybe I don't need a monitor to tell me about my earthly heart.

Maybe I need a monitor to tell me about my soul heart.

I think I care for it, I know I skip a beat sometimes, I feel irregular flutterings sometimes. But I keep going, keep bustling, keep moving on. I don't quiet enough to just listen to my soul heart sometimes.

So I ask God, *How is my heart?*

Because he doesn't look at our earthly hearts, does He? He looks at our soul hearts. And He's the only one who can monitor those. No machinery in the world could be strapped onto a person for a couple of days and tell the doctors how their soul hearts are, can they?

I know my family history for earthly hearts. Not great. And I know my family history for soul hearts - I've been reading through the Old Testament, tracking those Israelites with fresh eyes, seeing new things, learning about my soul family. Not great either.

Then I read about the few who followed their God, who chose Him above all others, who LOVED him. They used their soul hearts well and filled them with love for their God. There were a few kings like Josiah and David. The given names of our older son. The names we gave him to remind him of the good in his soul family. There were a few prophets like Elijah. The name we gave to our younger son, to remind him of the power of his God. Josh gave him the middle name Thunder just to make sure. There were a few Israelites like Caleb and Joshua. The names we chose for our middle son, who lives in the promised land before us. We gave him another middle name - Freedom - to remind ourselves of the ultimate freedom his soul heart lives in for eternity.

I want to be one of the few. No. I want to be one of the many. I hope and pray for many who choose God and love Him with all they've got. With all their hearts.

139

I drive to get my boys from school this afternoon, and the sun shines down as I listen to *How He Loves* in the van. Continuously playing the words over and over, like I just really need to hear them right now. The song says we are TREES. At church on Sunday morning I see the familiar words on the big screen up front, and I smile, and I sing the song with hundreds around me, and I worship like I haven't for a long time. My friend sends me an email with a link to the song, like God whispered to her heart that I need to keep listening to those words, like I shouldn't stop just yet. My soul heart hasn't quite heard them yet.

So I listen to them again as I drive in the sunshine. I pull up to a light with the windows rolled down, and I always wonder if I should turn it down or not (because I have it right cranked and I'm singing at the top of my lungs). I check to see if the cars beside have their windows rolled down too - yep, both of them. I stop my singing, and I turn the music down a little, but then I realize they need to hear the words just as much as I do, because that part of the song where he just constantly sings He Loves Us is coming up and don't we all need to hear that - always? Who am I to keep the words from flowing to those around me as well? But I keep my voice to myself and I let *David Crowder* proclaim God's love, just in case I'm off-pitch.

As I pull away from the light I feel a sudden gust of wind through the window. I could almost feel God's hand brushing my hair away from my face, patting me on the head just like my daddy always does when what he really wants to do is tell me he loves me. And I see how all these years my heavenly daddy was showing me love through my earthly daddy, with a simple pat on the head. It wasn't what he didn't do, it was what he did do. And he showed me love in his own quiet way, and those gentle pats on the head I hold dear in my soul heart, each one.

So how is my soul heart? I'll leave it with God to answer. He's the only one who can monitor each beat of that heart of mine.

But *How He Loves*, and if I let His love flow through my soul heart, that life-giving love can never cease to keep a steady beat.

## October 12th, 2011

### Butterfly Faith

I can't stop thinking about those butterflies. Elijah's class watched as caterpillars grew big and squirmy in their clear plastic cages this fall. Then they watched as each caterpillar formed its own chrysalis and their smooth, green bodies went into hiding. The anticipation built in the classroom. The teacher had told them what would come next.

The students made their own orange butterfly wings out of Bristol board and drew their own unique shapes on the replica wings.

They made butterfly headbands.

They rehearsed a butterfly play.

At last it was time. The monarchs emerged from their cocoons in all their orange, black and white glory. The students were thrilled. They knew it would soon be time to send their new friends to flight.

Monarchs travel to Mexico every fall to escape the cold winter weather. They vacation in warmer climates. Such smart little creatures.

The big day arrives, the day they've been waiting for, rehearsing lines for, creating wings for - the Butterfly Release Party!

Parents are invited, treats are baked, sunshine beckons the party to begin.

Josh and I show up with excitement. We snap pictures, nectar is smeared on student's noses, butterflies enjoy a nectar snack before their flight.

Each one released individually, students wonder if they will stay and visit for a while before they leave on their journey.

Then when the time is right, OFF THEY GO!

Soaring higher and higher, the children sing a goodbye song to the butterflies as they flutter out of sight.

There is sadness, but there is joy. Missing, but peace.

This is just the way it is for butterflies. And the children loved them anyways. Unconditionally. Beautiful.

Elijah gives me butterfly kisses at night, and the Bristol board wings and headband sit on our stairs. If we don't find an Anniken Skywalker outfit for Halloween, the butterfly gear is a back-up plan.

I think about the butterflies, about my butterflies. My Caleb took to flight long before any of us imagined. But I have two caterpillars to raise up for now. I am still a caterpillar myself. Still foraging, growing, preparing for my metamorphosis.

Ah, the faith of a butterfly. To enter that chrysalis state - do they have any idea what they will become when they emerge? Do they sense it at all - the utter beauty they morph into? The gift of flight waiting to be explored - to journey to distant lands, warmer weather - leaving friends behind in their sadness, their missing, their acceptance.

We know what awaits, unlike the butterfly. Though we can't really imagine anything like our emergence, our flight, our journey to the heavens - we still know it's coming.

How do we know? We know by faith.

*Now faith is confidence in what we hope for and assurance about what we do not see. - Hebrews 11:1*


## October 19th, 2011

### Washing My Son's Feet

I'm lying on my sister's couch, huddled under a soft, blue blanket, trying to beat the chill from hours out in the forest this morning.

I can hear the boys playing in the backyard, my dad is sitting on a chair close by, watching the rumbling and laughing from behind the window pane.

I can't keep my eyes open. I doze off, waking now and then when a boy comes in and slams the patio door. It is peaceful amidst the chaos, and I love hearing the cousins enjoying each other's company.

Josiah comes in for a few moments, and he tells me he's going to need to wash his feet when he's done playing. I realize he left his shoes inside for this round of play, choosing to feel the plush green

142

grass between his toes - he loves that feeling. And what Josiah does, Elijah often does, so there will be two pairs of boy's feet to wash. But for now I doze off for a few more minutes.

Finally it's time to come in for dinner. Boys are hungry anyways. My sister and I decide these boys should head up to the bathtub - now. She gets the towel and turns on the water and the boys step into the ceramic white bowl. I can see the dirt mixing in with the clear water, making mud that drains away.

I start to give them the soap to wash their own feet, then I catch this glimpse of a moment waiting to be lived. This time it's not hard to choose to live it. I wonder - when was the last time I washed my son's feet? Bath times are long gone, and these toes are kept clean by their hands instead of mine now. I don't think I've ever just washed their feet. I WANT to be Jesus in these next few moments. Will they pick up on it - the washing of the feet - just like Jesus with his disciples? When they came inside with dirt on their toes, when they were getting ready to sit down to a meal together?

Josiah says it as I start to wash. "Just like Jesus." I smile, I am instantly blessed right down to the core. He gets it. His faith is so quiet sometimes, he doesn't say much about God sometimes, it's just his way, and he gets it.

*Thank You God for giving me this chance to wash my son's feet. May I do this in so many ways in their lives as they grow. Help me to keep teaching them, showing them, living out for them, more of You.*

I never thought I'd find so much joy in washing dirt and muck from between a boy's toes. Motherhood truly is a wonder.


## November 2nd, 2011

### Finding Beauty In The Dirt

Me and the boys were visiting my parents recently. They have about 3 acres of land with forest and meandering river throughout - it's a beautiful haven in a country setting and we'll all enjoy it for as long as they are able to have it!

There is always work to be done to maintain this haven. This visit there was a heap of dirt that needed to be moved and levelled out to mark the beginnings of a roundabout driveway my dad is working on.

I don't know why, but I was so excited about digging in this dirt. Most likely it's the same reason my dad leaves the lawn for me to mow if he knows I'm coming for a visit, or the same reason he gave me that questioning glance when I clambered up on the roof to shovel off snow with him during a particularly hard winter. I just love it - the physical exertion in caring for the land, taking care of the simple basics of life, working with nature so we can live in community together, caring for God's creation - the first job He ever gave to us. It's something to instinctual in me, so pure and raw, I love the feel of dirt (but not worms), the smell of grass, the heaviness of snow in a shovel - to me there's real beauty in all that. There's farmer blood in me, I just know it. My father grew up on a farm in England for about 20 years, my grandparents worked the land and the animals for longer still. My oldest son would talk about farming once in a while. I think it just runs in the family.

So I invite my boys to grab a shovel from the big old shed and follow me out front. We look at the pile of dirt for a minute, make our plan of attack, and literally "dig in". We work as a team, one son chipping away at the top of the pile which has hardened slightly from the weather, another son moving the loosened dirt to its new location, me just digging and throwing, digging and throwing. Loving just about every minute of it, knowing I'll be sore tomorrow, and loving that thought too.

The dirt we dig starts to shape the roundabout my dad envisions, and we stand to look at our work every few minutes. We take pride in our accomplishment, we enjoy the comradery of our small team of diggers, and we laugh and help each other and it's all really, really good. For some reason, I am alive in all this, so alive, so born for this, and I wonder what that means for the rest of my life, this knowledge that I am a digger, builder, nature-lover to the core.

We are almost done our share of the task at hand. The rest we'll leave for Grandad. We imagine the surprise he'll get when he comes home and sees our work. We hope we've done a good job and we look forward to his reaction to our efforts. Always wanting to make daddy, grandad happy - I guess that never stops, does it? Same with the heavenly father - do you ever sense His smile on you? There is nothing else like that in the whole world.

As we finish up, Josiah brings me his dirty shovel and as he walks by he says, "I can see why you walked down the aisle to Dad that day. When we were digging, you walked by and I thought 'Wow!' You looked really good." He fills my heart up for years with a few words, and I'll put that moment immediately into my treasure box of motherhood, right where it belongs. I smile, I say thank you, I just revel in my son calling me beautiful in the middle of a dirt heap.

I think about it for a minute - why was I Wow in that moment? Probably because I felt so alive. It must be how God sees us - when we are using our gifts (even gifts of digging!) and using them to bless others and using them in community to serve together - that must be the most beautiful sight to God. It's why we're alive. He made us in His image. When that image reflects Him even for just a split second - it is pure beauty. And I think Josiah must have caught me in one of those seconds, reflecting the image of God. That makes me feel so amazing.

Beautiful as I dig up dirt, who would have thought?


**November 27th, 2011**

**I Am A Child Of God**

I wrote this article for the *Link & Visitor* - a magazine of the Baptist Women of Ontario and Quebec...

*Yet to all who received Him, to those who believed on His name, He gave the right to become children of God. - John 1:12*

Daddy, I need a hug. It's been one of those days that left me exhausted, confused, frustrated and lonely. I shut out all the people I love - AGAIN. I was grumpy. I was mean. I was anything but Proverbs 31. Forgive me.

*Come here child, I still love you. I always will. Today was good; it stretched you, your heart grew a little more and in the end you filled it with love. And you filled your family's hearts with love. Remember that part of the day, learn from the rest and forget about it. I already have.*

Daddy, can I have some money? The bills keep coming and there are extras this month and the budget is already spent. We're trying our best to use the money You give us wisely and we're giving money to the church and we're not buying things we don't need. But there just doesn't seem to be enough right now.

*Here child, never doubt my provision, you bless me by your wisdom in spending and giving. You are doing well, and I see that. Well done.*

Daddy, I need a band aid. It's not for me, it's for my friend. She's hurt. Real bad. She has cancer, Dad, and she has children and a wonderful husband, and I don't know how I can help. But I know You can help. Will You?

*Oh child, I see your hurt. I see your friend's hurt. I will heal her. It may not be in the way you hope for, but I am with her and her family. I am working out my will for them all. One day you will see how I will make everything better and there will be no more hurt.*

Daddy tell me a story. I love Your stories, and You tell them so well.

*Yes, child. I've written many stories for you. Every person you meet is one of my stories. You have to take the time to stop and read them. They tell of my love and adventure, sadness and joy. They tell of heroes and battles and romance. They tell of bravery and courage. They tell of your family. And there are many stories written for you and for all your brothers and sisters to read in My Book. Read them together, tell each other my stories.*

Daddy, thank You for Jesus. I love Him so much. I learn so much about Him as I read Your Big Book, the Bible. I just love that book. I love the stories, the people, and especially the happy ending. I want Jesus with me all the time, I know He died for me and I believe everything I read about Him in the Bible. The part I like best is when I read about living with You in heaven one day. I can't wait for that!

*Dear child, I can't wait for that day either. I can call you child because of Jesus, because you believe in Him, because you want Him in your life. You can come to me with all your happy times, your sad times and everything in between. I am always here for you. Never forget that. My arms are open wide to you - any time, any place. Just keep calling to me. I am so happy to be your daddy. If only you could see how much you bless me, just by being you. One day you'll see. That day is coming soon. For now, know I love you more than you can imagine, beautiful child, beautiful daughter of mine.*

## November 28th, 2011

### Sharing The Wealth

We received a letter from World Vision that asked us to sign a Christmas card for our sponsored child, Saowalak - in Thailand.

I asked the boys to sign their names, and Elijah went off to grab his wallet after he was done. The boys get an allowance every week and we're trying to teach them good money management skills - so far really good.

Elijah started counting money out of his wallet. I asked him what he was doing, and he said he wanted to give Saowalak some money so she's not so poor anymore.

I love it when it just flows freely from us, you know? That desire to serve, to reach out - I think it's growing in us - the certainty that we CAN make a difference. With whatever we have, whatever we can share - with people as close as next door or around the globe.

Such hope in this small act of Elijah's - not so small in God's eyes, and not so small in mine.

**November 28th, 2011**

**Trick Or Treat For Hope**

We've done some service projects in our family the last couple of months. It's been a wonderful time of connecting with each other and our world. Reaching out, trying new things - I've really enjoyed it. There is such a "filling up" that happens when we serve others.

And right now, yes, I plan out ways we can serve. But this is just to make sure we develop the habits. It is truly hard to develop some habits - especially ones that make us step outside our comfort zones, that take time out of our already-busy schedules, and that use up our energy and resources.

It's so worth it - the things we give up, the time we spend - it's so worth it.

My hope is that one day service will be so much a part of us, that no schedule need be done, it just happens.

My husband has run a food drive every Halloween since I've known him. He started Trick or Treat for Hope with his youth group way back and has carried on the tradition wherever he's been. Many versions and variations of this event have popped up over the years, and many of the major organizations like Free the Children have picked up on the idea in one way or another.

Every year at our church, youth from our congregation, their friends, and other youth from around the city gather to go out and take part in a different kind of trick or treating. They collect non-perishable food items for the local food bank, then the food bank truck comes and loads up at the end of the night. Groups compete to see who brings in the most pounds of food per person. It's all good fun.

Last year, my friend Amy challenged me to involve our children. Sometimes she challenges me like that, and I'm grateful for the push I need at times, and the support she gives.

It went really well last year, and our children collected a couple of wagon-loads of food, as well as tons of treats for their treat bags!

This year we tried again, and half-filled a grocery cart!

The kids really enjoyed this - they are getting very bold in asking people to donate as they were giving them candy. Most people responded in a very positive way, some didn't want to participate but were still very friendly, and we just had a great time!

After an hour or so, the kids (and us) were getting tired... and it was time to wrap up this Halloween night, drop our collected items back at the church, and call it a very successful night!

## December 8th, 2011

### No Room For Him

*And she brought forth her firstborn son, and wrapped him in swaddling clothes, and laid him in a manger; because there was no room for them in the inn. - Luke 2:7 (KJV)*

I get tears in my eyes. Every Christmas. I get so sad. I'm sorry, but I do. It's a new thing - just been happening the last couple of years. I'm not trying to be a stick-in-the-mud, I'm not trying to dampen anyone's Christmas spirits. Those who know me know how much I LOVE Christmas. As soon as I found out about Advent and discovered ways we could celebrate Christmas even longer (beginning in November!), I was a happy camper indeed. That meant putting up the decorations even earlier (!) if I wanted them up in time for Advent!

But the last couple of years, I can't shake it. Every December when I have to go do any kind of shopping, there are tears, sadness, loneliness.

I don't like shopping much to begin with, and definitely not in the craziness of the stores at Christmas, but as I think back to a few years ago, at least then I used to love the decorations (still lots of nativity items back in the day) and songs (still mostly traditional Christmas hymns way back when).

It's just so different now. I find myself hunting for anything resembling that first Christmas, anything remotely looking like a nativity scene. I snatched up a gift box that I didn't need today, just because of the manger scene painted on it - beautiful. But that really was all I could find.

149

And I miss Him. So much. It's His birthday and why can't we just celebrate it? I would hate it if someone forgot my birthday. I would feel horrible. And I think that's what makes me so sad. People are forgetting His birthday. Yes, there's lights and decorations and gifts and music and concerts and parties - but honestly, getting really honest here - He's usually not invited. I imagine how I'd feel if no one invited me to my own party. And if they invited someone else and it wasn't even their birthday. I would feel so unloved and rejected. And I think it just breaks my heart to think of Jesus feeling like that. My Messiah - He didn't get the invite.

Yep, here come the tears, I've hit the nail on the head. I am so thankful that typing out words helps me process life.

*Thank You God for the gift of words and how they help me so much to live out this life You've given me.*

*Jesus, I invite You to Your party this year, to this celebration of You. This Christmas, please enjoy every song with us, see Your children's faces as we share gifts. What do You want for Christmas? Ah yes, You want us to love You and love one another. Simple as that. Let Your love reign supreme in everything we do this year and every year to celebrate Your birth.*

*It's Your birthday. Happy Birthday Jesus. Let us make room in our hearts, our homes, our holidays, always, for You. May there ALWAYS be room for You. Help us not to leave You out in the manger anymore. Have the nicest rooms in our lives. Make Yourself at home in us.*

*I love You, Anna.*

# 2012

**January 1st, 2012**

**Day By Day**

I wrote this article for the *Link & Visitor* - a magazine published by the Baptist Women of Ontario and Quebec. I thought it would be a great one to share with you at the start of 2012. Happy New Year!

*Therefore we do not lose heart. Though outwardly we are wasting away, yet inwardly we are being renewed day by day. - 2 Cor 4:16*

There's a calendar that hangs on my wall. It's a special calendar, not like the others. The other calendars are full - one full of appointments and family commitments, another full of faith-at-home ideas and plans, an online calendar that reminds me of birthdays, anniversaries and holidays, and a fridge calendar full of menu plan ideas for feeding my family. But this one calendar that hangs on my wall is different. It's totally, absolutely, completely... empty. Blank.

I printed out a year's worth of dates by their months and taped them together to make a year-at-a-glance. A year of nothing. You might be wondering, *'What craziness, what madness, what strange new teaching is this?'* Quite honestly, I'd had enough. I was up to here with lying down to rest at the end of each day and only feeling a melancholy passing of time. I would weigh my efforts and actions each day and constantly come up short - with myself, my wifing, my mothering, my housekeeping, my Christianity - all of it. Never good enough. I was most definitely losing heart.

I would subconsciously hear the relentless tick tock, tick tock, tick tock of the time I had with this life, this marriage, this motherhood, and this sharing of the gospel. The ticking and tocking chased me to bed each night and woke me with a start each morning.

I looked in the mirror one day and took a really long look at myself. I saw what only my human eyes could see - the emergence of gray/white hairs, the increasingly more prominent wrinkles around my eyes and forehead, the waistline no longer visible after 3 big baby boys and years of neglect. Needless to say, I didn't like what I was seeing.

Then I asked God to please, please, please show me who I was in His eyes. One by one He showed me, blessed me, overwhelmed me with the beautiful things He saw when He looked at me. The mirror faded away and it was just me and my Maker, telling me who He made me to be. The blue eyes that can't help but see the beauty in His creation. The long hair that my husband loves, and my sons once twirled as they drifted into baby-sleep, each strand that God brushes and messes at will with His wind. The wrinkles that speak of decades of play and laughter. Frown lines that tell of occasional pain that He brought me through, pain that helped me trust Him more and made me more confident in His love and care for me. The waistline that is simply part of a still-very-healthy body that has the ability to enjoy life through all kinds of movement.

Everything changed in those moments, and suddenly I knew. When I look at time, at each day I'm given through my earthly eyes, there will always be lack. But when I gave my life to Christ I also gave Him my time. It is His, my days are His.

The ticking and tocking no longer chase me to bed, instead they lull me to sleep. They no longer wake me with a start, instead they gently rouse me to get going on a new day. I never know quite what the days will bring. They are His days. The tick tock is His way of reminding me that He's got things for me to do. Gone are the nights full of despair or the days full of drudgery. I still have to live out the appointments, commitments, plans, meal prep and special days on my calendars, but the one that hangs blank on my wall - that calendar is for God to fill however He wants. There is freedom, life abundant and countless blessings waiting on that calendar and I trust He will show them to me in his time and in His purpose.

*May I be open to all You have for me Lord, always leaving room for You in each of my days.*

How To Renew Day By Day:

- Leave extra room in your calendar and ask God how He wants to fill it
- Spend time with God and just listen to Him speak to your heart
- Look for God in the simple, timeless things of life
- Give God everything that makes you lose heart

**January 4th, 2012**

**Word For 2012**

I first read about the idea of naming a new year at a blog I've followed for a few years now.

Last year my words for the year were BOLD and CONFIDENT. And it was quite a year living in this new state of boldness and confidence. People really noticed - this new side of Anna - more sure of herself.

In 2011 I asked God for a clear vision of what He wanted from my life, what He wanted to fill the spaces that were left when my sons spent their days in school. He reminded me that first comes Him, He longs for time with me, spending all these days He's given me with Him, sharing everything - the tiny details, the big dreams and everything in between. After that must always come husband and sons. They are enough. If all I ever did was provide a warm and welcoming home for these men of mine, a place for solace and entering into God's presence - that would be enough. Always. And God brought me back to those basics and allowed me time to get used to the idea of it, of living such a simple, focused life. It was refreshing, so needed, a breath of sweet clarity.

Then I asked if there was more - *what about the writing, where does it fit in? What about the desire to teach the children, not just my own, to pour into the next generation? What about the longing to finish up my schooling? What about missions?* I hammered him with questions that needed answers once and for all. I needed to put so much to rest. One by one He helped me let go of the things that were not from Him, that had no place in my life, at least not for now. And there are so many things He kept in my life - there is always more than enough to do.

First and foremost, always, is teaching my children - more of Him, more of life, more of service, more of character - all these things I must learn first for myself - not easy, but so necessary - before I can pass them along to my children. So we learn - together. I look into schools and courses and online learning and how long would it take, what will they transfer in from the 5 post-secondary schools I've already attended (a symptom of never being quite sure of what I was

154

doing!). All the while, feeling this growing sense of confidence that YES, there is great peace boiling over in me about finishing my university degree! And YES there is still a longing to go on to Teacher's College - but the details I leave with God, for the closest school that offers that one year of training I'd need beyond my Bachelor's is an hour and a half drive - one way - away from my home and my family.

Confidence grows in wanting to pay for as much of the schooling as I can as I go, so no huge debt at the end. So I ask God for a job that fits with our family. He provides a bookstore job - perfect for me - with wonderful people to work for. A part-time job that I love.

Boldness comes as I learn to express what I need to be the person God is leading me to become. Trying to never be demanding, just asking, letting others bless me - not easy because I love to be the one to do the blessing - God gives me many opportunities to keep on doing just that. Letting others in - starting with husband and children - giving over control, sharing the load, recognizing it should have been this way all along, equipping boys to be men as they learn more chores, trying their unique ideas for solutions to problems, becoming more of a family in that instead of one woman trying to do it all and getting VERY tired in the midst of it.

First missions trip happened in 2011 - a dream since I was little. And I went with my hubby - AMAZING. I am changed, and thankfully so, and boldness and confidence come from staring to know my place in the global family. Hopefully many more missions coming, hopefully taking sons, hopefully finding our place around the world in whatever ways God asks us to serve.

And the writing will stay, can't help but stay - not really a question of it staying or leaving, just the amount of time I can give to it. It will be less for a while, but it will never leave. I am confident and sure of that. I ask God to use the words as He will because there will be less of them for a time while school takes the forefront.

I registered for 5 classes, started yesterday, and I'm feeling great about it.

Sons are now awake, the day begins before I'm ready, but I wanted to share my word for this year.... it's been brewing in me and I know it's the one....

FREE.

Free to be all I'm meant, all we're meant, free from fear, free from lack, free from... so much that I can't even name yet.

We are all free in Christ - even when life is hard and twisted and painful - we are still free. Easier to feel it when all is right and good and lovely, but freedom exists in any circumstance. And I'm so excited to learn that this year - 2012.

May it be your best one yet.

Blessings!


## January 23rd, 2012

### This Little Light Of Mine, I'm Gonna Let It Shine

I wrote this article for the recent edition of the *Link & Visitor* magazine - a publication by the Baptist Women of Ontario and Quebec.

*Have I not commanded you? Be strong and courageous. Do not be afraid; do not be discouraged, for the LORD your God will be with you wherever you go. - Joshua 1:9*

"Go upstairs and get dressed, Elijah."

"Will you come with me?"

"Why do you want me to come with you?"

"Because I'm too scared of the dark."

He's been saying this to me for almost a year now. There are two night lights in his room and a list of "Fear-Fighting" Bible verses taped to his wall. We pray for no bad dreams every night before bed. He used to crawl into our bed in the middle of the night - so cute and cuddly. Now he's too scared to leave his room until the light starts to peek through his window shade in the morning. My husband thinks it's great that he's broken the habit of these middle-of-the-night visits, but really he's just replaced the old habit with a new habit of fear. Besides, I miss those snuggle visits! Elijah is six now, so I know the mid-night snuggles had to end eventually, but what to do about all this fear that's crept into his life? The way he cowers at the darkness, the terrified look in his eyes - what's a mother to do?

I see myself in his cowering stance and his big, blue eyes full of fear. I ask my friends for advice. I ask myself, 'How does God handle me when I'm afraid?' I think back to the way God held my hand through the darkness of loneliness when I was single and lived far from family, the darkness of grief when our Caleb was stillborn, and the darkness of confusion when my dreams and plans seemed to disappear.

I'm scared of the dark too. I don't like it one bit. I want to help my sweet boy overcome his fears and be able to move freely through the home God has given him.

I tell Elijah this house is safe, that there's even Bible verses stapled in the walls. I tell him no monsters or ghosts are allowed in this house, only God's angels are allowed. I remind him that he is God's warrior and needs to put on his armour of God. He just keeps looking at me with those bright blue sparkles of innocence.

I pray a silent prayer for wisdom and have a moment of inspiration. I tell Elijah to grab his flashlight and I tell him to use the light to make the darkness disappear. The light will show the way. That should make him brave, strong, and courageous. That should take away the terror and the discouragement of fear.

He grabs his flashlight and fixes those beautiful eyes on me once again. "Will you come with me, Mommy?"

"But you have your flashlight to take away the darkness. You try to go by yourself now."

"No. I'm still too scared. Please come with me."

I think back to my Heavenly Father and the many times He held my hand in the darkness. I take Elijah's hand and his flashlight guides our path up the stairs to turn on more lights, bigger lights, stronger lights. Lights that drown out all the darkness. Then my son tells me he's OK now.

I come back downstairs to pack lunches for school. I think about how my presence, and a little light, make all the difference for my son. He can deal with the fear when he knows someone is beside him, when he can see a little light, then more light, and even more light until the darkness is gone. The light and the presence give him strength and courage to face the fear.

For now, I can hold his hand and keep encouraging him in his struggle with the darkness. There will come a time when he'll need to walk the path alone, with no hand to hold and no flashlight to shine, trusting in the Presence and Light within. The same Presence and Light that promises to be with us wherever we go.

"Fear-Fighting" Verses

- Joshua 1:9
- Psalm 23:4
- Psalm 27:1
- Psalm 34:4
- Psalm 56:3-4
- Psalm 91:4-6
- Isaiah 41:13

## February 11th, 2011

### Scenes From The Soul – Crossing The Tracks

She rides home in the family van, with all three of her men - one is her soul mate, two are her young men in training. Time is tight, swimming lessons start soon, young adults coming for dinner, assignment beckons completion for online university class. All this after waking early to finish up banking, read some pages for school and work at part-time job. She knows these are all good things, she is not bitter, just tired, wondering today how she can keep fitting it all in.

So she asks her soul mate to drop her off a few blocks from home. A walk is definitely in order, an opportunity to clear her mind, giving the boys a better chance at getting to swimming on time. It's cold outside, but not too cold for a walk.

The van stops at the corner, she hops out, waves to her three men, watches them drive out of sight, turns her head toward home. The sidewalk is clear, snow drifts piling up along the edges, there has been a lot of the white stuff this winter, but it has been so much fun when there are minutes of play found in the days.

She knows the path well. The path home. Along the lake, covered in white, smooth, untouched, beautiful. The sun is out, and its rays are so welcome as they shine on her face.

Her thoughts drift toward prayer as they always seem to when she is out walking alone. She meets with her Maker in these moments, always drawn to Him as she strolls in His nature. He is so ready to meet with her in the quiet, in the sanctuary of fresh air and outdoor sights. They talk about life, her thoughts becoming prayers. As she pours out her thoughts, her prayers, in the few minutes she has before she reaches home, He is always ready with His peace. So free in giving it, so generous, if only she'll receive.

Her street corner comes quickly, the walk is almost over, the quiet will disappear once again in to-dos. Her feet take her close to the train tracks she has to cross to get to her house. As she begins to walk across the tracks today she senses something important - He is trying to tell her something. Something wonderful, something for her heart alone, something encouraging, something sustaining, something full of peace and grace and truth. She is trying to listen, to open her heart to Him.

She takes one step over the tracks, then another - there are two sets of tracks to cross. As she steps she feels the sunlight on her, strong, bright, powerful, clear.

*You are crossing over, child. You are taking one more step, then another, and another. As you walk, one foot in front of the other, one step at a time, across the tracks, across the threshold of who you were, and into the realm of who you are becoming. I am always*

159

*making you more and more into my image, into the woman I created you to be, all for My glory, all for My kingdom.*

*One day you will look back over the tracks, over the threshold, and you will see this crucial point, this hard time when it feels like a train could run you over any second and you'd be left flat. I will get you across safely, you can trust Me, just keep your eyes focused on Me, feel My light on your face, keep taking one step at a time. I WILL get you where I always intended for you to be.*

*Try not to see too far down the road, there are many twists and turns, bends in the road, many corners to turn. Just like the corner you just turned, they will keep bringing you home - to Me. Make sure you just... keep... going. Enjoying the moments, living fully in them, sharing them with me. I gave them to you. I love you.*

She steps across the tracks, both sets of tracks, face-first into the sunlight before her, turning the corner home.

The walk was a good one, they always are, when she meets with Him.

She steps into her home, into the home of His love, picks up the to-do list once again, and starts to cross off another, and another item - giving Him the glory in each one, trusting He is using ALL of them to mold her more into who she was always meant to be.


## February 15th, 2012

## Fitting Dreams For Tomorrow Into The Drudgery Of Today

I have so many big dreams, and I can get lost in them sometimes, and lose my way with what's closest to me. I have to keep leaving the dreams with God, trusting He is getting me there, and living out the life He has me in TODAY with EXCELLENCE. So much easier to lose myself in the dreams sometimes, because sometimes today is hard and tiring and boring.

I trust that every day, even the hard, tiring, boring days, He is moving me one day closer to my tomorrows and the amazing things I see in my mind. I hope for those things, but I live in today. I live in the moments of today. And how can I use the moments of today in light of the tomorrow I hope for?

If I hope to be happily married in 50 years, how am I living that out today? How can I encourage and love my husband today? How can I forgive, communicate, connect with Josh today so that I can realize the dream of a life-long happy marriage for tomorrow?

If I hope for children, grandchildren who are following God and know Him in a most wonderful way, how am I making sure I know God that way, am following Him that way? How am I encouraging my two young boys to know God, follow Him today? God invites, never forces. How do I invite my children into Him without forcing?

If I hope to reach out and help others around the world, how am I doing that TODAY?

If I hope to teach, equip and love the upcoming generation, how can I keep going with my university studies today? What lectures to I have to listen to, what tests do I have to study for, what books do I have to read, what essays do I have to type, what research do I have to do, what courses do I pick next? All this to get me to a tomorrow of teaching in whatever capacity God has for me.

These are hard questions, but ones that need answers - TODAY.

Even if I can't see them quite clearly yet, the dreams are still alive and well, and I must leave them with Him. And focus on TODAY.

Destiny waits, calling, mission, purpose waits, dreams wait, but TODAY gets me one step closer on the journey towards TOMORROW.

So how will I use today? What big/small/tiny ways can I invest tomorrow into today?


## February 17th, 2012

### A Reminder To Live In The Moments – Will I Ever Stop Needing Them?

"To live now, *this instance*, is to welcome these three realities: ourselves, the external world, the universe of other men, and that over which our Lord reigns... [It means] that we refuse to escape into dreams either of the past, the future, or the unreal... One gains spiritual health when we are in possession of the present moment and no longer indulge in dreams of escaping from it but steps out into the daylight of Him who made all things and all life's passing moments and said that *they were good.* The cross of Calvary, which was a harsh but real moment, has transformed everything that harms us in this world into a source of perennial good. Do not be afraid then, to become a living being, to grasp the present moment with both hands, and to make it completely your own."

- From my devotional this morning - *Letters of Faith Through the Seasons, Volume 1,* James M. Houston. This is a portion of a letter written by Fr. Rene Voillaume.

If you've read my last two blog posts, you might realize, just as I am, that God is whispering something beautiful into my life... something very **free**-ing (free is my word for this year).

I posted about *Fitting Dreams Into the Drudgery of Today* - struggling with how to use the moments of today to invest in the dreams of tomorrow - like a happy marriage, Christ-following children and grandchildren, finishing university, ?teaching?, serving others around the world, etc. etc. etc. I could go on and on. And before that I posted about *Crossing the Tracks*, leaving who I was behind, stepping into what I am becoming - with the Light strong and warm on my face as He guides me ever closer to all He meant for me to be.

My devotional this morning continues to speak the truth into my heart that God has so much for us in TODAY. And it was good to put a label to my dreaming - *escaping.* There are so many ways that people can escape - I'm not sure that any of them are less harmful than others - whether it be the bottle, pills, adultery, shopping, eating, or living in dreams so ideal that any semblance of reality leaves people destitute inside and causes dissension in their relationships. This is the one that's got hold of me right now. All are crushing and destructive in their own ways.

162

I find that when I get lost in the dreams, when I escape, I find it almost impossible to see the good in my life. And believe me, there is a spilling-over of good in my life. A cup-overflowing of good. And yet I can't see it when I run away in my mind.

I pour out my heart to Joshua, tell him I can't see the good. I used to blame him a lot. I used to think if only this changed in our lives, or that, and why isn't he working on that RIGHT NOW? Can't he see it's just no good this way, that God has something else for us that's truly marvelous and we're missing out on it? Wow. Totally negates all the awesomeness of TODAY.

The thing is not to let go of dreams, but to leave them with God. Never stop dreaming, but don't let myself live in those dreams just yet, not until it's time. Trust God is moving me always closer to... whatever He has. I think He gives me just enough of a glimpse, so I don't lose hope and become discouraged - but then I grab hold of that glimpse and run with it in my mind and want to live in it NOW.

And I thought I was growing in my patience!! Ha.

What always brings me back, what grounds me once again... is to see the good. To see the God. TODAY. TO LIVE IN THE MOMENTS. It is my heart's cry - the name of this blog is so fitting, a vision for my life all unto its own. Something I must strive for on a daily basis.

I look forward to today. Being happy in whatever moments come from today doesn't mean I settle for a life of drudgery and dreams-never-realized. It means I honour God by enjoying what He has for me RIGHT NOW and look forward to whatever He brings later. I think I have some wonderful hints to keep me going, some passions and abilities that have always been there. And I'll wait to see which ones He gives first.

A wonderful lady once told me not to let go of the dreams in my heart, that they were probably ALL there for a reason and a season in life, but that I couldn't possibly live them all out at once, and that it's interesting to see which dreams God gives in what order.

But most of the time, I think the dreams He gives that are the most amazing are the ones we daren't dream, the ones we can't even put to words, the ones that go so deep we can hardly whisper about them, they're just too wonderful to even imagine, no escaping into them would do them justice...

Like the way I daren't dream about a Christian husband and children after years of walking far from God. And now I LIVE in that, in those moments that used to be but a whisper, deep down in the secret places of my heart. How can it be so easy to lose sight of the good?

*May I make my most passionate strivings today, Lord, to be to see the good. To live in the moments of today, whatever they may be. What happiness, joy, excitement, contentment, peace awaits in those moments. For that is where You are. Take all my tomorrows, my dreams, and do what You will with me. In Your son's name, Amen.*

## March 28th, 2012

### Imagine

I wrote this article for the recent edition of the *Link & Visitor* – a publication by the Baptist Women of Ontario and Quebec.

*I tell you the truth, he who believes has everlasting life. - John 6:47*

"You're so beautiful."

"I love you."

"You are such a good mommy."

"I'm so happy to be married to you."

These are words from my husband's mouth - he's been saying them to me over and over these almost thirteen years we've been together. My heart used to block them, believing these words couldn't be true about me. One day as my husband spoke wonderful words to me, as my heart began to choose to turn away from the good being offered, I heard Him ask.

*Why do you turn away from My words? I have put them in Joshua's mouth, so he will speak them to you, My bride, My love. I cannot hold you with human arms or speak to you with a human voice, but I have given you someone who can. Hear his words, for they are My words.*

164

*Open your ears to all My words. I've given them to many of my people to speak into your life. Believe them. I know no lies. Anna, these words are true, that is how I see you. Live in that truth.*

So I try, when my Joshua speaks wonderful words to me, when others speak words of encouragement and love, I try to really hear them and live in them and thank God for the gift of them. Thank Him for the words from beyond. Imagine a place where we only hear those kinds of words, an everlasting whisper in our ears of goodness and love and beauty... this is just a glimpse.

My older son has this laughter that bursts forth out of nowhere on occasion. It can happen anywhere, but it usually happens at the dinner table, as we're all gathered together and telling stories of our days. The days when we're all getting along and peace reigns among us and we're not rushing off this way or that. It starts with a giggle, on the surface of himself. We all join in on the chuckle. Then it spreads in Josiah, deep down into his being, until every cell must be full of it - this all-consuming laughter. He usually ends up on the floor, rolling through the moment, unable to sit on his chair or contain the joy for one more second. Pretty soon we're all laughing, and he's given us a round of smiles. I think back to my childhood and remember laughing this way with my sister. More gifts from beyond. Imagine a place where there is no more sadness... this is just a glimpse.

My younger son has these big blue eyes that sparkle even when no light from this world shines on them. I know the light that makes his eyes sparkle comes from another place, another world beyond this one. There's heaven-light in Elijah's eyes, and once in a while I get completely lost in them. That particular shade of blue must be made with a pinch of God's love, a sprinkle of God's grace and a dash of God's mercy. My dear friend has green eyes with the same sparkle - so beautiful. Imagine a place where the colours of the rainbow pale in comparison... this is just a glimpse.

My memory runs through the scenes of my life and pauses on the truly special moments. Moments when all is right, when life feels utterly rich, when all I can feel is all that is good. With family, friends, alone, at home, at the lake, in church - every scene is different. Imagine a place where there is no lack, in anyone or in anything - we live in perfect harmony, all the time... this is just a glimpse.

These glimpses of mine keep me going on the hard days and fill me to overflowing on the good days. They remind me of what is coming in the life eternal. This is God's promise to me, of a life with him, if I only believe... this is just a glimpse. Imagine.


## June 11th, 2012

### I Will Find My Joy In Him Alone

*Though the fig tree does not bud and there are no grapes on the vines, though the olive crop fails, and the fields produce no food, though there are no sheep in the pen and no cattle in the stalls, yet I will rejoice in the Lord, I will be joyful in God my Saviour.*
*- Habakkuk 3:17-18*

This is the verse that popped up on my desktop wallpaper for the month of May - courtesy of incourage.me. The verses often speak directly to me at whatever I'm living in that month or that season of life. Often I don't get it until the end of the 30 or 31 days. Often I don't hear what God is whispering into my heart until it's almost too late and almost time for the next verse. Often I barely keep up. These days. Not every day, not every season. Sometimes I run ahead of Him, sometimes we saunter through the days together, side by side. But when the lesson is a hard one, often I'm lagging behind, not wanting to keep up, not wanting to walk side by side. I want to keep to myself, alone, walking behind Him. I suppose that at least I'm still walking.

These verses in Habakkuk speak of rejoicing and being joyful in the Lord even when all seems empty. When the vision is unclear, when life is confusing, when it's time to lay it all down on the altar again (just like Abraham with Isaac) and see if He brings a ram instead of your dreams and hopes. Sometimes the ram is sacrificed, and sometimes the dreams and hopes. Then it is so hard to keep rejoicing and being joyful in Him. I can't see past the anger, self-pity and confusion.

166

Yet he lingers, always, never leaving me nor forsaking me, always lingering. He is ever-faithful. He can handle my emotions. He made me who I am, and who I will be. He will get me to the who I will be. I CAN trust.

This is what He brings me back to, time and again - to find my joy in Him alone, and to trust Him with everything. He never wants just a little of me, never wants me to follow Him just a little. It's all or nothing. I get that - He made me from the same stuff - all or nothing. Which is probably why it's hard to lay those dreams and hopes down again.

But when the dreams fade - some for a season, some for a lifetime - and all feels empty again... when the fig tree does not bud, when there are no grapes on the vine, when the olive crop fails, and the fields produce no food, when there are no sheep in the pen and no cattle in the stalls... I still have Him. I can still find my joy in Him.

If only I choose to keep up, not lag behind, and saunter through each day with Him.

Vision is renewed - sometimes totally different, sometimes slightly adjusted - and I start to see Him everywhere. In the smiles of my children, in the tender gaze of my husband, in the sunlight on the water, in the flight of a bird, in the dancing of the trees, in the people at church, at school, at the store. He cannot be contained. Not even by my dreams and hopes and visions. He will do His will and thank Him for it. I will find my joy in Him who is able.


**June 17ᵗʰ, 2012**

**Happy Father's Day Daddy!**

You will most likely read this tomorrow at work, in your office that overlooks the city you have travelled to - day after day, for more than 3 decades.

You travelled 2-3 hours every day to work this job.

We didn't see you at breakfast because you rose before 6am and were out the door soon after.

Many times we didn't see you at dinner either because you came in the door after 7pm.

Thank you.

For missing meals, for travelling so far, for filling the role of provider for so many years.

I remember the weekends. You would mow the lawn, maintain our homes and our cars, grow a garden, and take us for drives.

We always got a treat in the middle of the drive, before it was time to come back home.

You started showing me the world beyond our front yard when I was so young, and I never seem to get enough!

Vacations took us further still - Kingston, Florida, and England - still I wanted to see more.

And I have, all with your blessing, giving me wings to soar.

You drove me to dance classes and let me live my dream until the dream changed to something else. I still love to dance.

You drove me to church so I could learn the most important things about who I am - in Christ.

You cleaned the church for a time on Saturdays, to earn a little extra money. Karen and I rolled underneath the pews, played the piano, games in the gym, helped you a little, ate in the kitchen, climbed the trees outside, and became more comfortable with God's house as a place full of fun and adventure instead of a program for an hour on Sunday morning.

You drove me to the airport after I ran a lap around the house - me so dramatic sometimes - you released me into God's service that day - wherever it was He called me to go. Turns out He called me back home, back to you, at least for a little while.

You walked me down the aisle with my mum beside you. You gave me the blessing of my greatest adventure yet - being a wife to my Joshua and a mother to my Josiah, Caleb and Elijah. You released me yet again to become more of who God made me to be.

You were there when a grandson went home way too early. And you let yourself love him and you let him change you. And you make the most of the time you have with the four other grandchildren God has given you. You've pushed many a stroller and corralled many a grandson and played in the leaves, and watched them grow, and loved the one granddaughter in all her princess-ness.

You taught me to drive stick-shift (and promptly went home to ease your nerves with a little tobacco and alcohol!) and I'm positive this skill will come in handy someday in a jeep in a foreign land!

You step into my life whenever you can - now that I am 5 hours away (7 hours if you're driving!) - and my life is all the richer for it.

You put up with me when I was intolerable and rescued me from my own poor choices.

You have the heart of a wordsmith and when you write, I love to read.

You have been there for me, you have cared for me, you have given me roots and wings.

Thank you for being my daddy - I wouldn't want any other.

I look forward to many more adventures, to time well spent and to watching you grow more and more into the man God made you to be.

I love you and Happy Father's Day!

I wish I was there with you today!

# 2013

## January 1st, 2013

## My Hopes For 2013 And A Word For This Year

It's a whole new year.

I hope for so much this year.

I see God at work in so many areas of life.

It is truly exciting.

I love to ponder for a few moments on the coming year and search my heart for the word God is settling in there to best describe the coming months.

In 2011 the word was Bold (and confident seemed to go along with it). To ask boldly, to search boldly, to become confident in all that God had placed in my life and begin to discover how He wanted to use the gifts, abilities and passions He gave me. There was a lot of reflection, a lot of letting go, and a lot of grabbing hold. I also finally went on my first mission trip that year.

In 2012 the word was Free. Free to move ahead, to act on all He was showing me, free to be the person God created me to be. I began working diligently at completing my university degree online, I started a journey of reading through the whole Bible in one year, I came alongside Josh in the ministry to the young adults in our city and in the church-planting vision that is growing and developing in our church, and I enjoyed a part-time job at the Christian bookstore for a time.

And for 2013 the word seems to be **Plenty**.

The verse that comes to mind is *I know what it is to be in need, and I know what it is to have plenty. I have learned the secret of being content in any and every situation, whether well fed or hungry, whether living in plenty or in want. - Philippians 4:12.*

I am learning this verse means way more than material things - we can be in need in many ways in our lives, never having enough, never satisfied, never content. The journey was long, often hard for me to find contentment in Christ alone - to lay down hopes and dreams, ideas of what I thought my life should look like, and grab hold of all it is, all God has given me - because I know now and for certain - I have so much, so many good things, and it baffles me how easy it can be to lose sight of them sometimes. So I know that feeling of WANT, whether it is justified or not, whether it is my own doing or not, I get that feeling - to be HUNGRY, to be IN NEED - and Christ fills those holes to overflowing if only I let Him. He never forces His way in, we always have to extend the invitation. He is the Bread of Life, and we can never hunger again if we feast on His love. But to actually do this, remember this, choose this - easier said than done sometimes.

And this year so many amazing things are coming. There will be plenty to do as long-waited-for visions begin to live out in tangible ways, as I (hopefully) finish up a Bachelors degree, as visions become clearer and doors open wide in ministry, as boys grow into young men, my marriage is into its 14th year, and I finish off four decades of life. Plenty.

This year I will be busy - there is no doubt. But lately I find myself getting lost in the busyness, losing focus, feeling needy, feeling want, feeling hunger - this year I hope God will grow in me a contentment in the busyness. I hope I will only see that I am well fed and living in plenty. Fed with the Bread of Life and living in His promises. Plenty.

*Lord, help me find contentment in all You bring - in the **plenty**. Help me be encouraged as I take Your hand and walk in it all, knowing life is full to the brim, and it's OK for it to be that way, trusting You will give me all I need and more as we walk each step of the journey of 2013 - together. Whenever I hunger, may I feast on Your love and grace, whenever I am in need, let it be for more of You, and whenever I want, let it be for You alone. In Jesus' name, Amen.*


## August 14th, 2013

### Realizing A Decades-Old Dream

Sometimes dreams can sit on the shelf for a very long time. They get pushed back so other things sit front and center - sometimes GREAT things, sometimes unexpected things - but nevertheless... other things. Dreams can get found among the clutter once in a while,

172

taken down off the shelf and dusted off, held in our hands and coddled for a while - then put back on the shelf because for now that is their place. For now other things must sit where we can see them in full view, and that is perfectly OK. Really. Absolutely. As long as we choose to see it that way. Life is full of choices about what sits on the shelf and where it sits compared to everything else.

I started university when I was 18, and that was 21 years ago now. I left my home, my family, my town, and my friends to venture off to a university in Toronto and pursue a degree in Environmental Studies. I wanted to save the rainforests. I love nature, I love how God put it all together in His most marvelous way, I love trees and mountains and clean water. Somehow I wanted to help in all the efforts that were emerging to save our world.

Lack of finances meant I would take a year off after that first year of university (which had been almost completely funded by OSAP). I would only take one class the second year, I would live with my parents again, and I would work full-time at Subway. I became a "sandwich artist" instead.

I knew I wanted to finish my education, and I knew that university was way too expensive. So I went to college instead. I took two years to study to be an Environmental Protection Technician, and I loved the hands-on approach that college brought. I loved working in the labs and conducting field research. This degree helped me get a summer job at a local zoo, studying wetlands and writing wetland conservation newsletters. It seems that even when I wasn't looking for writing opportunities, they were still coming my way. God was probably trying to talk to me about that, but I wasn't listening to him much at the time.

No job in my field after that summer, now tens of thousands of dollars in debt, I took whatever jobs I could find as I tried to navigate my way out of my parent's house and into life on my own. Many years of administration work followed, which I surprisingly loved and excelled at. One of my jobs was reception work in a chiropractor's office. This is where I met up with God again after ignoring him for most of the previous seven years. This is also where I met my Joshua.

And this is where everything changed. The next decade plus of my journey was all about marriage, ministry, moving many times, and three baby boys. Talk about GREAT, unexpected things on the shelf of life. In a word - WOW.

I became a stay-at-home mom. The best ten years of my life - seriously and honestly. Also the hardest 10 years of my life. I learned about the best parts of myself and the worst parts as well.

Still the dream of finishing university lingered. I'd putter around on my shelf, take down a few things, dust them off, and see where they fit best in each new phase of life. I tried to take an online class when Josiah was only 2 - it proved to be way too challenging at the time, and I didn't have enough confidence or focus (or money!) to put that dream on the front of the shelf for long. But I did finish the class, and eventually would earn my degree from that university.

My post-secondary education was becoming very dusty and very complicated, so I let it rest for a long while and just had fun with raising my boys.

Side note: Before marriage I also took a few Bible college courses from a couple of different schools across Canada - but that's a whole different post!

Josh's journey led him to pastoring in the local church - first with youth, then as an Associate Pastor. The churches were very supportive of continuing education and he was able to finish a specialized Leadership course and then use that course as a head start to a Masters in Evangelism and Leadership. We all attended his graduation - the boys and I along with Josh's brother. It was AMAZING and I loved watching him grab his degree.

Then I just knew. I had been doing a complete overhaul of my life as the boys were heading off to school, and finally I knew it was time for me to put university at the front and center of my shelf. I had been really evaluating that dream, looking at the options, sorting through the possibilities for a degree, and settled on Liberal Arts instead of the original Science degree I was going to pursue.

As Josh was finishing his last course for his Masters, I was enrolling for undergraduate courses online. I decided to stick with a university that offered an amazing online program. This was the only way university was going to work for me - if I could set my own pace and work at 4am if needed (and it was - many times)! I was given credit for all the university, college and Bible college courses I had taken and I now had half a university degree under my belt. Another half to go. I wanted to finish in two years.

I got a part-time job at the local Christian bookstore to pay for my degree. I loved the job and I loved getting back out in the world. When the boys were both in school full-time my days had gotten considerably lonelier! And online schooling wasn't going to help with that very much, though I did enjoy meeting new people in discussion groups.

The job lasted almost a year before we finally admitted that our family life and ministry life were already full to the brim, not to mention how my schooling was adding to the mix.

When I wanted to give up and pack it in - I was 38 for heaven's sake and couldn't even see a job at the end of this journey! - Josh encouraged me to keep going. So I would enroll for another class or two or four at a time, and the number of courses required for my degree kept shrinking.

January 2012 - Fourteen to go

May 2012 - Ten to go

September 2012 - Nine to go

January 2013 - Six to go

May 2013 - Four to go

August 2013 - Zero to go

Zero.

That's where I am today. My last exam was written two days ago.

I was able to take a class on Jesus' life and the last exam I wrote was all about Jesus. A great way to end it all.

All being well, I will walk across the graduation stage in the fall and grab my degree - a Bachelor of Liberal Arts with a minor in International Studies. This pulls the last two decades of schooling together in a wonderful way - some of the Environmental Studies classes I took back in the day, mixed with some of the Bible college courses, and a few of the recent classes thrown in... and voila! International Studies jives so well with who I am today, and where my focus is headed in the future. And it's even similar to much of what I started to learn in Environmental Studies - except now it's about saving people rather than saving the trees. And people need the trees, and the water, and we're all in this together.

Amazing how things work out. How dreams can sometimes mix together so well, and more than one can be realized at the same time. That's God for you. Working things out as only he can. I love to watch him work.

I already see which new dreams are taking their places front and center. The shelf is already full. It was a little too full as the university dream was coming to an end, but I suppose it was best that way. It would have been very hard to let go of such an old dream, such a dear dream, without having new ones already poking their way through.

Maybe I'll post a graduation photo when I have one? With a cap and gown and a degree in hand? I still have my suspicions about whether or not I ACTUALLY passed Economics...

I suppose a little more time will tell.

I learned so many amazing things as I was living out this dream - I'll post a few of them to share with you tomorrow....


## August 15th, 2013

### 10 Things I Learned From Finishing University Later In Life

1. *Pay attention to the dreams that never seem to fade, one day it will be the right to time to live them out*

2. *When it's time to live out a dream, this doesn't mean it will be easy in the least - living out dreams often requires lots of hard work, and I mean LOTS*

176

3. *The hard work of dream-living can often last for months, years, decades even - and it is absolutely worth every second you gave*

4. *When dreams take a long time to realize, focus is key, and confidence in the dream*

5. *A strong support network really comes in handy when you lose your focus and confidence in living out a dream*

6. *Don't be afraid to share your dreams with those you love - dreams are an important part of who God made you to be, and running from them or hiding them from your loved ones means they miss out on knowing a wonderful part of you*

7. *Maintain balance in your relationships and keep your priorities in check - living out dreams does not mean sacrificing everything else that's important to you - it may mean some sacrifices, but it also means agreement, compromise, and patience*

8. *Big celebrations with loved ones are required when a dream has been realized, and if the dream-living journey is a long process, small celebrations are absolutely required along the way*

9. *Keep the end in sight and stay positive*

10. *Success is sometimes harder to experience than failure - sometimes living the dream means letting go once it's realized - but this also means grabbing hold of new dreams...*

## September 2nd, 2013

### Small Things

Yesterday at church our pastor talked about the importance of being faithful in the small things of life and faith. Often it's not the big things that make the biggest difference or have the biggest effect, it's the small things instead.

One of my favourite quotes from Mother Teresa says:

*We can do no great things, only small things with great love.*

I had that quote pinned up on my wall for years.

Every time I cleaned the living room, or washed dishes, or changed a diaper, or packed a lunch... I needed to remember these small things needed to be done with love. I was living adventures right in my home, or my yard or my neighbourhood - I didn't have to trek the jungles or climb the mountains to have adventures... not yet anyway!

With each blog post or magazine article or email to a friend, or family newsletter... I needed to remember these small things needed to be done with love. I was using my talents to encourage and reach others - I didn't need book deals or speaking engagements or conferences to attend.

I still need this reminder in every area of life, especially now that big things are coming. Fast.

When God spoke to Elijah on the mountain in 1 Kings 19:11-13 it was through a gentle whisper, and not the great wind, earthquake or fire.

*May I keep my heart tuned into your whispers, Lord, as I live in the earthquakes, fires and great winds of the coming days. May the echoes of Your still, small voice flow out into every area of my life.*

As our family heads into another season of ministry, the colours of this season look a lot different from the previous few. There will be a church plant on a local university campus, mentoring interns, reaching further north, becoming landlords again, and publishing Caleb's book.

All these big things could quickly overshadow the precious small things of our family's life.

And so I look forward to busy mornings getting everyone out the door, after-school down time, dinners full of stories and adventures of the day, swimming and judo nights at the YMCA, reading lots of books, exploring something of the world on Saturdays, and lots of potluck dinners with friends.

These are some of the small things in my life. Some of the rhythms that make the music in my life. And my life sings when I find the joy in these small things, when I am faithful in them, when I do them with great love.

**September 10<sup>th</sup>, 2013**

**What's Next?**

People are already asking me the question... but I think I would be asking it too if someone had just completed a major milestone.

"What's next?"

"After finishing your university degree, Anna, now what?"

Truth is... my next is the same as my was, my is, and my will always be.

When I set out to finish my degree - consisting of classes taken at 5 post-secondary institutions (I was never quite sure what I was up to and was not very good at finishing what I started) - I had wanted to go on to Teacher's College and find a job in the school system. I wanted to reach out to the next generation in positive ways and help to guide them into the awesome things they could be.

I live this out every day of my life already - with my two boys.

I also have a beautiful niece and exciting nephew, my friends and family have amazing kids, I volunteer at the school and know lots of kids there, I help out with the kid's ministry at church, once a year I get to teach during chapel for a week at a local children's camp, and there are often a few neighbourhood kids found floating around on my front lawn or in my house. I do what I can to pour into the kids right in front of me, every day, however I can. And some days I am certainly more sociable than others.

When I met Josh I was working as a receptionist at a chiropractor's office. He was a patient. As I remember it (and I may be romanticizing it just a little) he would burst through the door, arms wide open and full of life, have everyone laughing in seconds, and the whole place would light up just from his presence. It was magic - that's what my I-was-totally-in-love filter does to my memory sometimes. 14 years has matured me and our love, but I know I still want to be that guy's wife. And he still knows how to make a room full of people smile. Most of all, it doesn't matter if it's just me and the boys in the room, in fact some of his best work is done when it's just the four of us.

And that's been my What's Next for the last decade and a half.

It will be my What's Next for the rest of my life.

Thank God.

The degree is amazing, I loved it, everything I learned has added to my life and (hopefully) to those who know me best. Maybe there's a Masters in the future - I really enjoy school. Maybe teaching will still come - maybe in a college or university forum instead of an elementary classroom. Maybe in a foreign land with an interpreter, a mud floor, and a straw roof. I couldn't tell you.

Life is full, always, and school made it a little more full. The learning never has to stop - I've read almost 6 books in the past month since finishing school! Just soaking up some books that have been sitting on my shelf for too long, beckoning me to turn the pages.

For now, there is much to do with ministry and family life.

And maybe the most important thing that school taught me was that I never want to miss more than I have to of this full life I have been given. The blessings are right in front of me, new each morning, I just have to see them, recognize them for what they are, slow down enough to enjoy them, and as always, the thing I must keep on remembering....

LIVE IN THE MOMENTS.


## September 11th, 2013

### We Prayed For Joy… We Got Joy!

Driving to school that first day of the 2013-2014 academic year, we prayed for this new season of learning.

This is a regular in our family - praying in the car just before the boys are dropped off outside the school. We give God the day, we ask for fun and laughter for the kids, energy and patience for the teachers, love and encouragement all around.

Needless to say, some days go a lot better than others.

This time around, on that first day of school last Wednesday, Josh threw something new into the mix.

A unique request that I've never heard before in all our morning prayer times.

He asked for Joy.

He talked to God about the possibilities for us to find the joy in the year ahead.

We arrived at the school and unloaded boys and backpacks.

Josiah ran ahead in his usual style of anticipation and excitement (he's a seize the day kind of guy), and we sauntered into the schoolyard with Elijah.

Josiah fends for himself as much as possible these days - he's an independent, responsible, organized young man of 12 years of age. I love watching him go.

We found Elijah's friends and chatted with the teachers who were locating their students, and we met Elijah's teacher for this year.

Her name?

Joy.

We found Joy.

On that first day, before classes even started, we found Joy.

Elijah loves this story, he wants me to tell it to the world.

How we asked for Joy, and God provided it right away as only He can.

I love to watch Him go too.

Have a fantastic school year boys - learn from the hard days, enjoy the good days to the fullest, and I'll be there to watch as you both grow up a little more over the next 10 months.

**October 4th, 2013**

## A Different Kind of Friday Night

Wow... it's so weird... so quiet... don't know what to do on this Friday night...

For the past few years my Friday nights mostly consisted of making pizza and watching a movie with my three men.

We started out with those pizza kits when Josiah was just a toddler, then I thought I'd give the bread machine thing a whirl and homemade pizza dough made its way into our recipe box on a weekly basis.

I LOVE cooking from scratch (but don't always have the time to get it done)!

We'd rent movies from Blockbuster - one to watch with the boys, and one for Josh and I after the boys went to bed. Now we don't have Blockbuster, but we do have Netflix. And a local library that is always willing to share its cinematic delights with us for free.

Bedtime used to be 7pm for our sons... with naps in the afternoon as well! Those days are LONG gone.

The last couple of years watching a movie with the boys meant STARTING it at 7pm instead of finishing it up at that time. This also meant Josh and I had to stay up until the wee hours of the morning if we wanted to watch a movie of our own. Sometimes we did, sometimes we didn't. Depended on how exhausting the week had been or how much Pepsi we'd had with the pizza!

Now I sit here typing, processing, adjusting as quickly as I can to yet another chapter done.

Josiah is in Grade 7 this year and that means Friday nights are spent out at youth events.

A decade of Friday-pizza-and-movie-nights is a long time!

To be honest, I'm simply moving those nights over one day to Saturday... I just can't give them up altogether.

But I see the beginnings of time without boys in the house.

Just the beginnings.

And it's really... very... strange.

Way too quiet.

Even now I hear Elijah bouncing on the neighbour's trampoline, and I am glad for the noise.

The dishwasher runs in the background, and I love the sound. It reminds me that my house is normally full of people to share life with me.

The laundry piles upstairs are a different matter - I seem to have a love/hate relationship with laundry - I love sorting/washing/drying it but hate folding and putting away. Don't know what the deal is there. Maybe I know that really I'll just be washing them again in a couple of days... so why bother with the fuss of folding and neatly piling in closets? But I digress, that's another post!

I wonder what future Friday nights will bring... I'm trying to roll with the changes as much as possible... some seem harder than others...

I look forward to watching my boys grow, sharing what they will with me, giving them roots and wings all at the same time.

Not always an easy thing to do.

But I do love to watch them soar.

Even on Friday nights.


## October 7th, 2013

### The Final Lap

*Therefore, since we are surrounded by such a great cloud of witnesses, let us throw off everything that hinders and the sin that so easily entangles. And let us run with perseverance the race marked out for us. - Hebrews 12:1*

I love to watch you run.

You came home after that first track meet and told me how hard it was near the end.

How you felt like you couldn't breathe and the air couldn't get into your lungs fast enough.

That you felt sick from the effort it took to put one foot in front of the other during the last stretch of the race.

You weren't sure you wanted to run again the next day, at the next school track meet.

You weren't sure you were up for it.

I knew you were.

I've seen you run.

I've seen that look in your eye when a challenge comes your way.

You size it up and figure out if it's worth pursuing, and if it is - stand back!

And watch you run.

You decided the track meet was worth running, that you didn't want to quit, that you wanted to run the race you'd signed up for.

I was glad, because I love to watch you run.

I don't care what place you finish, I don't care if a million other kids cross the line before you.

I just want to know you are running your race.

In your time, with all that you've got, finishing however you finish.

Just run.

With that look of perseverance in your eye.

And so you took your place at the starting line with about 80 other young men...

You set a pace early on, content to run with your friends in the middle of the pack.

I saw more lime-green school shirts in front and back of you, and a couple of friends from other schools in the mix.

It was to be three times around the path that wound through fields and forests that overcast day.

At least there was no rain to slow you guys down or make the paces heavier with mud.

You were all free to just run, with a cool breeze on your face and beautiful fall colours surrounding you.

Two times around now, moving up the pack a little, your steps were still sure, your footing was still solid.

You were running the race before you, and you were almost finished.

Getting a little harder to run, but you kept at it. You couldn't see your friends now - they were spread out on the trail.

Sometimes it's harder to run when we can't see those we're running with.

But you knew they were there, somewhere on the same path, running the same race.

And knowing that makes all the difference.

There are others.

You are not alone.

Just keep running.

Third time around now.

We waited for you at the finish line, wondering how you were feeling on the last leg of the race.

Then we saw you, running towards us, steps still sure, footing still solid.

You were going to finish well.

You persevered and you ran your race.

We were so proud of you!

You joined the friends that had finished before you, and you waited for those who were still to come.

You were done.

Victory.

Then... a lime-green shirt comes around the bend... but he's not heading towards the finish line.

No... he's only on round two... he's still got one more whole round to run in his race.

He was pushed into the trees early on in the race... he was slowed down by others... you tell us his story as you run over to him.

You ask your coach if you can run with him on his last lap, and she calls out for teammates to join him, to help him finish his race.

A dozen lime-greens run over and run for a time with him.

Some fall back after a while.

I look for you, but you are long gone, running right beside him, helping your teammate to finish his race.

Helping with your presence, just being there with him, letting him see another runner, you know it makes all the difference.

And so you run your final lap.

You thought you were finished, but God had called you to a different sort of race that day.

One that didn't end with your three laps around the track.

When your teammate came around the corner, I saw the look in your eye.

You decided it was worth it to pursue the challenge in front of you.

To run another lap when you felt so tired from running your own race.

There was no hesitation in you.

You simply put one foot in front of the other and set your face to run - again.

And so we waited at the finish line - again.

Knowing this time you would really be finished.

Your race would end when every last teammate had crossed the line.

It was your final lap that inspired me the most that day, Josiah.

The lap that would never be counted in any official race records.

The lap you ran when only a few were watching.

The lap that made God smile BIG.

Yes, I sure do love to watch you run.


## October 9th, 2013

### Encouragement in the Grocery Store Line

I was just lining up to pay for a few groceries.

On my weekly run through the stores, stocking up on the deals, trying to ONLY buy the deals.

I'm at Food Basics and I see a special bin near the Express check-out.

Pre-packaged donation bags for the local Food Bank.

$4.99.

I've seen these at Metro as well - packaged in brown bags, so I have no idea what I'm buying for the food bank, but still I've put a few in my cart lately.

I'm trying to find practical ways to Live in the Plenty, to share the gift of Enough.

I have more than enough, others have less than enough - what are some realistic ways to balance it out a bit?

How do I do that in my daily life?

So the sharing isn't just saved for special occasions or group events?

So it becomes a part of who I am, a daily habit lived out in many different ways.

Because there are many times when I've said no.

Just this week I can count two.

Once outside Shoppers Drug Mart - a young man asked me for spare change. I truly didn't have any on me, but I suspect he needed a little more from others than some random coins. I suspect he needed a whole lot of care and concern.

I said no.

And at the intersection near DQ and East Side Mario's - a man stood there holding a sign that said he was hungry and could anyone help?

I drove on by.

With Elijah in the seat beside me.

I whispered, "Oh no... that man needs some help."

Elijah heard me, his mind raced for a while as we drove into the green light, and he said, "Could I have given him my doughnut as we drove by? Could we have passed it out the window to him?"

I answered weakly, "Yes, maybe we could have."

And I know I could have gone back, could have modelled compassion for my son, but...

I said no.

Maybe I'm tired of drive-by giving and throwing money at the problems.

Maybe I'm tired of doing what I've always done.

Maybe I want to find ways to do more.

Maybe I want to get right in there and make some sort of difference.

My husband will come home sometimes and tell me how he's helped someone.

How he bought someone some groceries instead of handing them change. How he treated someone to lunch and shared a great conversation with them instead of reaching into his pocket for random coins. How does he do that?

He's learning faster than I am. His extravertedness allows him to reach out so much easier than me. I am constantly running to catch up to him. He just gets it so quick. At times I lag far behind. As long as he is patient with me, as long as we both know I'm coming, that I will get there, as long as he holds out his hand to help me along, it's all good.

Because sometimes I do the same for him. In different ways.

He knows my heart, he knows I want this, to learn this, to make this a part of who I am, to get over whatever stops me - be it pride, laziness, fear, complacency, hopelessness, or a little of all the above - to learn right down to the depths of me about loving the least of these.

Then yesterday... I found such encouragement in the grocery store line.

Standing at the checkout, staring at those donation bags for the food bank.

These ones were plastic, so I could see the contents.

I just couldn't bring myself to buy all the processed food, so lean on nutrients, contained in the bags.

I know they are trying, they are jamming as much into these bags as they can for $4.99, and they are trying.

But I thought about all the cans at home, full of healthier options, and how I've been learning so much about getting these options for so little, and I realized I'd rather do that.

And I set my face forward, forgetting about the donation bin for now.

Then the man behind me starts rummaging through the bin, like he's trying to find the perfect bag to donate.

And I am convicted.

God was asking SOMEONE in that line-up to buy one of those bags.

And I said no.

With lots of self-righteousness thrown in as well.

Thinking I could do better than these donation bags.

The man behind me said yes.

And I watched as he bought one, and I thanked God for him.

I thanked God for the reminder that there are others on the same journey.

The man was elderly, he's been on the journey far longer than me.

Does it get easier to say yes as we get older?

I hope so, because I turn 40 soon, and there are many things I want to do differently for the upcoming last half of my life.

And then...

An elderly lady comes alongside me in line, she's asking if I'll move my cart so she can get by.

You see, she's got items for the food bank donation bin.

She packaged them herself, brought them in herself, made a special effort and a special trip to lay some items down in the bin.

And God says to me... *If you want to give healthier items, go ahead Anna, I've got people doing that as well. Nothing wrong with that idea! I put that idea into your head as well. Doesn't matter, as long as you give. That's what I'm looking for, hearts that want to give. I'll take care of the rest.*

And I am encouraged. So much.

We are all so different, we all do things our different ways, but as long as we're set on Doing. Something. That's what matters.

Big, small, wherever we're at, whatever we've got.

Just. Something.

And that's where I'll begin...

Long journey ahead...

One step at a time.

I'd love to share the journey with you.

And hopefully encourage you on your own journey.

## October 22<sup>nd</sup>, 2013

### Don't Give Up… You Are Not Alone

*Let us not become weary in doing good, for at the proper time we will reap a harvest if we do not give up.*

*- Galatians 6:9*

These two phrases are on repeat in my mind.

Don't Give Up.

You Are Not Alone.

It started at the race, then carried on to the grocery store, and it's busting out all over in my life, and I am so glad for it.

My God is reassuring me in His special ways, encouraging me in the journey, letting me know He is with me and it's worth all the effort.

Like on Thanksgiving weekend...

Elijah and I decide to go for a bike ride around the neighbourhood.

I ask him if we can visit a new spot; it's one that I've wanted to check out for a long time.

He agrees.

We buckle up our helmets and away we go!

A few minutes later we arrive at the lakefront. There is no sandy beach here, just big black rock leading into cool blue water.

We have to cross the tracks to get to the water. In Sudbury we always have to cross the tracks to get somewhere. I constantly feel like I'm crossing thresholds, entering new territory, stepping into something beyond myself.

Elijah and I make our way down to the water and he steps closer to get a feel for the coolness of the lake.

A small fishing boat drifts by with two passengers inside, and I get my first inkling that we are not alone.

There are others who venture out to enjoy the beauty of this place.

Then a solitary kayak passes us as we stand on the shoreline.

Another beauty-seeker in our midst.

We turn from the water and check for paths leading to different views along the lake.

We find one small path and we set out.

It doesn't lead very far, and along the way we see garbage strewn here and there, messing up the view, blocking the beauty of this once-pristine place.

We say to each other that someone needs to clean up and maybe next time we'll bring a plastic bag or two.

Just after we say the words two people come over the ridge.

Someone sent more people to enjoy the scenery.

Someone asked them not to come empty-handed.

Someone asked them to bring garbage bags and rubber gloves with them.

At first we don't clue in to what they are doing.

Then they start to pick up garbage and place the discarded items in their bags, and we turn to each other and smile.

We are not alone.

Never alone.

Don't give up.

Especially not in doing good.

We make our way back to the path that leads up and out of the lake scene.

We stop along the way and say a few words of encouragement to our fellow beauty-seekers.

They have a special eye for beauty because they can see it amongst the garbage and they are clearing the way for beauty to shine through loud and clear in this place.

We tell them how we were just saying we should bring a bag to help clean up next time we visit.

Then they arrived immediately after the words left our mouths.

The lady comments that it's a shame how people try to drown out the beauty that surrounds the lake.

She says that her friend and herself couldn't in good conscience just leave the place the way it was.

I get it.

I feel like that a lot.

And I know I'm not the only one, but sometimes I can't see the others. Sometimes I need a reminder. And He knows that.

Elijah walks by the lady and he stops to look her in the eye.

He holds her gaze and says with such a sincere voice, "Thank you."

She looks up from the task at hand and sees my son with the sparkly eyes and she says, "OMG, You are such a sweetheart."

And my mother's heart is instantly blessed.

I smile big.

We leave the lake and find our bikes and start the journey home.

It wasn't a long journey to the water that day, and it wasn't a long journey home.

Sometimes you don't have to look very far to know you are not alone.

Sometimes it doesn't take much to encourage a weary heart to keep going and not give up.


## October 30th, 2013

### I Finally Graduated!

Four days ago, I officially graduated from University of Waterloo with a Bachelor of Arts in Liberal Studies and a minor in International Studies.

I had a fantastic day, celebrated only with my immediate family, anything else would have truly overwhelmed me.

I can't tell you how hard it was to actually get myself to the convocation ceremony.

It was just so much to take in - that this was actually happening - after 21 years.

My mum drove with me, and the rest of my family followed. Josh and the boys joined us just before the ceremony began.

We left the house at 6:15am, all dawled up and looking pretty. I had been piecing together my outfit from amazing Value Village finds and things I already had. God even cares about finding the perfect black dress for grad in the perfect size and at the perfect price. But that's another blog post.

I've been launching into big changes from the comfort of my mum's house for most of my life. The morning of my wedding was spent in their living room, and now this. Graduation day. Who would have thought after three boys and 14 years of marriage?

I drove because, well, I've come to realize that driving on the 401 is not for everyone, especially not my mum, and I seem to be OK with it most days. It's like riding a bike. I reminisced about how I used to drive the stretch of highway from Ajax to Toronto almost every day while getting my college degree, then on Mondays when attending one class at York. I recall going about 140 in the fast lane, in my powder blue Omega Oldsmobile that my parents gave me - I called her Alice.

That was the beginning of my university journey, and here we were at the end.

My mum and I drove through the rain, her keeping me calm, letting me chat about anything and everything. We had to pull over once for my nervous stomach, but the important fact is that we DIDN'T get lost, and we were back on our way in no time.

We arrived in Waterloo just a little while after the sun rose to gray skies and SNOW.

We pulled into the campus and drove around a good chunk of it before finding the reserved parking.

After some psyching myself up to actually get out of the car and walk the short journey to the building where convocation was held, we followed the crowd to the right place. My mom held her purse over her head and tried to breathe in the freezing temperatures. The woman really is a trooper and I've always appreciated her doing her best to walk with her ambitious, driven daughter through life.

It also helped to know that Josh was close behind, bringing our sons and my father. Josh will always be there, as soon as he can, in any weather, I know he is with me, even if not in person. And my beautiful sister and niece were travelling the roads to be with me too - thank God her hubby was able to drive her - and that meant I would get to see my nephew after the ceremony as well. The only one who couldn't' t make it was my brother who was very sick at home. But he would be at the party later, and we were all looking forward to that!

Once I saw the thousand or so other graduates in their gowns, everything changed for me. I knew it would. Suddenly I didn't feel alone and that makes all the difference, doesn't it? After finishing half my degree online the last two years, never stepping foot into a Waterloo classroom, visiting the campus twice only to purchase textbooks, never meeting any of my professors or classmates - I finally saw with my eyes that they were here, and they were many!

I can't express to you how encouraging that was, how that experience will change me forever, how God's already been speaking this truth into my heart the past few weeks - You Are Not Alone.

Even when you can't see the others on the same journey, all running the same race, walking the same path, heading in the same direction - they are there.

See them with your heart.

So we line up and we filter into the gymnasium. There are at least a couple thousand in the space. Wow.

Three at a time they call us up on stage to get "hooded". There are three distinguished university persons waiting on stage to chat with us while someone else places our hoods over our heads. My hood is

195

green - my favourite colour. The man I talk to is pleasant, but he asks me the one question I don't want to hear right now... "What's next?"

I answer slow and tell him I'm a mother, and a wife, and I'm not quite sure. He gives me wisdom I'd hope for from someone of his position. He says to me, "Well then, what's next for you is LIVING your degree." And I think to myself that he gets it, and I am thankful for the encouraging words, right there in the middle of the ceremony.

We head off the stage, hooded and encouraged, and now challenged as well. Time to live out my degree. How? I trust God will direct. I can do nothing else but trust He will direct.

I see Josh, finally, I see him with my eyes and hear his voice. He steps into my graduation and I am so glad I can see him there now. He snaps a few shots, including my favourite one at the beginning of this post. He is my best friend. My greatest encourager in this university journey.

Making dinner, cleaning, caring for boys when I had nothing left and needed to study for four more hours at least. Listening to me when I talked through all I was learning. Catching my excitement as I discovered more of my interests and passions. And maybe understanding that a degree wouldn't mean clarity for me, it was just another step in our journey, and maybe wondering what I would be like after this graduation day... when there were no job prospects or new projects waiting... just more of everyday life and being challenged to live out my degree in that everyday life.

And after all the formalities are over I see the rest of my family and I get to hug them and we take lots of pictures.

My sister has been there in all the big and small events of life - from being my maid of honour to shopping for bathing suits to every one of my baby's births to cooking grilled cheese and Kraft Dinner together for our kids. I just love this woman who is not even two years younger than me. So glad I get to do life with her. We know each other inside and out, the very best and worst of each other, and we still love each other like crazy.

My amazingly intelligent, sensitive, beautiful niece Kara was there to share the day with me as well. I'm looking forward to sharing so much more with this young woman as we both grow up together.

And my boys who I love with my whole heart. Elijah did his best to sit still during a "boring" two-hour ceremony, but now he was ready to get out all his 8-year-old energy, so silly pictures were in order!

Then a more serious picture for Mom. The boys looked so handsome that day!

And my Joshua - sporting a rugged beard just now - it's a good look for him. He gives me roses.

And my parents who constantly support me and my ideas... wherever they take me!

And my brother who joined us at the celebration party later...

It was good to have fun with the day, enjoying the moments... living in them as best I can.


## November 9th, 2013

### Halloween 2013

Josiah had an amazing idea of being Everybody (attaching mirrors to black clothes) for Halloween this year, but it didn't work out like we'd hoped It was a great idea and I wish we could have pulled that off.

Instead we scrounged around the house and came up with a Krispy Kreme doughnut hat and a white apron.

Voila! Doughnut Boy emerged.

Elijah really wanted to be a Marvel Heroes something, and Superman was the favourite of all the choices available in his size 2 days before Halloween.

I loved the red cape - he had a lot of fun with that.

Me and the boys ventured out on Halloween night and made our traditional stop at Brenda's place.

Brenda is a very good friend of Team Sklar. We adopted her into our extended family about 10 years ago, right after we moved to Northern Ontario. We just love this woman!

Every Halloween we visit Brenda's apartment building and get our first stash of candy.

We walked into the apartment lobby and we were greeted by a familiar woman in bunny ears, carrying a duster.

I didn't get it at first, but Elijah points out, "Oh, I get it! You're a dust bunny!"

Awesome effort Brenda! She gave me a few chuckles that night.

With our first few tastes of candy stashed in our pillowcases, we headed off to the church.

I hadn't realized before... that there would be no more trick-or-treating with Josiah.

He will be participating in the youth group activities on Halloween night from now on. They go door to door and ask for food bank donations - a tradition my Joshua started WAY back when he was a youth pastor. The tradition came with us to Sudbury.

Slight sob for the ending of another chapter in my book of motherhood, and then we dropped Josiah off at the church.

Elijah and I decided to make our way back to our neighbourhood and do something we've never done before - trick or treat in our own backyard! Usually we go out with a couple of families and collect food bank donations as well (along with a good harvest of candy), but this year that just wasn't in the cards.

The slight drizzle couldn't slow down Superman that night.

He was faster than a speeding bullet and I could hardly keep up as he knocked on door after door and filled his pillowcase with goodies.

I managed to snap a few shots as we strolled down the street...

I had so much fun just watching my youngest son enjoy this night.

At one point he slowed right down and walked with me for a time.

I asked him if he was ready to go home.

He said, "No, I still want to go to a few more houses over by the creek. I'm just really enjoying this night - the rain falling, walking with you in the moonlight, and it's not too cold..."

My heart melted.

*Walking with me in the moonlight.*

Thank You God, I really needed this night with my Superman. I needed to see him living in the moments and know that life can still slow down enough to do that, and there are many more special times coming with these young men You've given me to raise.

We pass the creek and trick or treat at about 20 more houses. Superman is still full of energy and enthusiasm for this night.

We see many neighbours that we know, and it gives me a feeling of belonging to recognize so many faces as we knock on doors and wander the streets.

I loved the sense of community that night.

We see this pleasant surprise outside a house... "Happy Halloween - Please Take One" with a bowl full of packages of Halloween chocolates. This house was for sale, and the owners were out for the night.

After the last round of houses at the creek, it is time to head home. The pillowcase is full of goodies and we pour them out to sort once we walk into our living room.

Elijah calls daddy to tell him about the night.

Josiah comes home a little while later after a successful night of collecting food donations for the food bank.

Great news - Our church won the trophy for most pounds collected per person!

**November 17th, 2013**

## Goodbye For Now Aggie

My brother Benjamin couldn't say "Granny" when he was younger, but he **could** say "Aggie", so that's how our grandma got the nickname that stuck for about three decades.

Last Sunday, just after church would have ended for the morning, Aggie passed away.

She had sung her final hymns in this life and was moving on to sing with her beautiful voice in a place that I Can Only Imagine.

A place that I long for some days more than others.

A place that is starting to hold more pieces of my heart with every loved one that goes on before me.

I'm so glad my sister, Karen, called a few days before she passed.

"I think I want to go see her," she says to me on the phone. We knew the end was coming, and we didn't know how to deal with it.

We had seen her in August when she was still able to sit in a wheelchair for a while and speak on occasion.

The dementia and Parkinson's had taken their toll.

But we all gathered at the nursing home that summer day - there was 10 of us there to see her.

She may not have recognized all of us anymore, but she knew we were with her, that we belonged to her.

So when Karen called and said we should go, I booked a rental car and made the 4-hour drive first thing the next morning.

My sister brought her kids, and that was perfect. They bring such joy and laughter with them wherever they go, don't they?

Children always make life brighter, better, more real and alive.

Aggie was resting peacefully in the room in the nursing home.

No longer able to eat or drink, she was caught between worlds, almost ready to move on.

She opened her eyes as best she could a few times while we were there.

I stroked her beautiful salt-and-pepper hair (something she **never** would have let me do normally!) and told her it was okay, that I would see her soon. I hope she heard me.

I stayed with my grandfather long after Karen had to take restless children home.

We ate together in the dining room and we watch *Mrs. Brown's Boys* and we laughed. It was good to laugh.

He told me more than once that it was supposed to be him who was to leave this world first.

He who has had decades of heart trouble and illness.

He doesn't understand why he's still here and Lily is gone. I decide it's not the right time to mention to my atheist grandfather that I've been praying since I was a little girl that he would have salvation before he leaves the earth.

Instead I tell him he's not alone, and I know it to be true.

On the day of the funeral, we arrive at the nursing home for the service.

I am frozen at the door of the chapel.

Before me stands a woman from the funeral home - she's here to help with the service. She's been helping my grandfather to set things right for this day.

She looks familiar... "Josh, I think I know her. Isn't she the woman who helped us with Caleb's funeral?"

I'd know that face anywhere.

The one who cradled my baby down the hospital hallway after I gently placed him in her arms.

Yes, it is her. I'm so glad to see her. I tell her who I am, what she meant to me 10 years ago, how I tell about the memory of her in the book that I hope to publish **very** soon. She tells me she wants to read it. And so I see my Caleb speaking to hearts beyond those that hurt from baby-loss.

This woman has helped me say goodbye to two of my most dear ones.

The service is wonderful. The minister has been getting to know my grandfather and Aggie for a few years now. A retired Scottish minister and a retired Yorkshire *Becker's* owner. They joke with each other about their heritage, and their laughter makes me glad.

The minister talks about Jesus and how we can know him and be with those we love in heaven.

I know my Aggie is there already, playing with my Caleb, and I pray we will all be there together one day.

I read a Thank You list to my grandma.

We drive to the cemetery and lay her to rest in the almost-frozen ground.

We lay flowers on her casket.

My mum wanted us to play *10,000 Reasons* and we do this as we stand in the chill and say goodbye. For now.

We gather back at the nursing home and we talk about Aggie and we laugh and eat sandwiches and drink tea.

She loved her tea.

We talk about seeing one another soon - Christmas is almost here and we will be back to visit.

And then this morning... I stand in church, not quite myself yet... still thinking, processing, missing her, missing my family...

The worship leader tells us about the next song coming...

*10,000 Reasons*

Of course. Only You.

And I sing for her, for us, for You.

See you soon Lily, Aggie, Grandma.

I love you...

## December 1st, 2013

## My First Book Is Really Almost Done

I've been writing out his story, our story, for more than 10 years now.

10 years of sharing our journey of discovering hope after stillbirth.

What started out as a thought about creating a small booklet that could help others in the initial baby-loss has grown to a full-blown book.

All the first writings from 10 years ago are there - journal entries to Caleb during pregnancy and beyond, and practical ideas to help with the first few weeks - these were to make up the booklet.

But after writing those out, I knew there was so much more. I needed to share more.

Five years ago I mapped out chapter headings and created an outline for something a little bigger than a booklet.

And I got to writing.

A year later I had the first draft of a small book.

By then I had shared our story with so many hurting hearts, and I knew my Caleb had only begun to reach out in his own way.

God has such different plans for my middle son than I have. It all looks so different than I thought it would.

The book rested for a while, as I rested, writing these words out has been such slow going.

Journeying through healing after such deep grief is no small thing.

Every word of this book comes from the depths of me.

Even now... more tears... I have poured out my love for my son into these pages.

One of the few ways I get to tangibly love him on this earth.

My momma-heart has been opened wide to share with others.

This year marked the 10th anniversary of Caleb's stillbirth. His quiet entrance and exit.

I knew it was time to finish the task of sharing our journey of healing so far...

The book has grown to include more journal entries, poems, blog posts, articles and reflections, writings from others on a similar journey (emails exchanged with a friend as we both journeyed through pregnancy after stillbirth, poems, a song written for Caleb, and seven stories - all a little different - from wonderful women).

And it's done... at least for now... I keep saying that... maybe there will be more in another few years.

For now, our story can finally be passed along quite easily to others who may need the comfort of these words.

I found the greatest comfort in the knowledge that I was not alone.

Self-publishing has been an adventure all its own.

And trying to decide what price to ask, what to do with the proceeds, etc.

We have settled on the idea of asking a very reasonable price and donating proceeds to charity.

Charity could mean sending free copies to those who can't afford one. Or helping to build an education center in Dominican Republic. Or filling a medical clinic with World Vision. Or funding prenatal programs for mommies around the world. Or sending aid to children in Northern Ontario.

I've also had a dream of family mission trips for as long as I've been a mommy. We have a chance to live out that dream in the spring of 2014. Maybe some of the proceeds will help with those costs.

And that's as far as I got... for now...

I have a proof of the book in my hands. I've fixed the mistakes I could find and will order another proof. After I get that one, read it through to make sure it looks good, and fix any more mistakes I find, the book will be ready to order.

I will let you know as soon as I can.

My first book is really almost done.

**December 20th, 2013**

## Turning The Big 4-0... 40 Acts Of Kindness And a Year-Long Party!

Well, I turned 40 yesterday.

I knew it was coming, I've known it all year.

I think God's been throwing me a big year-long party, making so many of my dreams come true, just celebrating who He made me to be... there was meeting our World Vision child in June, my university graduation in October, and my first published book just this week. It's been quite a ride, let me tell you!

And now my 40th birthday.

I do love birthdays, but I'm not sure how I feel about being 40.

Silly, I know.

It's like I've been having this mid-life crisis lately - looking back to what is gone, looking forward to what is to come.

Am I doing a good job with what I've been given? Am I happy? What needs to go and what needs to stay?

I deep-cleaned the house a couple of weeks ago - got rid of everything that I couldn't justify or wasn't useful or was just plain clutter.

Emptying out, making room, dusting things off and taking a good look at them, making sure they should still be here.

And not just in the materialistic things of life - the emotional and spiritual things as well.

Religion (as opposed to Christianity), consumerism, the many masks I wear - I'm looking all of it in the eye and telling it to stay or go.

I'm probably just beginning.

It's a new phase of life.

The second half is wide open before me.

And I'm a little intimidated.

But growing more and more confident about what it should look like.

Then leaving the rest with God - for His plans and purposes.

Because, you see, they are so very different from my own sometimes.

And it's not such a bad thing.

Often times I am blessed way more than I thought possible if I'll just let go of me and grab hold of Him.

So that's what I did for my 40th birthday!!!

I'd been thinking it over for a couple of years, after a friend asked me what I would want to do with this milestone. She had just celebrated her 30th and had been challenged by friends and family to do 30 specific things before her birthday - they made her a list and everything! And for the most part, she loved completing the list and opening herself up to new things.

I wanted something a little different. I wanted to do 40 acts of kindness in one day. Yep, that's right - 40. In one day.

I think it's been changing me since the idea started growing two years ago. Like I figured it shouldn't be such a leap to think about doing that many kind things in one day. Shouldn't I be leaning towards that anyways in my life?

As the big day approached, I thought there was no way I could this - life is too busy, I'm too tired, I don't have enough money, blah blah.

But the idea wouldn't go away - I think it had been there too long.

I woke up a few days ago with the beginning of a list in my mind... and the list just kept growing... and I began to see that it absolutely was possible, that I did have a lot to give out of what I had already, that it could definitely be done.

And my Joshua had most of the day to spend with me, which made it even more possible (he's great at doing the extraverted stuff when required - have you noticed that about him?)

So here's a glimpse at my list of 40 Not-So-Random Acts of Kindness that was completed yesterday...

1. Treats for Josiah's class - Josiah helped make 24 cupcakes and I also made cookies (total of maybe $5 spent on all the treats for boy's classes - cake mix and icing on sale, cookie ingredients on hand at home). I DID buy special cupcake papers and trays to deliver them to the school without them falling apart - this cost about $8 more).

2. Treats for Elijah's class - cupcakes and cookies (costs mentioned above)

3. Card & World Vision donation for Josiah's teacher

4. Card & World Vision donation for Elijah's teacher

5. Candy canes for everyone at the boy's school (this was Elijah's idea, bless his awesome 8-year-old heart! Cost about $50 total - Elijah gave $10, a wonderful friend gave $20 and we gave $20)

6. Love note for Josh

7. Love note for Josiah

8. Love note for Elijah

9. Hang curtains at our rental property - I snagged these from my mum's house in the summer and I wasn't using them

10. 2 bags of food & 1 bag of hygiene items donated to the downtown mission (I love coupons - this stuff was just sitting around my house from recent stock-ups!)

11. Value Village donation (4 bags from the recent deep clean mentioned earlier!)

12. 2 Christmas plants donated to the mission - these plants didn't cost me anything

13. A few pantry items donated at the library - our donation meant our $2 fine was cleared - bonus for both sides!

14. Infant formula donated to the Pregnancy Care center - somehow I was put on a mailing list for new moms and received two cans of formula in the mail - so this donation didn't cost me anything either.

By this time, Josh is getting hungry and we need to rework the plan a little to get over to Costco for a $1.50 hot dog & pop lunch (I know, we're such big spenders, eh? We often joke about treating each other to lunch - just over $3 for both of us! Can't get a much better deal than that, even if it isn't the healthiest thing in the world...)

15. Returned a few carts in the Costco parking lot

16. Bought a hot dog & pop lunch for the next person in line to order that meal deal

17. Dropped some change in the Salvation Army kettle outside Costco

18. Toys R Us had this special Christmas tree in the front door - on it were ornaments with the names of children and their ages. These are children who will not be getting much for Christmas, so the local radio station organized a toy drive for them. I chose a boy aged 10 (in honour of our Caleb who would be 10 this year) and Josh picked a Lego set for him for Christmas. This item on my list cost much more than the others, but this is a new thing we are doing in our family - our boys get 3 gifts for Christmas, and so we'll be thinking of ways to do the same sort of thing in memory of Caleb. This Toys R Us gift was one of those gifts.

19. Returned one of Josiah's Christmas presents. How does this fit on my list? Josiah asked us to take back one of his presents so he could use the money as a donation for people in Africa, who just lost Nelson Mandela. Uh ya, I have awesome boys.

20. Donated change for someone to have a free load of laundry at a local laundromat - the lady who runs it is so generous and loving, and she called later to thank us personally

HALF WAY THROUGH THE LIST!!!

21. Donated all our Canadian Tire money in one of those bins inside the Canadian Tire store

22. Walked around Target and left coupons on about 20 items - really good coupons too!

23. Josh placed a free drink coupon on the shelf in a local Mac's store

24. Held the doors open for others to go ahead of me for much of the day

25. Used a Tim's gift card to buy a snack for a friend (Josh was given a $10 gift card from one of his judo students, and he graciously gave it to the cause today)

26. Used the Tim's gift card to buy a hot chocolate for a friend

27. Used the Tim's gift card to buy lunch for a person in line behind us

Time to pick up the boys from school and start our Christmas vacation!!

28. Surprised Elijah with a "dinner out at the restaurant of your choice" coupon, which we used while Josiah was at a friend's Christmas party - this cost about $12.

After dinner we took Elijah skating for the first time this year - he did great!

Finished the rest of my list online later that night...

29. Entered the special code from a Mars bar wrapper - gives $5 to Habitat for Humanity - and the bar only cost me 69 cents!

30. Went to The Hunger Site online and clicked on all the links to donate.

31. Bought a special Christmas ornament online in honour of Caleb - $10 was donated to the Make-A-Wish foundation.

32. Donated some of my Shoppers Optimum points to the *Jennifer Ashleigh Children's Charity* (this charity was started in memory of a baby girl who died at 6 months of age - her mom wrote out her story and shared it in my book that I just published this week!) - this donation didn't cost me anything, and the points were accumulated from recent purchases at Shoppers Drug Mart - a really good rewards program!

33. Earlier in the morning I had offered a coupon of $7 off my book to Canadians who I won't be handing a copy to anytime soon - this was to cover the cost of shipping until the book is listed on amazon.ca - hopefully in January or February?

And the last few items are all the same...

34 - 40 Ordered free copies of my book for my contributors.

And that's all folks! 40 acts of kindness in one day! All from what I had to give already, plus a few extra dollars - but nothing over the top!

There are so many ideas out there, I bet if you sat down and started jotting a few down, you'd have a good list going in no time.

I found out late last night that my Mum had emailed 20 people and invited them to do 2 acts of kindness each and tell me about them somehow - and that would total 40 more to add to my 40!

So I got some wonderful emails and texts telling me about how people were blessing others in their own ways - it was such a blessing - thanks Mum!!!! And thank you to everyone who played along - you guys are simply amazing!!!

And thank you to my Joshua, who goes along with my ideas, and helps me live them out when I don't quite feel like I can do them alone.

Now... on to the next decade of life... I wonder what it will bring?!

# 2014

**January 4th, 2014**

**My Word(s) For 2014**

I've procrastinated enough.

Every morning for the last 3 days, I've woken with the urge to share my word for this new year.

Then I start playing around with blog themes and I try to find fancy word art to go with the word I have in mind.

And I leave the computer with no blog post done - nothing accomplished.

I hope this isn't what the whole year will look like.

Me procrastinating, distracted, not really wanting to dive in to what is coming.

It's just that this word is not easy, and it's a bit scary to be honest.

A look back on past words tells me I've been leading up to the 2014 word for some time:

2011 - Bold (and confident) - I began a journey of discovering the gifts, passions, and abilities God had given me, and sorting out how He wanted me to use them.

2012 - Free - I moved ahead with many things that God was laying on my heart - going back to school, reading through the whole Bible in a year, getting back into ministry with Josh.

2013 - Plenty - SO MUCH happened... meeting Oliver, finishing university, publishing my first book, turning 40... and I became aware of the many blessings in my life, the **plenty** I exist in on a daily basis.

And now 2014...

The word is...

**Change**

There's another word lingering in the shadows as well - Crazy.

Maybe it's the combination of the two that scares me.

Crazy Change means something a little different than just plain old Change, doesn't it?

I'm praying that I will be open to all that God has for this new year.

There's scripture, a saying, a song, and an image that go along with my word for 2014.

It has all been coming together in my heart for the past few days.

The scripture:

*Therefore, I urge you, brothers and sisters, in view of God's mercy, to offer your bodies as a living sacrifice, holy and pleasing to God—this is your true and proper worship. Do not conform to the pattern of this world but be transformed by the renewing of your mind. Then you will be able to test and approve what God's will is—his good, pleasing and perfect will. - Romans 12:1-2*

The heading for this scripture is *Living Sacrifice* by the way. Maybe a lot of the crazy change will be from within instead of a lot of external changes.

Which leads me to the saying:

*Be the change you want to see in the world.* - Mahatma Gandhi

It has to start with me. I can complain all I want about the state of the world or how people should be doing this or that, but if I'm not willing to do it myself, I have no right to say anything.

And there's this song that's been on repeat in my van, my house, my mind, my heart - for almost two months now.

*Crazy Enough* by Mercy Me.

Recently people have been giving me gifts with a butterfly image on them... and I see now that it fits with what God is speaking in my life for this new year:

So there you have it...

**Change** - starting with me.

Crazy change - I might get some funny looks or "What is she doing now?" comments. Remembering to live out the change as a "spiritual act of worship", in love instead of in judgement of others - that just might be the crazy part.

And a cool song and beautiful image as well... what a way to end the year of **Plenty**.

Happy New Year and Blessings Abundant for 2014!


## January 7th, 2014

## How To Navigate Crazy Change

I was reading through this beautiful book during the weeks of Advent - *God With Us - Rediscovering the Meaning of Christmas.*

This book was a gift from the folks at *Arrow* - the leadership course Josh completed a few years ago.

I have read through this book for the past three years during Advent - it just blesses me.

I found a wonderful "nugget" in it the other day as I was contemplating this idea of Crazy Change - my words for this year.

What does crazy change look like?

Are there going to be big external changes? Are we moving? Will I use my degree in a new job setting?

Etc.Etc.

I really have no idea what God is bringing this year - do we really ever know?

It comes back to the truth that I cannot control what happens outside myself, but I do have something to say about what happens inside.

Like I mentioned in my last post, I think the crazy change starts with me.

Again, I don't really know what that looks like yet.

But I came across a navigational tool in this beautiful book I'm reading.

A direction, a guide, a sign post to mark the way...

It's a prayer found on page 162...

*Dear Lord, make yourself known to me, as you did to your followers, in the middle of ordinary life. I want to believe I can be changed through closeness to you, and to the community surrounding me. Protect me from sin and evil by the power of your grace, Amen.*

"... in the middle of ordinary life... changed through closeness to you... and to the community surrounding me."

Change starts today, this moment, right here, right now.

No big external differences are needed.

Just a willing heart, a gracious God, and a drawing near to Him and to those around me.

I am grateful for this nugget, this sign post in the middle of the haze.

There has been this desire to get back to reading through the Bible, to do it all over again this year.

I love this way of getting close to God.

Knowing more about Him through His Word, through the history of His people, through the life of His Son - Emmanuel, God With Us.

Just like the title of the book.

Shall we navigate crazy change together?

You are part of the "community surrounding me"....

And I do love to share the journeys of life with you.


**January 15th, 2014**

**Why Can't It Be Simple?**

I wanted my word for this year to be something a little different than **Change**.

And definitely different than Crazy Change.

When I was mulling over what my word might be, praying about it, asking God to show me a glimpse of the year ahead, to give me a focus for my heart as I stepped into 2014... I threw out the word "Simple".

Yes, I like that.

In 2013 we did a lot of simplifying around our house and started to work on simplifying our lives.

We are striving for more margin, for more time and energy to give to each other and the things we love in life.

We are asking God to grant us avenues to dive into our passions, to be able to give more of ourselves to what makes us tick, to dig into the God stuff instead of the good stuff.

Simple would be a great word for that, don't you think?

When I think of simple I breathe a little easier and the anxiety fades and I smile to myself.

But my word for this year is Change.

Not simple.

Is it?

I have to get through the changes, the crazy changes, to get to the simple.

Maybe simple will be my word for 2015.

Maybe God has given me words for the next 2 years, because to get through a year of crazy change requires a focus beyond the change.

If all I could see in this year was crazy change, well that might just drive me a little crazy.

Why the change? Why the crazy change?

To get to the simple life I dream about, hope for, long for, strive for.

And where does the crazy change begin?

With me.

That's the hardest part of this whole thing as I set out on this year.

When my world seems to be spinning too fast, I usually set about changing something in the environment around me.

I start a new habit, or clean up the house, or instill some new discipline for my children.

But as they grow older, I realize more and more that I cannot manage their worlds, or their schools, or their friends, etc.

I can only manage me.

When my husband has a hard day or when life crowds in so tight around us - all I can do is change me.

And what is the best way to do that? How do I navigate this season of crazy change - starting with me?

I draw closer to God. I ask Him for more. I trust Him more. I lean on Him like never before.

Crazy change has to come from Him.

My kind of changes are fleeting, depending on my mood for the day, how tired I may or may not be, etc.

His kind of changes move mountains and part seas and defy death and save an entire world.

Now that's crazy change.

*Do that in me, Lord.*


## February 23rd, 2014

### Are We Waiting On God, Or Is He Waiting On Us?

My husband says it feels like we're waiting.

But I'm starting to wonder if it's that God is waiting on us.

We've been watching Him line things up and put things into position.

He's given us fresh vision and pointed us on a clear path.

In life and in ministry.

We have been waiting for this for (it feels like) forever.

We've gotten used to the waiting, and comfortable in the waiting.

But it feels like things are flip-flopped around, like crazy change is happening, and now Someone is waiting on us.

Time and again - for the past THREE years - he's been playing this verse on repeat in our lives:

*Have I not commanded you? Be strong and courageous. Do not be afraid; do not be discouraged, for the Lord your God will be with you wherever you go. - Joshua 1:9*

Yep, it's a good one, eh?

It also happens to be my husband's life verse.

When God keeps throwing your life verse at you, in amazing ways, at just the right times, over and over and over again, you know something's coming, right?

We've had this sense of Him at work for a while.

Like on the hard days, when nothing made sense, and we couldn't see past the next few minutes, He was simply asking us to... wait.

It was really hard to learn to wait.

This verse helped: *...but those who hope in the Lord will renew their strength. They will soar on wings like eagles; they will run and not grow weary, they will walk and not be faint. - Isaiah 40:31*

Some days we just walked, sauntered even, through the confusion and the fog. Some days we didn't run at all, and we felt very weary and faint.

We learned to grab hold of the good, to live in the moments that filled our days with such blessings - if only we let them, if only we recognized them, if only we learned to see things through His eyes.

And I don't want to leave out my life verse either. Because for a time He was throwing this one at us from every direction as well:

*Ask and it will be given to you; seek and you will find; knock and the door will be opened to you. - Matthew 7:7*

My favourite hymn is *Seek Ye First*.

It's the only one I can play on the piano by memory - a version I created myself so that I can play it anywhere, anytime.

One song, just one song that has echoed in my soul for as long as I can remember.

Other songs have come and gone, but this one has always remained.

And we did learn to ask, to seek, and to knock.

Even when we didn't get the answer we hoped for in the asking, or when things weren't much clearer after the seeking, or when doors seemed to remain closed after the knocking.

It's all about timing - His timing.

And we continued to wait.

Somewhere in the waiting, in the watching for mountains to move and seas to part, we learned that the greatest mountains need to be moved in us, and the biggest seas need to be parted in our hearts.

God is waiting on us.

He is asking us, seeking after us, knocking on the door of our hearts...

Josh and I got married under a stained-glass window of Jesus knocking on a door with no handle...

I didn't get it until someone explained it to me...

How Jesus will never force His way into anyone's life, into anyone's heart...

He simply knocks, and it's up to them how they answer...

The door can only be opened from the other side...

He simply stands and waits for the answer.

And that's how it feels to me just now - like God is waiting on us.

We have done our asking, our seeking, and our knocking - now it's time to be strong and courageous, knowing that we don't have to be afraid or discouraged when things look a little crazy, because He is with us always.

After all the waiting, now I'm looking forward to running this next lap of the race with you, Joshua.

**February 24th, 2014**

**How A Writer Sees The World**

"Writer" is a new thing for me.

This label that's attached itself to me.

Honestly - I never thought of myself that way until recently.

I thought everyone scribbled things down on paper and felt words well up in them until they might burst and saw life's events through a lens of titles and paragraphs (or lines of poetry).

Seriously.

Doesn't everyone do this?

I remember playing a game in my mind as a child.

I'd picture my hands on a typewriter (because that's all there was in "those days"), fingers spelling out words as fast as I could.

I loved to write goofy poetry as a little girl.

Sometimes there were serious musings too.

It all started as poetry to me.

Maybe someday I'll share a few of the treasures I kept from the younger years.

As I grew up the poems became focused on friendships and boys.

Writing assignments for school were given good grades.

I was asked to read some of the writings out loud.

This was before I grew to be self-conscious, quiet, and painfully shy.

It was hard for me, but I did it.

I was chosen to represent my school and read a short story at a literary guild for juniors, and I made it to the city-wide semi-finals in a public speaking contest, and the cherry on top - Grade 8 valedictorian.

By then they were starting to recognize my fears of people looking at me and being the center of attention. They almost chose someone else because they thought no one would hear my voice from the platform. The solution of a microphone saved my spot on stage.

I was part happy/part scared out of my tree.

But it seemed to be easier to say yes back in the day.

And so I scribbled down what I hoped were words of wisdom, mixed in a little humour, and gave my speech one June night in 1987. I still have the speech tucked away in my memory box somewhere in the basement, along with my short story for the literary guild, and my cue-cards for the public speaking contest.

Words fill my memory box.

Life events that centered around words, cards from other life events, letters that travelled across the globe from my grandma in England, poems from my Joshua and scribbled words of love from my boys as they learned to write.

I have treasured words, played with words, worked with words, and shared myself with words - for as long as I can remember.

And no, not everyone does this.

I finally realized this truth a few years ago.

That's when the label stuck.

Writer.

It always meant something so grand and beyond my normal life - something like piles of books with your name on the front, and bookstore signings, and speaking around the world and...

Everyone watching you, and up on the stage in front of so many people, and what if there's no microphone?

OK... well... I have a little secret I've been keeping to myself for quite some time now.

There may be another way that I use the words in my life.

I may just use them to hide sometimes.

Pause... deep breath...

I once wrote in an email, "When I speak I have no idea who's talking. When I write I hear my voice."?

So true, so absolutely true.

But I've learned that sometimes people need an audible voice, a personal touch, a warm embrace, an eye-to-eye and face-to-face kind of connection rather than flipping through the pages of a book.

This is where it gets tricky for me and I doubt I have any of the right stuff for those situations.

There's something else I've learned, though.

I need the audible voice, personal touch, warm embrace, and eye-to-eye/face-to-face kind of connection too.

And without that connection, the words shrivel up anyways.

Because I shrivel up.

So it's time for crazy change again...

This really is a hold-on-tight kind of year!

And it's only February!

It's time to be open to coming out from behind the words.

To say yes if God asks me to take my place out front.

Even if there's no microphone.

A simple decision.

We'll see what it brings.

What He brings.

I'll continue to fill my days with words, because that's what I've always done, because I'm a writer, and because that's how a writer sees the world...

## March 19th, 2014

### Ash Wednesday

We write something on a piece of paper on the morning of Ash Wednesday.

Something specific we want to work on during Lent, something we want God to work on in our lives.

I've written down things like FEAR and WORRY in the past.

Though I still struggle with these in my life, they are loosening their grip on me as I grab on tight to God's hand in the struggles.

I know my word for this year, but I'll keep it a secret for now...

Then we burn the paper...

and make a cross with the ashes...

and watch the "something" turn to dust in light of the cross.

In previous years we've drawn crosses on our foreheads, but this year we painted with ashes, and Josh made a beautiful picture out of what was once our secret "something"s.

God knows us, He knows our struggles, He made us from ashes and one day we will return to ashes.

He came to us, to take our "something"s and turn them to dust with His grace.

And at Lent we especially remember this.

## March 5th, 2014

### Losing Light and Gaining Perspective

We ventured out into dusk. The sun was slipping behind the horizon and the moon was yet to make its appearance in the night sky. We had just enjoyed a warm meal together and now it fueled our efforts to snowshoe on the trail of snow and ice. Our friend's cottage faded into the distance as we skimmed over the Muskoka landscape before us.

It would be a quick trek on the trail tonight. We were losing light fast, but the pinks and oranges of the sky had beckoned us through the big bay window in the living room. And we raced to answer.

Now we raced against the darkness. Each of us trekking at our own pace through the now-murky night. The youngest of us needed extra help to gear up and even then we didn't know how long the broken gear would hold. Yet still he wanted to venture out with us. Another had raced ahead, leaving poles and warm gear behind, anxious to get on the trail and grab all he could from the moments of light we had left. The biggest and tallest and strongest of us equipped all the others before starting on his race. His steps always sure and steady, his pace only slowing to help others, he gave us confidence to see the race to the finish. Then were was me, always bringing up the rear, making sure everyone else was running the race well ahead of me, never wanting to leave anyone behind, loving the view of watching others as they ran.

Through the darkening sky we raced against the blackness. The beautiful colours that only moments before had beckoned us out of the comfortable cottage, now gone from our view.

The youngest lost a snowshoe long ago, now carrying it in his arms along with his two poles, excited by the humorous story he had to share with friends back home. This smallest of runners loves to find his own pace and enjoy the moments of his race. He grabs what he can from his surroundings, finds the beauty in what he sees, and invites others to enjoy the treasures of life with him. He shows me a whole new world if only I stop to listen and watch with him. The other was far ahead, still in sight, stopping now and then to point out a new discovery or wait for those of us who lagged behind. It has always been hard to keep up with this runner. He is fast, he is fearless and he is full of life. I love him this way. Once in a while I find the courage to run side by side with him in his race. The biggest

224

and tallest and strongest was in front of me now, turning back at times to give me a smile or wait for me to catch up to the team. As long as I know this runner is still in the race, this gives me energy and patience and perseverance like nothing I've ever known as I put one foot in front of the other on the trail ahead. And then there's me, taking it all in, enjoying the view from the back, knowing that one day, soon enough, the youngest runner will out-pace me by far.

We come to a small fork in the trail. The cottage is back in sight and the trail provides two paths to the front door. I notice that the youngest members of the team turn off one way, and the oldest members turn off the other. So it should be. We each have our own races to run, our own paths to take, all leading to the same place eventually.

No matter that the trek was quick that day, or that we raced against darkness, or that we each raced is such different ways - what mattered to me most was that we set out in the first place, that we answered the call to enjoy the beauty of the trail before us, that we finished strong, and that we gathered together again when the race was done.


**March 31st, 2014**

**Riding The Waves**

Feels like it's been a while.

Feels like I have so much to share and no idea where to start.

What a week, what a month, what a year!

I've been waiting for a time of quiet so I can think and write it all down.

But even when there is no audible noise, there is soul-noise.

Yesterday it seems I may have found a place, a time of rest.

Because this morning it is a little quieter in my head, my heart.

Can I share?

This year has been one major event/change/transition after another.

225

Don't we all have years like that?

Sometimes the big things are not good things.

This year they have been good things - thank God.

Because of course there will be times that are the opposite.

But not right now.

This year there was Meeting Oliver, Graduation, Turning 40, and Publishing My First Book.

But I don't think I've mentioned much about church planting or the Northern Ontario focus or the Dominican focus.

Not to mention I am watching my boys grow up more and more every day. It's a whole new phase with one of them in youth group and the other finishing up primary education soon enough.

And my husband will soon join me in entering another decade of life - he will also turn 40 next month. We really are growing old together.

I find myself leaning into the song *Oceans* more and more every day...

I remember finding this saying at my mum's house a few years back - I keep it in my wallet…

*I can trust the waves, for I know the One who made the ocean.*

Ya, exactly.

Lots of waves, not big horrible waves of destruction...

But waves that knock me over, flip me upside down, spin me around and around, and make me search for which way is up.

My husband tried out surfing in Mexico when I was five months pregnant with our first son.

We were much crazier then, in different ways, and didn't mind hopping on a plane with 5 days' notice and travelling across the world to catch a few days of adventure - with a baby coming we knew life would be spinning us around in many ways.

I remember sitting on a beach near Los Cabos, with a woman I barely knew, trying to spot Josh and this woman's boyfriend on the horizon.

They had this crazy idea to try surfing.

Josh with his long wild hair and his fearlessness.

Me with big baby belly, red kerchief on my head, sprawled on the blanket on white sand.

They told us at the surf shop where we rented the boards that it was dangerous to go out on the waves that day.

Some of the walls of water were 12 feet high they said.

But still Josh went out, having never surfed before.

Back then I reveled in his craziness instead of trying to tame it (oh my, why do I even try to tame this in him?).

I remember scanning the horizon, not seeing the soon-to-be-father that I'd been married to for not even two years.

I stood up and searched some more.

Trusted.

I knew he was there somewhere, that God had him, that he would saunter back up the beach to me with that smirk on his face.

And he did, but not for a while, and not without a fascinating tale of adventure to tell.

He'd been knocked off his board, tossed into the waves, spun around and upside down, couldn't tell which way was up.

Good thing he had tied off the board to his ankle.

Good thing he had something to pull him right-side up, to show him the way to swim.

Ya, good thing!

And I looked at him and knew I loved the craziness in him.

Always have.

And here we are, almost 15 years later, and I still love that in him.

But I've started riding the waves with him more and more.

I'm not sitting on the beach anymore.

Not wrapped up in a cozy blanket, watching life happen - now out on the waves alongside him.

And it's spinning me around and upside down, and some days the waves seem way too big to be trying to navigate.

So instead I let them wash over me, and I pull on the rope that shows me the way up, and I come up for air, and get ready for the next wave.

Knowing that the seas do calm, the waves do still, and it will get easier to catch my breath - eventually.

Really, though, I wouldn't want to miss the ride - waves and all.

What crazy changes this year is bringing so far...


## June 4th, 2014

### Hungry For More

*I wrote this article for Live magazine - a publication of the Baptist Women of Ontario and Quebec...*

Fasting has never been something I want to do. I fight it all the way. Why would anyone want to go without if they don't have to?

I have only fasted a few times in my life. There was the couple of times I joined in with World Vision's *30 Hour Famine* as a youth group volunteer. Or that short stint with fasting for breakfast every Tuesday. Poor planning on my part also meant I was usually grocery shopping on Tuesday mornings. It didn't take long for the fasting habit to break under those circumstances!

As I contemplated writing an article on fasting, I knew the one question I wanted to answer was *What do I hunger for when I choose to go without?* This is what I discovered as I started to answer that question in my life...

**Sweetness -** When I fast from food for a time, I miss the sweet side of life that I usually experience through my taste buds. I am forced to look for the sweetness in other areas of my world. Once I start looking, once I fix my gaze on the search for the good, the positive, the uplifting, and the encouraging things of life, I find they are not so hard to spot after all. The way my husband looks at me across a crowded room, my oldest son's mischievous smirk when he's teasing me, my youngest son's *I love you* that melts my heart every time, my mum's voice on the phone when I really need to chat, my sister's laughter, my dad's insightful emails, my brother's amusing blog posts. All of these and more fill my heart to the brim with the sweetness of life.

**Fullness -** I crave a life that is full of good things, great things, God things. I long to know I am living in His will, I am on the right track, and I am accomplishing at least some of the things He hoped for me when He knit me together in the womb. Am I living out my days with purpose? Vision? Direction? These questions taunt me even on the good days at this point in my life. Looking back just four days ago, I walked across the graduation stage to receive my Bachelor's degree. This milestone was 21 years in the making. Looking ahead less than two months from now, my fortieth birthday looms in the foreground. Have I lived a life that is full so far? Have I made the most of the opportunities given to me? What about the next forty years? I want them to be full to the max with the things of God.

**More -** I hunger for more when I go without. More to receive from others, and also more to give to others. I yearn to be given more love, more attention, more relational sustenance, more purpose, more direction, more vision, more assurance that I am exactly where I'm supposed to be, doing exactly what I'm supposed to be doing. On the other hand I also yearn to give more love to others. I rediscover the lack in myself when I fast. There is an emptiness in me, a space that only God can fill with His love for others. I would never be enough

to do the things He asks of me, and I would never have enough to accomplish His purposes for the days of my life. Not without Him.

Fasting makes me abundantly aware that I do not like to go without. As I live in the moments of lack I am acutely reminded of all the hungry faces I've seen on television, on mission trips, and in magazine articles. When I look in the mirror I know my face is not a hungry face. Yet I do know hunger. I hunger for the sweetness of life, the fullness of life, and I hunger for more. Always I want more.

If only I could point this longing for more in the direction of things that would be worth the striving, the sacrifice, and the pursuit required to obtain them. Then the fasting would be well worth the hunger it takes to set off in the direction of the longings in me for more.

## June 9th, 2014

### It's Definitely Time To Celebrate... Anything!

My mum is the queen of celebration. When I was growing up there was always a cake or a card or a dinner out to celebrate the small things as well as the big things. The woman never marked the calendar, she just marked life. Often I never realized there was cause to celebrate, never thought **that** would be something that should render any kind of attention, but she saw the potential for a party in everything.

I used to roll my eyes at it, but secretly I loved it. She made me feel special, time and again. She still does. I love my mum.

When I show up to visit her house with my boys, often there are little surprises waiting for them on the bunk beds she keeps in her spare room for us. She sends care packages in the mail now that I live a few hours drive away. She never forgets special days. Never.

Is celebration a spiritual gift? Probably not, but I'm sure she would have it if it was.

I've inherited some of her zest for a good party. The first time my husband and I celebrated a Christmas together (just a little over a month after our wedding), imagine his surprise when he came home from work to our newly rented townhouse and stepped into a winter wonderland. I had gone all out and there were decorations **everywhere**. I had a whole big tote full of things I'd been collecting over the years, mostly from the dollar store. Money was always tight, but the dollar store provided endless possibilities for broke students and young workers to celebrate just about anything!

Josh wasn't used to celebrating. He usually chose to skip it all and hide out somewhere far from the party when it came to birthdays and Christmas. So when his birthday rolled around a few months after the winter wonderland scene, he came home to balloons and streamers and a scavenger hunt to get to his present and a Dairy Queen cake with candles and... it was all a little much for my Joshua.

I have learned to tone it down to what he can handle, and he has learned it is truly important to celebrate life however you can.

Often celebration means hard work. Like the potluck Thanksgiving dinners we host every year. Some of the minor holidays can get a little lonely because we live a few hours away from family. So a few years ago we decided to invite other lonely people out to celebrate with us. Every year we gather, we give thanks, and celebrate together. Some faces around the table are familiar, but usually the majority of faces are new. It's always a good time. The preparations are always worth it in the end.

Preparation means discipline. Something I'm not always great at. But when I sit down to type out the invitations, I catch a vision of the people behind the invitations, and the faces that I am preparing to bless. Some faces are unknown to me at the time of preparation, and I know that soon they will be a part of the vision too, when it's all over and the celebration is done.

Community is all around us, if we can have eyes to see it. We can find it in the small things as well as the big things. When we step out the door and greet our neighbours, we celebrate them in our lives. When we congratulate someone who has reached a milestone, we celebrate their accomplishments. When we host a party for friends or family, when we buy Christmas gifts, when we invite people over for any reason at all, when we send a card or an email in honour of a special day, when we bake turkeys for Thanksgiving and hams for Easter - this is all celebration.

There are times when I look up silly holidays that people have created, just so I can find a reason to celebrate on the days when it's hard to see the good. How about celebrating *Look for Circles Day* or *Eat a Cranberry Day*? People are crying out for celebration.

I am proud to say I am one of them. It's a choice we make every day, and it's often hard work, but it's always worth the effort.

Go on... find something to celebrate today.

## June 14th, 2014

### Happy Father's Day To The Father Of My Children

*I'm posting this one for you today, Joshua, because I have a special one coming for my Daddy tomorrow...*

I know your heart, Josh, your father's heart...

You long to be a good father to our boys...

You've been discovering what exactly this means over the last 13 years...

Skimming through articles online I read a few things about being a good father...

But I don't need to read any more articles to know what I've always known...

Ever since before Josiah entered the world...

You would be a really good father.

I was not wrong, Joshua.

You care for us with all you've got, you put us first whenever possible, you work less so you are present more, you try so hard to do the right thing, you provide more than enough for all our needs (and many of our wants as well), you dare to dream big dreams, you cheer us on and build us up and give us roots and give us wings.

You are outrageously spontaneous and wild and crazy and free.

You are fun and fun-loving.

You love to make us laugh.

You hold us when we hurt - if we let you.

You value tradition.

You love to try new things.

You fix things that are broken.

You protect us.

You give us freedom to discover who we are.

You love to rap and dance and play guitar.

You invite all kinds of amazing people into our home.

You open the world to us and show us there's no place like home.

You sit in silence when we need it, and you chat with us about life when we need that.

You listen.

You learn.

Always more learning when you're a father....

Thanks for putting in the time, the effort, the creativity, the prayer, and the love needed to be the father you are today.

We will love you more tomorrow, and the next day and the next.

Just as we know you will do the same for us.

Happy Father's Day Joshua.

Hope you like your presents tomorrow!


**June 19th, 2014**

**It's Been a Good Couple Of Days**

I've just been regrouping for the past two days...

Being quiet, praying, looking past the chaos that sometimes comes in our family schedule...

This verse has come to mind quite a bit...

*Be still, and know that I am God - Psalm 46:10*

It's so good to know how He loves us, that He cares about every area of our lives, that He's always trying to help - the good Father that He is.

Lovely people have been sending me lovely words of encouragement and support...

So many people willing to walk alongside me on the journey for a while...

This journey towards health after a long season of fatigue and sleeplessness.

Thank you for walking and talking with me...

It's good to have some company.

Sleep has come easier for me - last night I finally managed to get just OVER 7 hours.

I feel like a new woman.

What if I could get that kind of sleep every night?

Ah, but one day at a time is what is helping right now.

I managed to get through another book that's been sitting on my shelf for a few months...

This one really helped with affirming that I'm on the right track with just getting back to basics and knowing that being healthy isn't rocket science.

It's all the things I already know, updated a little since I learned them.

It's whole grains and lean meats and fruits and vegetables and lots of water and exercise.

At this point in my life it's also a little weight training (this is a new one for me, but I've been lifting weights off and on for years - 5 or 10 pounds that is!).

It's being active with the boys (I always suspected this could be my best exercise regimen!) and my Joshua (no, I'm NOT getting on the judo mats Josh!).

It's getting back on my bike and going for walks and hiking the Rainbow Route trails and finally using the canoe paddle Josh bought me for Valentine's Day YEARS ago and swimming in the Northern Ontario lakes (once it warms up just a LITTLE bit more!). These are all things I absolutely love to do.

I've been recruiting family and friends to walk and hike and ride bikes for decades. Did I ever mention my dream to bike across Canada one day? That dream never fades, so I trust it will come when the time is right. Josh says he'll drive alongside in the van and set up camp every night. Thanks sweetie. Maybe our sons will ride alongside me on the journey?

One thing I know for certain is that God is with me on the journeys of life... He has always been with me on the journeys...

I remember one of the biggest journeys of my 40 years...

I'd always wanted to see the Rocky Mountains... and so when I felt like heading off to Bible college after re-dedicating my life to Christ when I was 23, guess which school I chose... That's right - Rocky Mountain Bible College in Calgary, Alberta.

And what a journey it was... I flew out with a good friend about a month before school began. We stayed in hostels and drove through the mountains to Vancouver. We left the rental car behind and met up with another friend who was living on Vancouver Island at the time. One friend went back home to job and family, I stayed with the other friend for a few weeks in Victoria. During my stay I joined in on a Wilderness Expedition for 3 days - travelled in a van across the island with 11 people I didn't know...

Canoed in Rocky Mountain lakes...

Sauntered through the West Coast Rainforest...

Walked among 600-year-old trees in Cathedral Grove...

Hiked through the clear-cuts of Clayoquot Sound...

And swam in the Pacific Ocean at Long Beach...

Mmmmhmmm... really good adventures...

Then back to Calgary to start school.

Again, I didn't know a soul, didn't know how I'd pay for school, didn't have a place to live or a job.

Found a room to rent on the bulletin board at the school. The renter's name was Mary-Catherine and we had the same birthday. I figured it was destiny, that God was working it all out in His special ways - I wasn't wrong.

And when a whirlwind romance with a fantastic man came her way and she married soon after I moved in, her family who lived two doors down took me in and cared for me like I was one of their own (they already had 4 girls! I still call them friends and visited with them just 2 years ago on a church-planting trip to Calgary - but that's another post for another day...). They hadn't been expecting a boarder, but this family has always done their best to follow God's leading, and I'm so glad God led me to them for a time. They fixed up a lovely room off their den and let me choose the wallpaper and it was home for 4 months.

I found a job at my favourite restaurant - Swiss Chalet - and walked back and forth to work after school was done for the day.

I got some OSAP to help pay tuition.

I got a couple of friends to hang out with.

God was with me every step of the way.

He was with me on the nights I walked home from work, the crisp fall air rustling the leaves as I prayed - a lot.

He was with me on the bus rides to school as I explored the strange surroundings of a new city.

He was with me when I signed up to spend a week at the Mustard Seed as part of a course at school - I never doubted my safety, even when we walked the streets as the homeless, or lined up for food, or slept in the old church, or ate with people who yelled obscenities at me. I was scared, I was far out of my comfort zone (couldn't even see it if I tried!), but I never doubted He was with me.

The journeys He brings us through are never what we imagine - always a little better or a little worse, I've found.

But they are always good, and always just what He intends.

So this journey of health is no different. Some days will be better than I think, and some days will be worse.

One day at a time, one day being "different" at a time.

And learning, step by step, how to do "different."

I'm sure I'll have some cool snapshots to share along the way - maybe not in pictures, but in experiences and memories and realizations.

I'll keep sharing the journey... I can't help myself... it's just who He made me to be.


## July 15th, 2014

### "Stop Sitting On The Premises"

I heard this from a preacher on the radio in Chicago a few years ago.

We were there for Josh's graduation from Wheaton College.

First we had visited Josh's brother in St. Louis for a few days, then we brought Uncle Jay with us and piled into a rented Jeep to drive to Chicago for the graduation.

It was a grand affair, visiting Wheaton was a magnificent experience, and the ceremony was inspiring to say the least.

On our last night in Chicago we were winding down in the hotel room with the boys.

Josh went for a swim in the hotel pool, and I tucked the boys into bed.

They used to listen to music as they fell asleep, so I was trying to find something soothing on the radio.

I found a preacher.

One of those southern gospel preachers, you know?

With the booming voice and the beautiful lilt to his words.

They always sound like they have something amazing to say.

I've always wanted to visit at least one of those churches - maybe one day.

That day the radio was enough.

I just couldn't change the station.

I can still remember one line of the preacher's sermon.

Just one line that has stuck with me and changed me in different ways.

One line that applies to so many areas of life.

"You got to stop sitting on the premises and start STANDING on the promises."

Ya, I just LOVE that!

Don't you?

This one line has grown my faith immensely.

It has encouraged me to step out of my comfort zone over and over.

And now it is encouraging me in areas of health.

You see, my body is sore - EVERY day.

Not just sometimes anymore.

ALL the time.

It started about a year ago, when I was writing my last exams for university and I knew the book would be published within a few months and church planting in Northern Ontario was the new

direction we found ourselves on.

There was a whole heap of new things, big things, wonderful things going on.

And I'd gotten really used to sitting on the premises.

When big things loom in front of you - it's not easy to stand up.

It's much easier to just keep sitting down.

I'm not talking physically here - I can go through the motions as good as the next person.

I'm talking spiritually.

It's this verse that sticks with me...

*As the body without the spirit is dead, so faith without deeds is dead. - James 2:26*

I've been working out the "faith without deeds is dead" part for a couple of years now, and it's been motivating me to "start standing on the promises" all over the world! In my own neighbourhood to Northern Ontario to Dominican Republic. Such great adventures, with more coming I hope.

It seems it's this part that I have to work on next - "the body without the spirit is dead".

Going through the motions and neglecting to live in the moments of them is proving to make me worn and tired and sore.

I think I tend to leave my spirit at home when it's time to stand on the promises.

I think I leave a chunk of me behind - to keep sitting on the premises.

It's safe there, it's under control, it's familiar and warm and comforting.

Standing on the promises is often unfamiliar, cold, strange, confusing.

But it's time to start moving.

The more I sit, the sorer I get.

The more I hurt.

It's three simple words that have been on repeat for a while in my heart, but I've forgotten them the last little while.

*Just... keep... going.*

But not just physically, it's got to be spiritually too.

It's got to be all of me that stands up.

A wonderful lady sent me these words recently - she has Parkinson's and this simple phrase is highlighted on one of the Parkinson's exercise posters...

STAND UP

SIT LESS

MOVE MORE

Yes, that sums it up nicely...

## July 16th, 2014

### A Very Special Email

Sometimes I sell these Lunchbox Jokes that I made a few years back.

I have a little Etsy Shop that I don't normally mention much - there's not a whole lot in there right now - just 3 things at the moment.

It will often be weeks or months in between sales from my shop, but then I receive a notification that someone has purchased one of the creations listed.

Last week I got such a notification.

This one was a little different, though.

This one came with such an enormous blessing attached.

Can I share the comment I received from the purchaser?

*I am a volunteer with an organization called Blue Skies that provides families with children who have cancer a week of vacation at the beach. My plan was to use these cards at night as little surprises when I turn their covers down for them while they are out at the pool. I know how much children love jokes so I thought it would be fun. Thanks so much...*

Mmmhmmm.... a very special email... blesses me to no end.

**August 17th, 2014**

## A Time To NOT Write

Sometimes I don't have the words.

I can feel them piling up inside of me, getting all jumbled together, with nowhere to go...

But sometimes it's best NOT to write them out.

Not here on this blog, not in my bedside journal, not anywhere.

Because life can get busy and confusing and loud.

And for me the words come from such a quiet place.

There are times when I can't get to them.

Not the ones that should be written down and shared anyways.

Sure, there's a lot of words floating around in my head and my heart that are crying out for a spot on the paper, on the screen, on my lips.

But words are the overflow of what is inside of us, and what if the inside is just too messy?

Like inviting someone over and there is no place to sit because every surface is cluttered, and there is nothing to eat because the pantry is bare.

Sometimes I give all I've got in ways that empty me out fast, and there is no time or energy to get ready for the next "thing" before it comes.

These are not bad times, not unhappy times, just different times.

I wouldn't change them.

When I'm this tired and the words are this jumbled and it's time NOT to write - it means I'm really Living in the Moments.

Sure, if I had to keep going at this break-neck speed (by my watch, which tells time much differently than you, or you, or you), I would burn out like crazy.

But I know a different season is coming, a slower one, that will bring much time for sorting through the mess inside and the jumbled words.

241

It's already starting.

This morning I see some words floating to the surface.

I see which ones come first, then second, then third, and so on.

They are still there.

Sometimes when I don't have them for a time, I worry they won't come back.

I sort of need them to figure out my days, my place, my roles in this world.

But for now, for another little while, they will remain inside.

More will heap on the pile, will come to rest in their rightful spot in the mess, to be sorted in the coming season.

I do love to sort out messes.

I'm weird that way.

I love to take things that are all over the place and make some sense out of them.

So it is the same with the words.

I hope you are enjoying the weeks of summer - there are still a few more to go!

I'll be back when it's time to write once again.


## September 4th, 2014

### Just Keep It Simple Anna

I need to have these words on repeat in my head and my heart this year.

When I see so many options, so many "good" things to fill my life, so many paths before me, I need to remember to *Just Keep It Simple Anna*.

It helps to revisit the beginning of things.

Like what were the first words that were whispered in my heart, before I dared to speak them out loud, before I shared them with others, before I wrote them down and they became a "real" part of my life?

Every fall it seems I need to go back to the beginning.

And look at things with fresh eyes and make sure I'm still on track with what God whispered in my heart way back when.

Make sure all that has been spoken out loud, or shared with others, or written down and become part of "real" life is still in line with those first whispers.

Remember Elijah on the mountain? When he was waiting for the Lord to pass by? He recognized God in the gentle whisper.

Not in the powerful wind that tore mountains apart and shattered rocks, not in the earthquake, and not in the fire.

God was in the whisper.

So when I go back to beginnings, to the first whispers, I have to look past the loud things of life, the distractions, the noise - I have to listen for the gentle whispers.

Not always easy, is it?

The loud things are so loud, the distractions are so many, and the noise is everywhere.

But if I wait for it, listen with my whole heart, the gentle whispers never fade, and they out-last the others - always.

What are the whispers in my life?

Writing and encouraging have been there as long as I can remember.

When I rededicated my life to Christ at age 23 and travelled out to Rocky Mountain Bible College for a semester, the whispers were a question...

*Will you give me your all Anna? I want to use you for the kingdom - will you let Me Anna? Will you trust me?*

Because He never forces us to do anything, does He?

It's always our choice, and it's a choice I have to continue to make in different seasons of life. A choice that comes easier some days than others. A choice that comes particularly hard when I don't get a single thing about what He is up to in my life.

Then as I was getting to know a certain strapping young man named Joshua, the whispers were really girlish, childish, goofy, yet simple...

*I'm going to marry Josh Sklar and have his babies.*

Ya, told you, and we weren't even dating yet!

Then when our second son was stillborn...

*Focus on what you have, not what you don't have.*

Caleb in the Bible - he told the people that the giants who currently lived in the promised land were no match for God, and surely the Israelites could move on into the land God had promised to them. He focused on what they had (God!!) and not what they didn't have (mighty armies, huge warriors, etc.).

And going back to our dating days, Josh and I have always headed north. It's like a magnet that draws us constantly. It's only fitting that is now our home.  The whispers God has for us are so simple...

*Reach the north.*

And more and more He shows us how to do that.

If I can just remember these few gentle whispers in my life...

1.  *Will you give Me your all Anna?*

2.  *Marriage to Josh and mothering Josiah, Caleb, and Elijah are top of the priority list.*

3.  *Reach the north - however He leads us to do that.*

4.  *Writing and encouraging others are big on my personal to-do list.*

5.  *The only way to keep going is to focus on what I have, not what I don't have.*

It gets quite simple if I can just tune my head and my heart in to the whispers.

So many things can fall to the wayside and it's OK.

Really.

This lifts the weight so much.

What are the whispers in your life?

**September 14ᵗʰ, 2014**

**The Longest Journey**

In the wee hours of this morning, I fell asleep with a Bible pressing into my forehead.

I kid you not.

It was a Superhero Bible with a red and blue cover, with tabs inside to mark each book - so that it's easier to find verses when you're looking them up.

The Bible belongs to my youngest son, and he had a bad dream last night.

The most scared he's ever been.

He crawled in with us (the second time in as many weeks), and I prayed with him and cuddled up next to him, and then moved back over to his bed with him to do the same.

Back in his room, we were finding it hard to go back to sleep.

Every little noise seemed bigger and scarier than it actually was.

So he asked if I'd read from his Superhero Bible.

We've been reading through it together, slowly but surely, for at least a year now.

Page by page, chapter by chapter, book by book.

We've been reading the stories in the Word of God since he was born.

But now we're reading them as they are (with some parts skipped over for age-appropriateness!).

And I smiled when he asked me to read, because I knew which story was next.

I knew that we had just read about God's provision for Elijah as ravens fed him by a river and a widow fed and housed him from the little she had.

Next was Elijah's battle against the false prophets.

And Elijah's victory.

God's victory.

And rain after a long drought.

And the defeat of the most wicked queen in the Bible.

So yes, yes, yes, we can read Elijah.

We didn't quite make it through the whole story - it's a LONG chapter and we usually break those down into 2 or 3 nights of reading.

But my youngest knows the story, and he remembered that God is bigger than anything.

And our hearts quieted down, and the noises of our old house faded into sleep, and there was just peace and safety and knowing God is on our side.

This always makes all the difference, doesn't it?

I have struggled with nightmares most of my life.

Ever since I was a little girl, bad dreams were often a part of my nightly routine.

I had some amazing people pray for me before Joshua was on the scene.

That seemed to calm them when they were at their worst - out in Calgary while I was at Rocky Mountain Bible College - I was 23 years old.

The strapping young man I married told me to wake him whenever the nightmares came - he prayed for me and held me and I felt safe and loved.

So when Elijah came to our bed last night, I told him about his daddy's talent, and Josh prayed for him too.

Then Elijah felt safe enough and loved enough to go back to his room - as long as I would go with him.

Gladly, my son, gladly.

I am becoming more and more aware that these times will come to an end as he just keeps getting older and older.

Growing more and more into a young man - right before my eyes.

So we lay under cozy blankets, we try to settle our hearts, we read about Elijah in the Bible, and I fall asleep with the Word of God pressed into my head on the pillow.

You see, I'd told Elijah about a secret trick I used to have when the nightmares were really bad...

I would fall asleep clutching my Bible to my chest.

Not always comfortable if it was my hard-cover Bible!

But absolutely always - this trick helped me every time.

So the Bible stayed on the pillow as we drifted off to sleep.

He'd tried my trick for a while, clutching the red and blue Superhero Bible to his chest.

Then he'd laid it on the pillow beside him.

My pillow.

And I woke up feeling like something was on my forehead, and I remembered the Bible, and I smiled.

And I remembered hearing a preacher out in Calgary say that "Sometimes the longest journey is from our head to our heart."

Even though the literal distance is so short.

Sometimes all our Bible reading and all our knowledge about God just stays in our heads.

Never makes it to our hearts.

Never changes us.

Never changes our world.

And so I'm left wondering, praying, pondering this morning...

Where am I at with the journey?

The Longest Journey... from head to heart.

*Where have I got you perched in my life right now, Lord?*

I suppose that's a good question to wonder about every once in a while...

## October 30th, 2014

### Clear Your Plate Of The "Good" Stuff, Make Room For The "God" Stuff

I constantly feel like there is not enough time to get everything done. And you know what? THERE ISN'T! Not when you are simply trying to do more than any one person on earth should be doing.

As I first realized I was tackling just way too much in life, I started to try and figure out why I was in so deep. Was I trying to escape? Was I trying to prove something? Was I trying to find worth in things that I shouldn't?

These are all very valid questions, and I'm sure it's a little of all of the above, but instead of drowning in introspection, I simply got to work. Clearing, sorting, organizing, seeing results, fulfilling tasks, knowing that some of the things I was doing were for the LAST TIME. This got me moving in a positive direction, helped me see more clearly through every step, and now, just a couple of months

later, I am in a much better place, sleeping more than I have for years, feeling somewhat healthy again (spiritually, emotionally, physically - all of it!).

I wanted to share a general plan with you - to start to clear the plate of the "good" stuff and make room for the "God" stuff.

**1st Step** - List the things you are currently involved in - work, volunteer, household, activities for the family, hobbies & interests - what are you up to these days?

*Caution: This step might make you dizzy or cause your vision to blur, but just - keep - going.*

Mine looked something like this for Fall 2013 - Fall 2014...

Household - Cooking from scratch MOST of the time, couponing and shopping flyers, finding deals on EVERYTHING to lower expenses, most of the cleaning, gardening, child care (for The Youngest), dropping off/picking up boys from school, finances and budgeting, drive boys to many of their activities, drive hubby to work-related appointments (we have just the one car).

Volunteer - School field trips, help at school events, Parent Council, help with reading club, Co-lead a church plant for university students at the local campus (meets on a weekly basis through the school year), help to create vision for church planting in Northern Ontario, most of organizing for international mission trip and local mission trip with church (took two teams of 12 people on each trip), help out at Sunday school, help out at local children's camps for 2-3 weeks in the summer, and a few other odds and ends.

Writing - Self-publish first book, maintain personal blog, submit bi-monthly articles for women's magazine.

Hobbies/Interests - these really took a back seat during the past year... tried to get out for walks, sewed pillowcases for us and curtains to take on one of the mission trips (after clearing the dust off my sewing machine that had accumulated from years of neglect!), got together with friends for a women's dinner every month for a while, attended a women's conference out of town that I LOVED.

Other - administrate rental income for one property

That's what I can think of right now.... there's probably more... and I used to wonder why I had trouble sleeping!!

WHEW!

This step was actually really freeing for me - to see and understand that it's not lack of time management skills or organization or motivation, it's just trying to do too much all at once!

**2nd Step** - Ask yourself - Why? Why am I doing all these things? Are they truly important? Is God in this at all?

This is where the dizziness fades and the blurred vision clears.

If you can't give a good answer to WHY? then you can let it go... seriously.

Like if you're doing a ton of things because you *should* be or because others tell you they are important, it's absolutely time to reevaluate. This is your time to answer to GOD and YOU - no one else.

**3rd Step** - Start to clear your plate - what can come off the to-do list?

Like I let go of growing my own vegetables for now and started ordering local food boxes instead.

Like I let go of trying to eat vegan and started making a few recipes for the family that are meatless instead.

Like I started to sort through the very long list of amazing volunteer opportunities I am involved in, and I'm learning to say no to even the good things. I'm praying a ton and asking God to guide me to only the things He'd like to see on the plate when it comes to volunteering.

Like I found an easier way of doing the household finances and budgeting that works for ME.

**4th Step** - Focus on what's left on the plate - what does GOD want to keep on there? What do YOU want to keep on there?

Health is very important - my favourite work outs are not in a gym, they are outside in nature - a walk, hike, swim, bike ride, playing with the boys. So I started walking for about 30-45 minutes almost every day (be it a hike up a hill with one of the sons to see the fall colours, or a stroll down the street with Hubby to the lake, or discovering new trails with a friend, or just a saunter by myself) and I feel much better, and life is much richer because of that one small thing.

Eating good food is very important. Learning the basics of eating well is NOT EASY when there are so many conflicting views out there. Time and again I am drawn back to food in its natural state, even full of fat (good fat) and calories (good calories) and learning to

250

eat less food that packs more of a nutrition punch. And I'm trying a ton of new recipes with ingredients I have ON HAND (so no pressure to run to the store!). We are also learning to freeze and can and look for free sources of local food (we picked a TON of apples from trees in our neighbourhood this fall and Josh made lots of jars of yummy applesauce!).

Keeping a functional household is very important for all the members of Team Sklar to run at full capacity - I am learning to delegate much more, focusing on getting the basics done and realizing it's OK to leave the rest until it's really needed.

For me, writing/blogging is very important and is becoming more of a priority than ever before - and this is a GOOD thing! It's not a distraction, it's actually a huge part of what makes me tick! I am setting goals and deadlines that will help me see accomplishments with this area of my life, so I can know I am getting somewhere with all the words in my head and my heart.

And my love of words extends to **reading** books - I am doing this every day - even if only a few pages or a chapter each day - last night I started a book I've wanted to read for a while (Anne of Avonlea), only got 2 pages done before I couldn't keep my eyes open anymore, but it's a start!

So... this is all a good start. A God start. I'll keep asking Him for guidance as I go along on this new path of LESS and MORE. Less busyness and exhaustion and emptiness. More health, fullness, generosity.

Another part of my life that was due for some Crazy Change this year.

And it always comes back to Living in the Moments.

## December 17th, 2014

## Wrapping Up The Year Of Crazy Change

My first posts about this year of Crazy Change mentioned ideas like "Maybe a lot of the crazy change will be from within instead of a lot of external changes... It has to start with me... Change starts today, this moment, right here, right now. No big external differences are needed. Just a willing heart, a gracious God, and a drawing near to Him and to those around me."

The verses were *Therefore, I urge you, brothers and sisters, in view of God's mercy, to offer your bodies as a living sacrifice, holy and pleasing to God—this is your true and proper worship. Do not conform to the pattern of this world but be transformed by the renewing of your mind. Then you will be able to test and approve what God's will is—his good, pleasing and perfect will.*
*– Romans 12:1-2*

The inspirational quote was *Be the change you want to see in the world* – Mahatma Gandhi.

The image I used as a reminder was a butterfly.

Through the year I posted about things like Food, More on Food, Employment, Vision for Ministry, Being a Writer, Sleeplessness, Basics of a Healthy Family, and Good Stuff vs. God Stuff.

What do I want to say about this year?

It was needed, folks, absolutely needed.

There were so many things I was doing on auto-pilot. The verse talks about not conforming to the patterns of this world - this year I started to realize just how many areas needed work, needed a fresh breath of God, needed to - change. A crazy kind of change.

And to look at everything with a renewed mind, to let God loose in all areas - even the "Christian" areas - not easy at all.

So much letting go to do, so many safety nets to rip apart, so much security to chuck out the window. And to fall into Grace. That kind of fall is far-reaching, ever-lasting, and it can shake you to your core.

Free falling into Grace can make the craziest changes in you.

252

Try it out and see what happens.

When you let Grace into your home, your family, your friendships, your religion, your schedules, and your routines.

And what about letting Grace in to the depths of your heart, mind, and soul?

Like I said, that's the craziest part - when it starts with you, when Grace gets right in your face - and you *hear I still love you without all the patterns, without the conformity, without the masks and the rules and the traditions. On the bad days, when you're at your worst - I'm never going to stop loving you. I just want you - in all your mess, your doubt, your confusion, your baggage, your failures - I love you just the way you are. ALWAYS.*

So crazy. That kind of Grace will change you, no doubt.

That's what my name means - Grace - I carry it with me everywhere I go. And I'm starting to recognize it. Every time I sign my name, hear my name, read my name somewhere - it's all Grace. And I can be that to everyone I meet, everyone I live with, everyone I'm friends with, everyone in my family. God asks me to live up to my namesake every day for Him. To give back what I receive freely every second of my life. To be Anna, to be Grace in the world.

To take the Grace I receive on a constant basis and spread it around as much as I can to whoever is close to me that moment. Living in the moments. Bringing Grace into the moments. Not expecting others to conform to any patterns, just as I am called to non-conform. Letting others be whoever they happen to be, just as I am called to be the person God made me to be. Loving others, accepting others - instead of judging others by the standards and patterns of this world - just as I am loved, accepted - by Grace Himself.

There's been a lot of remembering during this year of crazy change - when you strip away all the patterns and the conformities - when you go about renewing and transforming - you remember a lot of who it was you started out to be - before the masks and traditions and formalities. It can be very freeing, but it can also be very scary, or depressing, or lonely, or sad - if you find yourself far from the person you once thought you would be. Never forget about that Grace that is offered every second our lives. Never let go of that Grace - no matter what you find when you start to remember.

There's a lot of testing to do as well - testing God's good, pleasing and perfect will. We might not look at all like we thought because God's been at work in our lives - rearranging and changing and molding us into something beyond what we could have imagined originally. Yes, there's a lot of testing to see what we have put in the mix ourselves and what God put in the mix intentionally. When you can sort through all that, the picture looks much clearer.

In my life, I am learning to recognize the dreams, hopes, desires, and passions that never change. These things never leave me alone, no matter how many times I give them back to God. I can just hear Him saying, *Yes, thank you for laying that one down AGAIN, and now I'm going to give it back to you AGAIN. Live this one out Anna - I have great blessing waiting for you as soon as you start to live in it - I gave this one to you from the start!* Doesn't mean it will be smooth sailing, but it means I am free to pursue it - when the time is right. That's another thing - He's great at letting us know the right timing for things as well - in a way that is so clear we couldn't miss it.

These things that never go away, these things that always stay - these are the ones to listen to. For me it's writing, travelling, cooking, frugality, playing piano, singing, walking, spending time in nature, sewing & weaving. And doing these things in the context of being married to Joshua and being a mother to Josiah and Elijah. There is also a very strong pull to encourage others in their faith, minister to children, and help with social justice issues both near and far.

Josh and my boys were the biggest surprises of my life - I never saw them coming. Yet they are also the biggest blessings. Beyond what I could have imagined - God put them in the mix and I'm so glad He did!

And it has taken much renewing to get back to these basics. There has been much to sift through, to declutter, to rearrange. It has been worth it.

I come to the end of this year feeling renewed - but it has been a very hard, long road. I had accumulated so many patterns and conformities that were never mine to carry, and they were weighing heavy on me. I have started to hold everything up to God, ask Him if it stays or goes, and He is so faithful to help me on this journey to...

My word for next year - I've known it all through 2014, been excited to get to it, been encouraged by its impending arrival...

**Simple**

I couldn't get to this word until I'd gone through some crazy changes. There are more crazy changes coming, I've come to realize they may never stop coming, but with Grace all things are possible - even riding out the waves of change, even when it starts with me.

## December 22nd, 2014

### "Let's All Help At Least One Person This Christmas!"

That's what the stranger says to me, as he runs out the FedEx depot door.

I'd been asking myself a question about Christmas for years, desperately trying to find an answer amidst the busyness, the consumerism, and the traditions of the season.

The question that started lingering in my head, my heart, and my soul a few years ago is this: *What Does Jesus Want For Christmas?*

It's a celebration of his birthday after all, right?

No matter what it has become through the centuries, no matter if the exact date is correct or not, Christmas Day started as a celebration of the birth of Jesus.

So what's the best way to celebrate this most special day of the year?

Don't get me wrong - I LOVE Christmas trees (I drive my family nuts getting our 15-year-old artificial spruce to look "just right"), and twinkling lights hanging on my house, and yule log cakes, and stuffed stockings on Christmas morning, and a new tradition for our family - Chinese food on Christmas Day (as per the movie *A Christmas Story)*.

But still the question lingers...

And I find myself standing in the Fed Ex depot, waiting for the clerk to tally up a price for my four boxes for family afar, and print the shipping labels that will get the boxes to their destination in 2-3 days ground shipping. The prices are great at Fed Ex, and the service has been wonderful on this busy holiday night. I'm grateful for this, for less stress in crossing this task off the to-do list.

A man comes in the depot behind me, and I see he's only got one small item to take care of, and I say it's OK if they help him - I'll wait. That's probably something Jesus would be happy about, right?

The clerk goes in the back for a few moments, and the man sighs and starts talking to me.

He says something like this:

"I don't know about the way we're doing this holiday. I don't have much, and I don't get much, but it's more than most, you know? I heard about a lady who just started inviting homeless people into her home for a meal, and it started as only a few, and now these dinners happen all the time and lots of people come and she's got donations from Costco and others to put on these dinners. I think that's what it's really about."

I feel a God moment coming on here - like the answer to my question is within reach - like God is talking to me through this Fed Ex "angel" (aren't angels simply God's messengers - whether they're spirit or flesh and blood?). I want to listen, I want to get it. I try and choose my words wisely, try to share a little of what's on my heart in response to this man who's searching for the same answers as I am.

"I'm convinced it could all be much simpler than this. I don't think it has to be so crazy at this time of year."

I wait for him to share some more, and he does.

"I got this list from someone in my family who is 30 years old. I can understand getting a list from a child, but not when you're over 30. They don't need any of this stuff. I'd rather give money to the lady who is hosting all those dinners."

I keep nodding my head, listening intently to the sidewalk preacher in front of me. I feel like yelling "Preach it brother!" But I hold those words inside. There are a few others in the FedEx depot now, they came in after our conversation had started, and they look a little confused. I don't want to scare them off, and I think this "angel" has a message to share with the world.

I knew I would be sharing it here as soon as I heard the next words that came from his mouth. I knew this message was one to spread around the world however I could.

It was the answer to my lingering question about what Jesus would want, summed up in few eloquent words thrown back over a stranger's shoulder as he ran out the FedEx door...

"Let's All Help At Least One Person This Christmas!"

Yes, keep preaching it brother!

"Sounds good!" I yell in reply. I hope he heard me. I hope he knows that at least one person was listening that night.

It doesn't mean I'll pitch the Christmas tree or stop stuffing the stockings or never buy a yule log cake again. We'll most likely keep visiting the Chinese buffet for years to come.

It does mean that helping others goes at the top of the Christmas list, instead of somewhere in the middle or the last-minute gift idea. Finding ways to help others will take more and more priority as the years progress.

Help at least one person this Christmas season - yes, I CAN do that. Yes, I WANT to do that.

Happy Birthday Jesus.

I love you.

# 2015

**January 17<sup>th</sup>, 2015**

**2015 – The Year Of Simple**

2014 was the year of Crazy Change for me.

Turns out that most of the change needed to come from within.

I still see the scripture from last year popping up all over the place - Romans 12:1-2 - so I know God's not done with the changes. I realize that getting to the simple means going through change. And the simpler I want, the crazier the changes need to be.

But the calendar tells me it's a new year, and it's time for new beginnings. And it's OK to step into what is next, into what is coming for 2015.

I've been excited about the word for this year, I've been feeling it grow in me for quite a while.

**Simple**

I've prayed and asked about the verse that goes with it, and if there are any songs and sayings to add in the mix. This is just the way I work - you give me words and you give me life. Give me one word to focus on and that word will start to spread and spill over into everything.

For me **simple** means getting back to basics, taking it from the top, re-grounding, minimalism even. This is how it looks so far in my life...

Have you ever picked a life verse? Or a marriage verse?

My life verse is Matthew 7:7 (and I just realized this lines up amazingly with the fact that my favourite number is 7).

*Ask and it will be given to you; seek and you will find; knock and the door will be opened to you.*

There is ONE song that I just had to figure out on the piano without any music sheets to help me. This goes back to when I was a little girl - this one song I had to know how to play ANYWHERE, had to carry it with me wherever I would go, had to know it by heart. It goes perfectly with my life verse.

259

### *Seek Ye First*

Do you sense a theme here? I have been so excited to catch on to what God has been working in my heart for most of my life - this focus on Him, this turning to Him, seeking after Him, trusting Him with all the rest.

And there's another song that has been on repeat in my soul for decades - but mostly it's this one line from the song...

### *All I Ever Have to Be is What You Made Me*

Just like the picture I shared at the beginning of this post (me at 23 years old, walking among the tall trees of Cathedral Grove in BC, under rays of sunshine seen clearly in the photo!), my desire is to be a woman who is walking in the light, on the path God lays out for me, taking in the beauty of life that surrounds me.

I am now 41 years old than the young lady in the photo, I have been a wife for 15 years and a mother for 13 years. The path has gone in directions I never dreamed, and the scenery looks so different some days than I thought it would. But the Light has always guided me true, bringing me to places of such blessing, even when the forest around me seemed thick and heavy with darkness. The beauty of life has been far greater than anything I could have imagined - simply because He has been there always, in everything.

And this year of simple starts with Him... with asking, seeking, knocking on His door...

*What would You bring to this year Lord?*


### February 23rd, 2015

### My Joshua

When I walked into my friend's house a few days ago, I knew I was in for something good.

I had attended the *IF Gathering 2014* in a small town 2 hours from home. This year I would get to enjoy snippets of the *IF Gathering 2015* in my friend's living room, gathered together with about 10 other amazing, godly women.

I didn't even know the theme of the Gathering, I just knew it would be good. So when the DVD started and I found out the theme was Joshua, I just sat there and smiled.

I smiled because I could see another glimpse of what God was up to in me - this theme has been running through our lives over and over for years, and especially the last 3 years. Every time it comes up it's time to take another step into the Jordan, not seeing how the water will part, just trusting we'll make it through to the other side... somehow... in God's will.

I think I already had an idea of this next step to take... but I'll get to that in another post...

It's funny, when God plunks down His will in the middle of your life and leaves the choice up to you.

It's like coming to a wall, right in front of you, and you can go either one way or the other, but you can't continue going forward - not in the direction you were heading.

Because you are never the same person after God presents His will to you.

No matter what choice you make, whether yes or no, you will go either one way or the other, but never be on the same path again.

You will always know that either you followed God or you didn't. And either one can change you forever. You will never be the same. Going forward on the path you were following is impossible.

And so it was with My Joshua. I met him in a chiropractor's office in 1997. He was a patient, I was a receptionist. His personality would consume the entire office space as soon as he walked in the front door, I would keep the office running smoothly in the background. He would have every single person laughing and connecting in a matter of minutes, I spent quality one-on-one time with the patients as I led them down to their treatment rooms. We had such different gifts and abilities, and we used them to minister to those around us in different ways, neither more important than the other.

I checked his file soon after meeting him.

*HHmm... just a few months younger than me.... this could work.*

Except I look younger than my actual age, and he kept inviting me to the youth group he was pastoring at the time. I kept telling him I'd let my YOUNGER brother know about the group.

Then I went off to Bible college for a few months, thinking I would never return. I had these grand plans of missionary work and being a jungle bush-woman. Marriage and children were NOT on my radar.

I returned home for the Christmas break. I never went back to school. There was such a tug on my heart to stay. My mission field was here first, with my family and friends.

I needed to find a church I could plug into (I had grown up in the church, wandered away for many years, and my own faith developed while working for the chiropractor - a man who served on the international mission field for 45 years, practicing his chiropractic methods for free on whoever needed them). I remembered My Joshua (just Josh at the time) was a youth pastor at a local church. After a little shopping around, we started attending his church.

Within a few months my YOUNGER brother was part of the youth group, My Joshua (still just Josh) now knew my correct age, and I was volunteering as a leader with his youth group.

Then came the wall.

I had prayed that if God ever had marriage in mind for me, I would only be attracted to that person, I was done with the emotional roller coasters and mind games of dating. The more I got to know My Joshua, the more life was changing for me.

I had a choice to make. I could go in one direction or the other. I could follow the plans I had for myself and go to the mission field. Or I could stay and most likely marry My Joshua (I knew he would still have his own choices to make once God presented him with the wall that was Anna).

I struggled and prayed and pleaded with God to show me His will. Now I realize He already had. Now it was my choice. If I chose marriage, Josh was the man.

I chose marriage, and left the missionary work in God's hands, knowing He may or may not give that to me also, hoping He would. Josh seemed to have a pretty big heart for it as well.

We started dating soon after, we were engaged not even 3 months after our first date, we were married not even 3 months after our engagement.

What a whirlwind romance! But when you know, you know, and we knew.

My Joshua has lived up to his namesake in the Bible many times over. He has listened to God and marched around many strongholds and brought them down in God's timing and God's power. He has served leaders well and led others well. He has met with God in the desert time and time again and done his best to follow whatever it is that God says to him there, no matter how ridiculous it may sound to everyone else (including me, maybe even especially me).

My Joshua has seen the promised land and brought back reports of its amazing bounty to others who longed to live in that kind of a land. He has offered to lead them there. Giants don't distract him. He is a fighter through and through. I love to watch him fight for the things God lays on his heart. (Especially when it's me and the boys he's fighting for!)

My Joshua also has a Caleb in his life, someone else who has seen the promised land and brought back reports of its bounty to us, whispers of what heaven must be like. This Caleb is our son, who was stillborn in May 2003. I will write more about that soon...

And My Joshua's life verse is Joshua 1:9 - *Have I not commanded you? Be strong and courageous. Do not be afraid; do not be discouraged, for the Lord your God will be with you wherever you go.*

For now, even though the Gathering was just starting, I knew that God would be speaking to my heart about marriage to My Joshua and about going into the promised land. Over the last few months God had shown us a vision and direction for Reaching the North, and I knew it was most likely time to take another big step of faith.

I also knew that for me the step might just be from within.

**March 3rd, 2014**

**A Day With Elijah**

Dear Elijah:

You stayed home from school yesterday. You had a bit of an upset stomach and you were feeling a little queasy, so we decided to let you ride this one out at home.

First you read *Bridge to Terabithia* in your cozy bed with the red and camo sheets. You are in a reading club at school called Battle of the Books and you are reading through your list of books pretty quickly. You'll be ready to help your school's team battle it out against the other schools next month. You'll be an amazing contributor when they quiz your team on what they've read. I love being an assistant coach for the team and I enjoy stepping into your school every week to meet with the small group of kids who love to read.

Then you chatted with your dad and I after we had our in-house ministry meeting. You heard us discussing what's on the agenda this week for church-planting and mission/service in our lives. You didn't really want to talk about that stuff too much, although it does interest you to know what your parents are up to.

Mostly you wanted to talk about sports. You love to watch sports these days. Just about anything - basketball, football, hockey, even curling seems to excite you. You love to watch the plays of the week and chat with us about the players. I can't believe the knowledge that seems to be growing inside you - you could be a commentator or a coach no problem! It makes me wonder how this new-found passion will fit into your future self.

You played some sports video games while your dad and I finished chatting and your dad headed out the door for the rest of the day. I got a few things done on the computer, then we had some lunch together. For you it was something light - peanut butter and banana on English muffin.

Then we went for a walk together. I told you that was part of the deal if you stayed home yesterday. This would be my first official walk in months, since somehow I had really twisted up my back & hips in recent months. You have been so concerned for me, helping me when I needed it, telling me you hope I feel better soon. And I do. The physiotherapy and chiropractic treatments are doing wonders, and finally I am getting better.

We ventured out into the winter wonderland around our house. It was only minus 5 when we left our home, the sky was blue, and the sun was shining bright. Not even one minute into our walk, you proceeded to throw your Nerf-style football over the neighbour's fence and we had to figure out how to get it back before continuing on our journey. We put our heads together and discovered a solution. We were on our way again.

We crossed the train tracks by our house and headed to the main road that led to the view of the huge lake in our town. I have walked this path countless times in the last 10 years - first pushing strollers, then hauling bike trailers, then walking alongside bikes with training wheels, then riding my own bike alongside boys and BMXs or scooters, and now walking side by side with young men taller than me or just about as tall as me. Wow, sometimes it hits me, how things have changed.

You love this, Elijah. This walking with me in the winter sunshine, looking out over the ice-covered lake. You point out to me all the landmarks you know so well - the ice-fall over the rocks, the place where you skated first this year, and the building where the corner-store used to be. You remember going there for licorice so many times, and the people who used to live & work there, and their little dog who used to greet us customers. You have really good memories of growing up here, in this neighbourhood in Northern Ontario. I am so glad for this.

You tell me to look at where we live. You ask me if it gets any better than this? No, of course not, Elijah. This is your home and you love it. Thank God. You dream about buying our house and living in it yourself one day. It is the only home you have ever known. My heart is so full to the brim to know that your childhood has been a good one, here in this tiny piece of the world.

We sit on the blue bench that someone has cleared a path through the snowbanks for people to get to. I've been coming to this spot, on this huge rock, since before the benches were added to this scenic lookout. We would throw rocks from this spot, hoping to get them onto the train tracks below. Beyond the tracks are a few trees and then the lake. You tell me how beautiful it all is, that you love to look for a long time at the scenery and notice new things about it. Ah - there I am, I knew I was in there somewhere! You sound just like me when you talk like that.

Then you say the most wonderful thing. You tell me that these moments with me, or your dad, these special times - they make all the bad stuff in the world fade away. And you fill my heart to overflowing, and I look at your sparkly blue eyes and the freckles on your cheeks, and I thank God for you. I thank Him for the reminders that came from you today - that life is wondrously good, that healing does come, that family is what truly matters, that beauty awaits just outside our door, that God can meet with us anywhere and anytime.

Neither of us wants to leave our moment in the sun, but the winter chill comes and it's time to head back. Not before snapping a picture of a train coming out of the rock, with you smiling your goofy smile in the foreground.

Your headache starts around dinner time, and that means we won't be joining your dad at the university church plant. So we stay home and enjoy some fresh-made bread (thank you for asking me to make that - I love knowing how to do that!) and eggs with your big brother.

As I chat with you before bed you have more wonderful words for me - you tell me about the beauty you see in me and how much love you have in your heart for me. Oh Elijah, if only you knew how much I need to hear those words from your not-even-10-year-old lips.

It takes you a while to fall asleep, but you lay under the woven blanket that took me years to make - first a baby blanket for your crib, and then a big-boy blanket to cover a double bed. I loved weaving all those squares together for you. A rainbow of colours for a rainbow personality. That's what I thought of as I wove the blanket for you.

Thank you for today, for unexpected time together and sweet moments in the sun. I will cherish and treasure whatever times we have together.

I love you my youngest son,

Mommy


**March 17th, 2014**

### It Can Be So Easy To Help People

I was at the library with Elijah the other day. I had just picked him up from school, his brother had basketball practice, so it was just the two of us on the drive home today.

We headed over to the local library I frequent at least once a week to pick up free goodies in the form of books to read or movies to watch. Have I mentioned before how much I LOVE the library? I love the sight of shelves of books, I love the book displays, and I also love the smell the books... but that's another post for another day...

After picking up our books and videos from the library clerks who have come to know us by name, we head back out into the freezing winter air. Our car was in sight, just a few more steps to at least a little more warmth!

I notice an elderly man with a cane, chatting with someone outside the car parked next to mine. The car leaves, but the man is still there, looking slightly confused.

Hhmm, I wonder what *that's* about?

I go to duck into my car, and I hear a voice.

"Excuse me!"

It's the elderly man I just mentioned.

"Can you please give me a ride to the bus stop?"

Pause... mind racing... let a stranger in the car with me and my 9-year-old son?... well, he looks extremely harmless... I could put him in the front and Elijah in the back... it's only a 2-minute drive to the bus stop downtown... it's so cold outside...

"Sure!" I come around the other side of the car and help him in. He looks as surprised as I feel. He mumbles something about getting old and doing foolish things. I ask him if he missed the bus or was lost. He says he just got confused and needs to get back to the bus station.

We drive and chat about the weather. We ponder on the ways the town is changing. We arrive quickly at the bus station, but he asks me to drop him off across the street at the mall instead.

I stop on the busiest street imaginable, receive a honk from a frustrated tailgater, let out the man I just met 5 minutes ago, say a prayer for his safety, and drive on, back to "normal" life.

Sometimes it's so easy to help people. They are literally right in your path, every day, asking for help in many different ways.

Do I always hear them? No.

Do I always want to help? No.

For me, it seems easier to help others half way around the globe than in my own neighbourhood.

But I am learning. There are so many to help. With as little as a ride to the bus station and 5 minutes of my time.

I was really blessed by the man with the cane outside the library.

Be on the lookout for unexpected blessings in your life today.


## November 2nd, 2015

### Scenes From The Soul – Just Look To Me

She walks.

Along the often-forgotten boardwalk that follows the shoreline of the lake.

Its cobblestones and wooden planks and concrete pourings all meld together to make a special path.

A path that allows for sightings of beauty.

Beauty in nature, and beauty in people.

Red squirrels scamper along the forest floor that parallels one side of the path.

They jump in the tiny trees that decorate the shore on the other side.

She comes face to face with one that seems to be looking for a handout.

They must be so used to people passing by every day, generous with peanuts for squirrels to store for winter use.

But she has nothing for them, so she watches them jump from tree to tree and burrow in the pine needles on the forest floor.

She never knew about their burrowing.

There is always so much to learn.

She thinks back to the baby red squirrel her dad found on the garage floor about 20 years ago, how her family nurtured it to full health, how they gave it the name Morgan, and eventually released it back into the wilds of the old, tall forest surrounding her parent's house.

She has an affinity for red squirrels now. She sees Morgan in every one of them.

Seagulls gather on the sandy beach area, they squawk for a minute in loud chatter with one another and take to flight over the water. She sees a rare beauty in the all-too-annoying birds today.

She was only going to walk for a few minutes, that was all she thought she could do. It's been a long autumn already, with many anxious thoughts swirling around in her mind. Today was an experiment, this walk a test, to see just how bad or how good she's doing.

She comes to the gazebo on the hill, the spot where she was originally going to turn around and head back to the car, but she realizes she is not even close to done today.

So she walks on, further along the path, drinking in the sunlight's reflection on the calm water beside her.

She has always found peace by the water.

Now completed almost the whole lakefront path, it will be time to turn around whether or not she is ready. There will be no more path to walk soon.

A bridge. No one else around. A view that makes anyone feel lucky for a glimpse.

She stops. And stares at the sight. And listens.

*Just look to Me. When everything crowds in and the worries come, when nothing makes sense and confusion gets loud - just look to Me.*

She thanks God for the moment of clarity, for the truth that she can take home with her, for something to grab hold of in the chaos that comes.

Her mind starts to wander already - what if someone sees me standing here, alone, looking out over the water? Will they know something is wrong? What will they think of me?

*Just look to Me.*

Peace returns, and she knows she is ready to head back home.

Along the way she greets fellow walkers on the path, many of them retired, walking their dogs. Their kindness fills her heart - every smile they send her way, every "Good morning" or "Hello" seems to lift her spirits. She must have received at least 20 of them in her 40 minutes on the boardwalk today.

She gets back into her car, sips her still-hot jasmine tea from the travel mug, and already looks forward to the next walk - maybe tomorrow? maybe the day after that? Who knows what she will find on the boardwalk then. Maybe rain, maybe snow, maybe another dose of sunshine.

She'll have to wait and see what comes next.

# 2016

## February 23rd, 2016

### Forward To "Normal"

It won't be back to normal.

I might not even recognize normal.

Moving forward might look completely different than looking back.

But it's time.

It's actually been a long time coming.

The last couple of years were a slow descent into increasing anxiety.

I've been learning lots, reading tons, praying, searching, questioning, listening, pondering, being more than doing... which brings me to here.

Today.

Now.

A totally different scene than a few months ago.

Back then it was sleepless nights, worry upon worry, fear run rampant, confusion, doubt, sadness, pain, and loneliness.

Now it's... better.

Much better.

Now I can sleep.

Now I can relax.

Now I can hear God's voice in the noise of my world.

Now I can leave more with Him - He actually LOVES it when I do that!

Now I can laugh.

Now I can find joy.

Now I like to spend time with people.

Now I also appreciate the quiet days at home.

Now I can let my boys go a little easier.

Now I can remember bits and pieces of who I am.

Now I can catch glimpses of who God created me to be.

Instead of who I should be or who others want me to be.

Refreshing - ya.

Renewing - yes.

Encouraging - absolutely.

I'd love to get back to some writing.

It's still a big part of me.

Always has been.

Always will be.

And as always, it's good to share the words with you...


## March 8th, 2016

### Maybe It's Me

*Written for the March/April 2016 edition of Live magazine...*

You ever get this feeling that change is coming? That it's just around the corner? And sometimes you catch a glimpse of it out of the corner of your eye, just out of sight, waiting to come into focus in your life?

I knew change was coming. But I really had no idea what it would look like, or what it needed to look like for me. I only knew there was no way my life could continue as it had been.

Waking in the night for longer and longer periods of time, reaching for the junk food at every opportunity, shying away from almost all social engagements, feeling like I couldn't attend another Sunday morning church service, dropping ministry commitments, fighting with my husband, and losing all motivation to write or clean or cook or budget or care much about anything.

Something had to change. Many things had to change. So I set to work trying to bring whatever change I could muster into my life. I tried to change my roles in ministry, I tried to change my household duties, I tried to change my husband and children, and I tried to change my ideas for writing. There was temporary relief at times, but always there was this nagging feeling that I was missing something. Something my ideas and plans weren't catching. What could it possibly be?

What was it that kept holding me back? What was keeping me from getting on track? What had I overlooked?

Then I caught a glimpse of what lurked in the background – in every situation I was trying to change – the same thing popped up every time. Me. I was the constant. And I wasn't changing much at all. I had been so busy trying to change everyone and everything else that I had skipped over the hardest part.

Picture a jaw-drop and a head-shake.

That was two years ago, and I've been on a roller coaster ride of realization, renewal, and restoration ever since. I'm getting a sneaky suspicion that it might just never end. And instead of dreading the next uphill ascent and subsequent drop into thin air, I'm starting to learn to throw my hands up in the air and fall into Grace. There is no controlling Him or changing Him, no matter how hard I might try.

There have been many layers to peel back. Every layer uncovered reveals another layer to give over to Him. Like one layer was admitting my lack of interest in just about everything instead of putting on the smiley mask yet again. This revealed the next layer - my struggles with anxiety. This revealed yet another layer – my fears and negative thought patterns. I have no idea what the next layer will reveal.

I do know that He is renewing me, from the inside out instead of the other way around. That everything is being held up to the Light and tested against His will for my life. That if I'm going to continue on the journey with Him then anything goes. And it most likely won't look like what the world tells me it should look like. I won't look the part of the world's standards or patterns. Most of the differences will be invisible to the people I pass on the street, because only God can look at the heart.

But we'll know the differences are there, and what a lovely secret to share. What a wonderful way to worship Him. By letting Him loose in the deepest parts of ourselves, underneath all the layers, where true renewal can happen in our lives.


## March 15th, 2016

### To-Do Today

I've been clearing the plate and simplifying.

I've been listening and looking.

I've been trying to keep things flexible.

I've been NOT writing, letting the words simmer and swirl within.

But in case you haven't noticed, I do love to plan.

After a while I go a little insane without deadlines and to-do lists.

And sooner or later the words catch up to me, and I burst at the seams with them, and need to share them.

So...

As I move forward this year...

As I take the exit door on anxiety and depression...

As I look ahead to an all-around healthier life...

This question lingers...

### What is it that I want to put INTO my days?

I made a visual... laid it all out on the table (literally)... and took a step back.

YES.

A good start.

And a list to share with you... I do love lists...

In no particular order... (yet)

- Time with God

- Time with Josh

- Time with the boys not in front of TV

- Time helping, serving, contributing to others - Volunteering at school, social justice issues

- Time relaxing - Reading, playing piano, baking is often relaxing, watching TV or movies, visiting or chatting with my friends/family.

- Time working - Some of the writing is work (like computer stuff - ugh, and publishing books and resources - the tasks involved there I mostly enjoy. Writing makes a tiny income every month). And then there's making grocery lists/meal plans and cooking at home most of the time (this saves us the equivalent of a part-time job every month). Also there's property management on rental houses (also makes a nice little income every month), household finances (having a plan, and a budget, and tracking everything also saves us tons by keeping us accountable and giving us goals and dreams to aspire to).

- Time creating - A lot of the writing falls into the creative category. And some of my household stuff like home decor. I'm also into sewing quilts and weaving large squares of yarn for blankets right now. Josh made me this wooden loom that makes 1 large square (the equivalent of 4 of smaller squares I use to make on a plastic loom) - also in less time. Josh surprised me with the loom one day last year - my man is very creative himself! And I love the efficiency factor!

- Time on household duties - Cooking, cleaning, laundry, delegating chores - not so interesting stuff like that.

- Healthy eating & drinking - This one is the hugest challenge for me - so many issues wrapped up in this... but I'm.... getting... there.

- Exercise - Also... getting... there. Keeping it simple, finding activities I enjoy in the place I enjoy most - outside. Skated when I could this year, walked a few times, looking forward to getting my bicycle out and trying some longer routes this year.

That's it... for now...

A basic plan.

Flexible but precise.

We'll see how it goes...


## May 31st, 2016

### My Word For This Year

It's been slow around here.

It's been nice to be slow around here.

It's given me time to think and listen and let things settle.

It's given me a chance to figure out a tiny bit of what lies ahead and a bit of confidence too.

That there are things in place in me that stay put and need more of a focus in my life.

That I can let go of many of the driftings of my heart and the flutterings of my soul and set my sights on more solid things.

Although sometimes a little drift and flutter can lead to new solids :)

For now, I've finally made a plan for the rest of 2016.

A plan to put a few things in the works and fix my attention on a to-do list.

A bigger to-do list than the daily list I'd set for myself a couple of months ago.

I never told you my Word for this year, did I?

Drumroll... Fireworks...

**Stay**

Stay close to God, stay close to the important people in my life, stay focused on who He made me to be.

Not as easy as it sounds, actually!

But I've been trying.

And it's been good.

I'm excited about it :)


## July 16th, 2016

### What a Broken Picture Frame Taught Me About Family Life

There's a series of collage pictures that hang in the carpeted staircase leading up to the second floor of our house.

Each frame holds pictures for one year of our family's life.

About 6 hang of them hang in our home so far.

For a while there were only 5 - one of the frames had gotten knocked off the wall and smashed when our oldest son was moving something upstairs.

I wasn't sure what to do - replace the frame? That would mean searching for something that would hold the exact amount of photos I had in the frame, and in exactly the same order.

Do I try to make some sort of a new frame that would hold the miraculously-unbroken glass front?

Do I find a completely different collage frame that might prevent me from including the already-carefully-chosen pictures from that year of our lives?

Nope. Nope. Nope.

None of those options worked for me.

Then it hit me...

This is life.

Especially family life.

And especially with two wonderfully rambunctious and full of life young men in my home.

Things will get broken - it's a wonder more hasn't been broken through the years.

These young men of mine have actually done quite well in containing their rambunctious-ness and vitality to certain areas of the house or the outdoors.

Do I want a perfect, pristine home?

Nope.

Just tidy once in a while.

And well-organized and free of a lot of clutter.

But mostly that's my job to keep it that way.

Their job is to simply live here, truly live here, in the moments, whatever they bring.

To laugh, love, learn, grow, respect, relax, and LIVE.

So I hung the collage back on its spot on the staircase wall - with sticky tack on the back.

The matting was still fine.

It was still good.

It's all good.

If I choose to see it that way.


## July 28th, 2016

### It Has to Bring JOY or It Has to GO

I promise to share what I can if you promise not to judge...

DEAL?

Deal.

You see, I have some OCD issues.

Like there's this one plate in my cupboard that bugs me every time I open the door.

Upon first glance you might miss it sitting on top of the other plates.

But it's there, not fitting nicely in the stack, always needing to be moved as I put away the other clean plates, just bugging me and my OCD.

It's this plate...

An old-school Swiss Chalet plate.

I keep it because I absolutely love it.

The joy it brings when I see it definitely outweighs the amount it bugs me by not fitting in with my organized cupboard.

I need these little reminders than not everything needs to go as planned, and not everything needs to fit in nicely with everything else.

Some things should just be fun and spontaneous and mess up any kind of plans I might have had.

Like moving out west on my own for 5 months to attend Rocky Mountain Bible College, like meeting my Joshua, like finding out I was pregnant for the first time, like moving to Sudbury, like our family trips to Mexico, Dominican, and Cuba.

So many amazing memories than I hadn't planned for, so many incredible changes that I didn't see coming, so many ways my life has been surprisingly enriched.

Like the Swiss Chalet plate.

Swiss Chalet was our family's favourite restaurant when we were growing up. Birthdays and milestones were celebrated there. My go-to meal is still the chicken on a kaiser with white meat and fries. YUM.

When I moved out west on my own I got a job waitressing at Swiss Chalet in Calgary. I loved that job - I loved the activity of the restaurant, having a job that required constant movement, meeting so many new people, and half-price meals! I could now enjoy a chicken on a kaiser with every shift I worked - even as a struggling student!

And when I moved back home suddenly instead of pursuing my Bible College degree, and started dating Josh a few months later, Swiss Chalet was often where we would hang out - especially after church on Sundays with a big group of people.

Josh and I also had many date nights at Swiss Chalet. On one of those occasions we discovered the old plates would be replaced with new ones very soon. I remembered this happening in Calgary during my time there - how the plates got much bigger and heavier - I could only carry 3 now instead of 5! More trips to the kitchen and back!

One night Josh asked if he could have an old plate before they would become obsolete. He's quite a charmer and had no problem convincing the waitress. She tucked our plate into one of the old foil containers they used to give for doggy-bags - you know, the ones with the cardboard lids? His request was never discovered by upper management, and we escaped the restaurant with the plate - no problem at all.

And that's why I can't seem to part with the plate - because it has memories of so many different chapters in my life. It's from the exact same restaurant I used to frequent with my family as I was growing up, many celebrations were there, I remember so many dates with Josh there, so many times with friends, and it also reminds me of a special time in my life that I spent out west - just growing up and figuring things out.

That odd plate can stay in my cupboard as long as it likes - no matter what my OCD has to say about it.

Why?

Because it brings me joy :)

If it didn't bring me joy, it would have been on the way out long ago.

I just finished reading a book called *The Life-Changing Magic of Tidying Up: The Japanese Art of Decluttering and Organizing.*

These sorts of books really appeal to my love of all things organized and efficient.

One thing that stood out for me in the book was that we should only keep things that bring us joy. We shouldn't hang on to clutter that has bad memories, or guilt - things that have been passed down to us that we don't even like, even things that are attached to memories of long-ago chapters of our lives. We can still have the memories without the things - I'm always telling my youngest son this - he's a bit of a clutter-bug. We replaced his massive bookshelf with a much smaller one last week, and the first thing he said was, "Yes, more room for posters on the wall now!" I'm just not sure I got through to him when I was trying to encourage him to declutter :)

I find most of my clutter comes from wanting to hang on to special memories - like when the boys were young. But I also feel like maybe this stops me from living in the moments of NOW - this is one I'm figuring out still and haven't touched the "Memory Tote" I have for each boy. Totes they've never looked through (and neither have I to tell you the truth). It's just stuff, stored away being of no use to anyone, so I can hang on to a phase of life that has long passed. I'm sure I'll hang on to a couple of items, but I'll have to limit myself I think :)

Even my wedding dress is potentially on the chopping block - I'm still not sure. It was specially-cleaned as a wedding present and packed into a storage box. I have moved this box a few times, never opened it, never gazed on my wedding dress since the one day I wore it, I don't have any daughters, and I'm not sure I want to inflict any unnecessary pressure on potential daughters-in-law.

And I'm trying not to pressure my item-attached husband too much to find another home for his family momentos. We all move at our own pace. And he's done well with often coming home to find things moved around in the house and piles of boxes and bags to discard. (Thanks for understanding Josh :) )

So there it is - when you look around your home - do the items that currently live there bring you joy?

Or do they weigh you down in some way?

Those are the questions I'm answering as I sort through my house...

Apparently when the things that surround you are of your own choosing and bring you joy - this helps you uncover much about who you are and things that you love to do.

And the absence of clutter can restore and renew your passions and dreams.

Looking forward to it!!

## August 28th, 2016

### "Be More Heart and Less Attack"

While I was taking a break the last couple of weeks, I went away on vacation with my family :)

We listened to a lot of music in the car, and I found myself belting out this tune whenever it come on - *More Heart, Less Attack* by Need to Breathe.

The song lyrics went along with this nugget of wisdom I found in the first few pages of *Personalized Promises for Mothers* by James Riddle (I always take a pile of books to read, and usually get through a good chunk of pages before the vacation is over):

"The Word says to train our children in the nurture and admonition of the Lord. (*And, ye fathers, provoke not your children to wrath: but bring them up in the nurture and admonition of the Lord. - Ephesians 6:4 KJV*) Notice that nurture comes first. If we show our children love, spend time with them, become involved in what they are doing, and teach them with a heart of compassion, we will eliminate most of the need to discipline them."

**I really resonated with these words.**

The Merriam-Webster online dictionary defines discipline as:

- *control that is gained by requiring that rules or orders be obeyed and punishing bad behavior*

- *a way of behaving that shows a willingness to obey rules or orders*

- *behavior that is judged by how well it follows a set of rules or orders*

This is how I used to mother my boys when they were younger. Rules, order, obedience, punishment, control.

It was a struggle to figure out what I heard about this verse:

*Whoever spares the rod hates their children, but the one who loves their children is careful to discipline them. - Proverbs 13:24*

And this verse:

*Even though I walk through the darkest valley, I will fear no evil, for you are with me; your rod and your staff, they comfort me. - Psalm 23:4*

When my kids were going through their darkest times - trying to figure out the world around them, their place in it, all their emotions, temptations, and relationships - I was expecting even more of them in blindly following social norms. Somewhere along the way I started to realize this was how their whole world was revolving - at school, on sports teams, even when it came to faith.

They were constantly measured by how well they were adhering to the norms of whatever environment they found themselves in.

**And I was missing out on just getting to know my sons.**

Don't get me wrong, of course some rules are required, and there are some social norms that just need to be followed in order to live in our world, but there's this other Bible verse that has grabbed me and just won't let me go. Now I'm at the point where I hope it never does. I think freedom and full life are waiting in this verse...

*Therefore, I urge you, brothers and sisters, in view of God's mercy, to offer your bodies as a living sacrifice, holy and pleasing to God—this is your true and proper worship. Do not conform to the pattern of this world but be transformed by the renewing of your mind. Then you will be able to test and approve what God's will is—his good, pleasing and perfect will. - Romans 12:1-2 (NIV)*

So I've learned that a shepherd's rod is usually used to gently guide the sheep, that a shepherd would never hurt his flock intentionally, that I am a sheep myself and my Shepherd loves me in the humblest ways, and that my Shepherd is so patient as He guides me on the path He has laid out for me.

**I want to be the same for my children.**

I've learned to pick my battles. I've learned when to stick with something and when to let it go. I've learned that children are full of wisdom and good ideas, and often compromise is OK. I don't need to be right, I don't need to be perfect, and I'm human too. And my boys need to know that. They also need to know they are loved, respected, important, and valued - no matter what age they are.

*Don't let anyone look down on you because you are young, but set an example for the believers in speech, in conduct, in love, in faith and in purity. - I Timothy 4:12*

I was trying to be someone else with all the rules and rigidity. I was trying to be my personal concept of what a good mother & pastor's wife would be.

It was getting pretty complicated, and I was liking myself less and less.

So I decided to remember more of who I was instead of trying to be someone else. To remember how much I loved children and loved their fresh perspectives, their honesty and openness, their caring, generous, and forgiving hearts. I let them show me what their world looked like - it was often so beautiful.

*Jesus said, "Let the little children come to me, and do not hinder them, for the kingdom of heaven belongs to such as these. - Matthew 19:14*

It's not about winning or losing, or being in charge, or getting my way. And it's not about letting my kids have the upper hand either. It's about doing life together.

As far as I can tell, they know I still get the last word, I'm still the parent, and somebody needs to make the final decisions if no common ground can be found.

For the most part, they respect that. There might be some complaining and sometimes there's still a "punishment", but they can usually see it coming a mile away if that happens.

Sometimes they even choose the punishment. And sometimes it's harsher than what I was thinking!

But I think it's all a part of raising young people to be old people who will one day make all their own decisions, and live their own lives, and be totally self-sufficient, and contribute to the world around them.

Not conforming, not cookie-cutter, not always what is expected, free to be themselves, change the world as only they can, and have lots of fun along the way.

God made us all so unique, and I don't want to miss out on truly knowing my sons.

*I am the good shepherd; I know my sheep and my sheep know me - John 10:14*

Just as I can trust and rely on my Shepherd, so I want to parent my boys in a similar way.

I want to gently guide, humbly correct course when headed for danger, share the path ahead, reminisce about the path behind, look for green pastures and blue skies, pay attention to any fences that are in place for our protection, and explore the wide-open fields together.


## September 13th, 2016

### What About When Life Isn't So Simple?

Sometimes life is complicated. Sometimes it's anything but simple. Sometimes the answers are a long time coming, and it's really hard work to get to them.

It's harder still when you don't even know the answers you're searching for.

Sometimes it's confusing, and frustrating, and seriously trying.

The farthest thing from simple.

I've been on a very complicated, confusing, frustrating, and trying journey for about 5 years now.

And for now, the journey has taken a new turn, a stop at simple, at least for a time.

Wow - I'm relieved - to put it mildly!

I feel like I could fall down and sleep for a year.

In fact, in quite uncharacteristic dramatic fashion, I lay down on the kitchen floor last night as my oldest son was trying to tell me something about his day.

He looked at me in exasperation because I wasn't listening in the least.

All I could say was "Don't you see? It's all OK! At least for now - there's nothing else to do about it! And it might be OK forever! It might just keep getting better and better!"

He mustered a "Ya, that actually is pretty cool" and just kept on walking past his crazy mother.

A similar conversation happened in the car after a doctor's appointment with my youngest son yesterday afternoon.

He just couldn't grasp the great news we'd just received - that no more appointments were necessary - no more physio, no more special orthotics, no more hospital tests, no more doctor's offices.

I tried to make him understand - but I got the same look of exasperation and amusement all mixed together in one facial expression.

Both my boys think I'm nuts.

But really I'm just totally and completely relieved - shoulders drop and I put my head back on the chair - I look up and close my eyes and... Thank You Lord.

You're probably wondering what in the heck I'm talking about...

Let me share a story with you...

Five long years ago my youngest son woke up screaming in the night. He was 6 at the time, and he had intense pain in his legs. After three hours we were able to settle him into sleep again.

A visit to the doctor suggested growing pains. I was less than impressed. I did the online research and found out growing pains can be very, very horrible for some kids (our oldest son just had a mild bout at around the same age as his younger brother), and learned some of the coping techniques like warm baths, massage, stretches, pain relief pills, etc.

Over the next few nights I tried them all. Plus a visit to the chiropractor.

The pain didn't ease up for Elijah, and it became a nightly occurrence, and it lasted a very long time.

On one of my less-than-stellar-mother days I threatened to take away all the things he loved in life - TV, toys, video games - ya, great mommy moment. I was absolutely done, hubby was away for work, and my parents were staying the night to help me drive the boys back to their house for a few days while Josh was away. We were having car trouble as far as I can remember, because usually I'm just fine to drive the few hours to my parent's house on my own!

So... at this point I was giving Elijah children's pain relief every night, giving him a soothing warm bath, and doing stretches and massages on his legs. It was quite a process every night, but I knew there were families dealing with a lot worse (the year before we had spent a week at the Children's Hospital in Ottawa because Josiah had a very rare, very bad infection in his eye - ugh - let's not get into that just now!) so I kept going.

After a couple of months the nightly pain seemed to taper off, and I was so glad to say the least. I chalked it up to a bad case of the growing pains.

Fast forward about 6 months and suddenly the pain returns, but only in one leg, and he feels it in his toes as well.

He's a little older and can explain things a little better to me, and he tells me it feels like butterflies behind his knee.

WHAT?!

288

No, not this again, and what's with the adaptations?

So we try the old routine until we can get in to see the doctor.

We discover that a heating pad wrapped around his knee does the trick (and one around his toes too).

This seems to hold the discomfort at bay when he tries to lay down to sleep (thank God!).

The doctor recommends a round of blood tests, x-ray, and ultrasound.

We do them all, me wondering about all sorts of diseases and illnesses, trying to keep Elijah calm about it whenever it came up in conversation.

He's my new hero because of all he goes through - usually smiling at the doctors and nurses, bringing out the best in them.

Then there's me with white hairs growing in by the second and worry lines forming on my forehead :)

And after all the tests... nothing.

Nada.

Zilch.

*Maybe he's playing it up for attention, Anna. Maybe it will pass shortly Anna. Maybe there's really nothing there Anna. Time will tell Anna.*

This is what I hear from the experts. I try not to be bitter. But I sort of am.

And I buy into it for a while - that there's really nothing wrong. That he's just trying to get attention. That all this effort and worry is for nothing.

I go back and forth for quite a while.

Because the nightly discomfort goes on for quite a while.

And it starts to creep into his days whenever he's sitting for too long or resting for too long.

Activity makes it better, sometimes he even has to get up and walk around at night so he can fall asleep.

I hear him turn the heating pad back on if he wakes up in the night, and when he gets up in the morning and reads in bed.

This constant reminder that something is not right.

And no one knows what it is.

Not even the experts.

And some days I waver more than others in believing there really IS something wrong.

Then one day - he's now about 8 years old - yes, this has been going on for a LONG time - Elijah tells me about how he wishes he could just fall asleep like a normal person.

Without a heating pad, without discomfort, without worry.

I look at him and think to myself - *Why can't he have that? Why can't we figure out what's wrong and solve this problem for him? It's obviously not going away on its own. Time to go back to the doctors. This time we push it until there's answers. Something IS wrong. Elijah doesn't go around lying for no reason, or seeking attention without reason, and especially not for THIS long.*

So we chat about it, about going back to the doctors, about more tests, about more questions, about maybe them not believing there's anything wrong and how we would handle that - and he agrees to try again.

When the doctor finds out Elijah is STILL in nightly discomfort she agrees to more tests. She agrees it's not just growing pains. She agrees he's not making it up. A good start for sure.

We don't have to redo all the tests, we just have to wait for an appointment with a pediatrician. This takes a few months, but we get in to our favourite pediatrician. He's the one who sent Josiah to the Children's Hospital for his eye (we believed he saved his life that day), and he's the one who ordered a chest tube for Elijah just after he was born to get rid of the air pocket that was forming outside his lungs (he definitely saved his life that day). He's basically our hero. And here he was again, helping our boys live to the fullest.

By the time we get in for the appointment, Elijah is 9 years old. It's been three years of discomfort now - but at least the screaming discomfort was only the first few weeks of this whole ordeal. At least it's manageable at this point. It's not slowing Elijah down at all. Just not helping him sleep at night. Just worrisome, frustrating, tiresome, annoying, confusing.

The pediatrician calls for an MRI. Oh man, we've never had to deal with one of those before. And we'll have to wait.

In the meantime, he notices one of Elijah's legs is slightly shorter than the other (possibly due to a nasty fall on the growth plate when he was 2) and orders a lift insertion for his shoes and physiotherapy.

The lift we get very soon from our footcare specialist. The MRI we get within a couple of months. And the physiotherapy we get... on a waiting list. A LONG waiting list.

The MRI shows nothing wrong with the hip. And Elijah was so brave - such a little guy in that big, loud machine.

But the MRI shows something else might be wrong with his upper leg - there's a mass that needs to be re-examined.

WHAT?!

So he goes back into the MRI machine a few weeks later and... it's all good - just a cyst - pediatrician says nothing to worry about.

WHEW.

Elijah is now 10 years old. The heating pad still works wonders at night, but he's developed a strange web-like appearance on his leg.

A trip to the doctors tells us it's from the daily use of the heating pad - bringing the blood more to the surface of the skin. When he's able to stop using the heating pad, the skin discolouration will disappear. Nothing to worry about.

WHEW.

Elijah continues to be a very active, healthy, growing-like-crazy boy. This brings me so much joy, but the nagging unknown gets to me every night as I hear the heating pad turn on yet again.

Then I need physiotherapy for consistent hip and back pain, and I discover our sons are covered under Josh's benefits for a few physiotherapy visits each year.

So I book Elijah in with my physiotherapist while we wait for free physio offered by Ontario health care. But it's been over a year now, so I'm not holding my breath.

My physiotherapist does her assessment, Elijah is very patient, and she gives him some exercises to try at home. He's pretty excited at first, and he's pretty diligent - he knows this should help with the knee. After the covered benefits run out, I consider just paying the quite-expensive fees out of our pocket, but summer comes and we'll be travelling, and he says it's not really helping anyway.

Another lull in progress.

The fall comes and we get a call from the pediatric physiotherapist that works for our city, and I ask Elijah to keep trying, to go see just one more health care worker. He agrees, and he goes through another assessment. This young man has now officially gone through more poking and prodding and tests and assessments than I can even count. I marvel at his patience.

This physiotherapist is trained to work with children, and she's amazing, and she's thorough, and she becomes the major key in our quest for answers. We didn't know this when we scheduled our first visit with her.

She gives Elijah exercises to help with his now-aching back, his sore shoulders, and his extremely tight hamstrings. And she notices he needs an adjustment to his orthotics. And wants to send him for one more MRI to check on the area behind the knee instead of the hip. Elijah is less-than-thrilled about all of it, but he keeps trucking along in an effort to get to the bottom of his dilemma. I marvel at him some more.

I watch him leave the house with his daddy at 6am on a dark, cold winter morning - for another MRI appointment. Josh says he's a super-star, and the noise didn't bother him this time, and he's a charmer with all the nurses. That's my boy.

The MRI results are the final piece needed to solve the not-in-the-least-bit-simple puzzle of Elijah's 5-year leg discomfort.

He's got an old injury. They say it looks like a sports injury. The ligaments behind his knee don't join up properly.

WHAT?!

How many times have I asked that on this long journey, I don't even know.

My now 11-year-old son has an old sports injury that's been causing him trouble since he was 6 years old. But that does explain the "butterflies" he used to describe to me.

I wonder to myself... *What did you DO Elijah?*

I run through all the nasty falls, bumps, scrapes, bruises, etc. of the last few years - BEATS ME.

Could be anything really - take your pick - there's LOTS to choose from!

But I'm so happy for the results, and I gush over the physiotherapist, and I thank her repeatedly, and I hug Elijah when we leave, and I smile big smiles.

But the hard work of getting better continues.

Every day there are exercises for Elijah to do to strengthen around his knee, and exercises to ease his sore shoulders and back and tight hamstrings from carrying his body a little funny these last few years.

He keeps at it, and I keep nagging when necessary, and I do the exercises with him to try and get a smile from this weary fella of mine.

It's been a long journey - it's gone on for about half his life - he probably can't even remember a time when he DIDN'T have leg problems.

(And let's not even mention the barracuda slicing his other leg and needing 10 stitches on a recent family vacation to Cuba - it's just been INSANE with leg problems for Elijah. That's one scar he'll never get rid of and may need cosmetic surgery if it doesn't heal right - we won't know for A YEAR - ugh!)

But there is such good news at the end of this story - or at least this time of calm in the storm (he may need minor surgery if it gets worse as he gets older) - we went to the doctor yesterday and Elijah is...

CLEAR for no more physiotherapy (his shoulder and back aches are gone, his hamstrings are much looser, and his knee discomfort is much better!)

CLEAR for no more heel lift (his hips are the same height now!)

CLEAR for no more appointments, or tests, or anything for 8 months!

YES! NICE! CAN I GET A HIGH FIVE!

So as Elijah sat across from me in the car in the parking lot at the doctor's office yesterday, looking at me like I was crazy, me asking him how he wanted to celebrate, congratulating him on the excellent effort he'd put in to get better these last few years, marveling at him for going through all those tests, reminding him of all the days I'd had to pull him from school from appointments (not sure he minded that one too much :) ), explaining to him it was ALL OVER for at least a while - he just smiled at me in his relaxed way, told me I was getting really excited for nothing, and we didn't need to celebrate, and la la la la la.... it struck me how this has all become so normal for him.

What was not-simple-in-the-least for me, was simple for him - get the answers. Do what you have to do. Focus.

Maybe he was just reminding me what I'd told him a million and one times through the last five years? What I'd lost sight of in the complicated and confusing and frustrating?

Just... Keep... Going.

Eventually you get there.

Thank you Elijah for all you taught me the last few years on this journey of the Mysterious Pain That Wasn't Really Pain But More Discomfort.

I'll have to come up with a shorter title :)

**October 11th, 2016**

**My First Royalties Cheque!**

There are new books are on the horizon...

They make up a *Jesse Tree for Advent* series...

They should be ready to purchase on Amazon in the next couple of weeks - in plenty of time for the Christmas season.

The *Lunchbox LOL* series has been doing well on Amazon. This is so encouraging for me - I've never had a book that sold consistently like that.

I actually received my first and second royalty cheques from Amazon. Wow, what a feeling!

It's pretty cool to watch something you created get scooped up by so many others - a real treat for sure.

I have learned a lot about the business of writing to earn money. I have made a lot of mistakes along the way as well.

One thing I know is that I'm not a marketer, I don't like the spotlight, and when I write something it's as much for me as it is for the reader.

So when I tried to host a book launch in July for the *Lunchbox LOL* series, I really didn't have much fun with that at all. But when I saw my first sale through Amazon I had ALOT of fun with that! It happened by accident - I had to check on another project I was working on, and when I visited the self-publishing site (CreateSpace) to get the information I needed, I saw a few sales listed on my account. Not just one - a few! After that I couldn't help but check every day (sometimes 2-3 times a day) - it was just so encouraging to see some success. My best day yielded 10 book sales on Amazon - so cool!

And I learned a lot about my style of writing and publishing these past few months - I love to make easy-to-use-resources for the family, I love to try new things, and I love to introduce something unique to the market. I love to keep this all very simple, I love to have fun with it all. I don't love social media or being on the computer for long periods of time, but both are necessary to write and publish these days.

So I'll keep writing and publishing and sharing the moments of life with y'all. As always, I am so thankful for my readers :)


**October 17th, 2016**

**"Love Pushing Pedals"**

"Love pushing pedals"

That's what my friend wrote on Facebook one day. I was so excited to read her words because I love pushing pedals too.

I could spend hours riding my bike. I have done just that in the past.

When I was younger, I would ride along the lakeshore trail of our small town. I would ride so long and so far that I'd reach the next small town. I was lucky enough to grow up along the shores of Lake Ontario, in a town called Ajax, and I would bike all the way to Pickering or Oshawa. The scenery was amazing - the lake stretched all the way to the horizon with cliffs and beaches and parks and marshes to satisfy all my senses for hours on end.

And I would never feel tired. What would stop me and turn me around back home was time constraints, or thirst (I never thought to bring a water bottle), or hunger.

If I didn't have those reminders, I would have pushed the pedals forever it seemed!

When I was really young I would ride everywhere - to friend's houses, along the bike trails around our house, across town even when I was a preteen. My first bike was a pink "banana" bike.

I remember riding my bike in the town parade every year - anyone could join in and decorate their bikes and ride through town behind the floats.

For high school graduation I asked for a good bike, and that one lasted me for a few years. Early in our marriage Josh and I went to a police auction and scored two really good bikes for really cheap. Our oldest son is still riding around on one of them - a green Bianchi (sadly the other didn't make it through one of Josh's bike accidents a few years ago :( But at least Josh made it through the accident!).

I've tried buying a couple of bikes from Kijiji, but they don't seem to last long or they are in such bad shape that it's not worth it to fix them. But that green Bianchi allowed me to take the boys pedaling with me in a bike trailer until they got too big for it. Then I bought them their own sets of wheels - tricycles, then training wheels, then teaching them to find their balance on our unusually long driveway. I love all those memories of pedaling with my boys. They still join me now and then for a ride, but mostly they like to venture off on their own or with friends. I am glad for the independence that pushing pedals allows them :) My oldest will be navigating a new set of wheels next year when he turns 16 - WOW! How did that happen?!

So when my friend shared her love of biking on Facebook a few months ago, I was actually really excited - a kindred spirit! I hadn't found that many with a similar love of pushing pedals - a lot of runners in my sphere of friends - and I am anything BUT a runner. I know this for a fact, and I'm comfortable sharing it with the world :)

I have something else to share - a dream of mine - to bike all the way across Canada one day. I have hope in realizing this dream since I know of people in their 60s who are just getting to it. I hope to live the dream before my 60s, but I know it's still at least a couple of years out.

And a dream that big needs to be broken down into smaller dreams, beginning with bike rides that are a few hours, or a weekend, or maybe a week long.

When I saw Anne's post, I decided to share my love of biking with her. We decided to bike together whenever we could and share our adventures with one another when we couldn't.

And then my friend Amy decided to join in as well!

Oh joy :)

Over the last few months the three of us have biked on our own, with our husbands and kids when they were willing and able ;), and even managed to meet up a few times to ride together. We all live in different towns, but only about 1/2 hour away from each other, so sometimes we could swing it. We checked out the routes that the others were biking on and got to show off our favourite spots to ride.

Anne loves to ride along the highway, and she loves to take pictures of the scenery as she goes. She is not intimidated by long rides and dreary weather... and she finds the good and the beauty around her each time she puts her feet to the pedals.

Amy has overcome so much in her determination to get on the bike. She even rode with tires that needed a good shot of inflation for a few weeks! Nothing can stop her :) She rides when she can - with kids riding alongside her, without kids, with bike trailer in tow, uphill, downhill, through gravel and bumpy roads. She is a survivor, that one.

And me... I asked everyone for bike money last year for any kind of event where people might buy me a gift - Christmas, birthday, Mother's Day - anything. Then I went out and scored myself a purple

Schwinn with shock absorbers for 1/2 price at Canadian Tire. A brand-new bike. All mine. No touchie. I have let my boys try it out briefly, then I put my arms around it to protect it from any possible threats and say "Mine!" Just kidding... mostly. I also got a water bottle holder so no more dehydration, and a little pouch that tucks under my seat to hold my car keys and phone. That way I can still be mom if needed, even when I go out for an hour or two for a ride. It gives me peace of mind.

It's been a blast this year - being able to ride a nice bike, taking it on family vacations and testing it out on many different trails, often with at least one of my guys.

Thanks for those three simple words, Anne! Thanks for joining me on yet another journey, Amy! Looking forward to more biking in the future!

**October 20<sup>th</sup>, 2016**

## Discovering Hope Leads to Surprising Joy

I had the most amazing dream. I was invited to a night out with my Joshua. We were at the event, people were singing a beautiful song, they were happy to be there. Then the guest speaker was being introduced. It was me. I was off in the background of the location, puttering around with something, but I was holding a stack of *Discovering Hope* books. I wasn't going to take the microphone. They were waiting. Josh knew I was terrified. He went to the podium and started to explain why I wasn't responding to the invitation to speak. Something in me decided it was time. Even though I didn't know what to say, or what words would come out once I put the microphone to my mouth, or how they would sound - I took the stage. And started talking. And stumbled. And did my nervous

laugh. And didn't make any sense. And then talked some more. And eventually I got to the point, the reason for speaking, the message that was on my heart to share with you...

I have been surprised by joy.

As I have pursued the discovery of hope - set my sights on the good, my focus on what HAS come, my vision on what IS YET to be - I have also found joy.

It can only be God.

Where once I could only see the bad, I could only focus on what HAS NOT come, I could only envision what was LOST - now there is so much more.

There is life in place of death.

There is light in place of dark.

There is hope in place of despair.

There is joy in place of sorrow.

Joy is new for me when it comes to Caleb. I have discovered ways to hope, ways to celebrate, different perspectives, restoration, and renewal.

But I'm not sure there was ever joy.

Just like in my dream as I was surprised by the invitation to come forward and share with the audience.

Just as I was so unprepared for what was coming.

Just as I had to decide to put one foot in front of the other and see what would happen.

So it is with Caleb - I am surprised by what he shares with the people who meet him, I'm unprepared for the ways he touches this world, and I'm in awe of every step we take as we decide to grab hold of God's plans for him.

My son surprises me, my God surprises me - I am so surprised by joy.

Now that is a message I can share any day.


## December 22nd, 2016

### Merry Christmas & Happy New Year!

I had a few more blog posts I wanted to write before the holidays begin, but you know how the busyness of this time of year can sneak up on you... so the posts will have to wait for now :)

I did want to make sure to wish you all a very Merry Christmas and a Happy New Year as we close off 2016 and welcome in 2017.

I love to invite people into my home, and my home looks particularly festive right now, so let's pretend you've just pulled into my driveway...

And seen our Christmas disco house :) We have an outdoor disco light positioned right on the front deck, and I really enjoy coming home at night to see the fun has already begun :) And we have some lights around the front door, framing our Christmas tree in the front window. I just love it.

The snow has been falling like crazy this week, and the snowblower and shovels have been very busy making clear paths into our home. If you try and use the front door, you might be disappointed... the tree gets to take over this door for a month of each year :) You'll have to use the back door for now...

300

By the end of the night the BBQ and deck will be full of another fresh falling of snow. There will be about 6 inches of sparkly, fluffy whiteness perched on top of the grill by morning... But we clear a path every day to make sure visitors can get into our home safe and sound...

Come on in! I've just done some grocery shopping, stocking the fridge and pantry for another few days...

Make sure to stomp the snow off your feet...

An indoor perspective of the Christmas tree... it's full of decorations my mother gifted to me throughout my childhood - the oldest ornament I have is dated 1975... that's right - almost as old as I am :) I've carried on the tradition for our boys, and they each have at least a few ornaments signifying special events or character traits from each year of their lives. And the lace angel perched on top was purchased on our honeymoon at a midnight madness sale in the small town where we were staying. Notice the 3 presents under the tree... they're all for me :) My guys tell me not to put their gifts under the tree until Christmas Eve - it's too tempting for them to shake and squeeze and guess what they're getting... and they like to be oblivious until they get to tear off the wrapping :)

The stockings are hung... on the curtain rods with care :) Josh and I made these stockings our first Christmas together. Josh bought the supplies and brought them home to his extremely new wife (we'd only been married about 3 weeks!) who was sick in bed for a few days... The star ornament hanging on the lamp is something Elijah made this year at school.

And the boys' stockings I weaved for them for their first Christmases. Each has their name sewn on the front. Alongside their stockings is a wall hanging of the manger scene. A beautiful piece of fabric picked up on clearance sale at Fabricland, hemmed and attached to a small piece of doweling.

And a beautiful wooden decoration from a dear friend, highlighting my favourite name for Jesus... MESSIAH. This hangs in our home year-round since I love it so much.

301

I hope and pray your holiday season is full of love and wonderful memories. But if not, I hope and pray you catch at least a glimpse of how much you are loved by God, and how welcome you always are into the life He has for you. It's not always easy, it's not always happy, but there can always be joy, and there can always be love. That's what Christmas is all about - spreading the love. First with Jesus bringing God's love to this world in such a real way, and now with us spreading that love around in His name.

# 2017

**January 9th, 2017**

**My Word For 2017**

**Still**

That's my word for 2017.

And I love to have a Bible verse to go with the word...

*Be **still** and know that I am God.* - Psalm 46:10

And I love to have a song...

*Oceans* by Hillsong.

And this quote I LOVE... I remember grabbing it from my mum's house years and years ago... she had it in a daily quotes package... I carried it around in my purse for about a decade...

*I can trust the waves for I know the One who made the ocean.*

I mentioned that quote and song in a blog post almost 3 years ago.

I've been drawn to that song for so long.

So I'll grab hold of it for this year, to go with my word, to anchor me in the rising oceans and the waves that will inevitably come this year. Don't they always come? Isn't there always waves in life? Would I want it any other way?

Sometimes.

Be they good waves or bad, easy or hard, I will focus on **Still**.

I know this requires trust. I know this requires submission. I know this requires obedience. But most of all I know this requires love. Knowing that I am loved. Beyond anything I can imagine. And it's OK to **Still** when I'm loved that way.

I will try to remember.

Do you have a word for 2017?

I'd love to hear it :)

**January 11th, 2017**

**One Foot Forward - Walking Through the Pain Instead of Avoiding the Pain**

I watched this documentary on Netflix the other day - *Finding Traction* - it was about the ultra-runner Nikki Kimball. In 2012 she decided to attempt to break the record for completing the 273-mile Long Trail in Vermont. The record had been held by Jonathan Basham who completed it in 4 days, 12 hours, and 46 minutes in 2009. He was 31 at the time. Nikki pushed so hard to beat the time and kept up the pace so well until the last day when she simply had to take a rest. She came away from her attempt with the absolutely amazing achievement of instead breaking the women's record by a full two days. Nikki's time was 5 days, 7 hours, and 42 minutes. She was 41 at the time.

A major bout of depression hit Nikki for the first time when she was in her early 20's. She learned to adapt and then to thrive with running. She can outlast the best of them and has gone on to claim many records for her efforts. I find her to be very inspiring :)

She found a way to put one foot forward during the darkest times of her life - when everything was confusing, when her hopes and dreams were slipping away, when she had to adapt everything and find new meaning in life.

I'm sure it started with just simply getting out of bed. Putting one foot on the floor, then the other, slipping on her running shoes, and stepping one foot out the door, then the other. One foot further down the street, into something new, facing each step as it came, one at a time, then the next, and the next.

It's like living in the moments. One thing at a time, what's right in front of you, taking it all in, just one moment, then the next, enjoying what comes.

Pain will inevitably come - physical and emotional and spiritual - all sorts of pain. Confusion will come even as you take one step then the next, out there beyond the safe walls of your house, beyond the safe comfort of your family and friends. Out there in the unknown. But all you have to see is one step. And once you've taken that one step, all you have to see is the next step. That's all. Looking too far down the road, too far beyond the comfort, too far beyond the safe, will only make the first step that much more impossible to take.

Which is probably why I've struggled for so long with getting back to walking. I can't seem to take that first step. It sounds so silly to me - not being able to open my door, and step outside, and put one foot in front of the other. But this is a pretty annoying hurdle to face - being one who loves to go for walks, one who needs to get some sunshine even through the looming winter sky, one who thrives on glimpses of nature to lift my moods.

When I watched Nikki run her Long Trail race, it was about putting one foot in front of the other. And I saw that as she did that, she gained confidence in her ability to take the next step, even if it was slower than she hoped, even if it was cold, even if she hurt in ways we couldn't see as we watched her race. I also saw that she knew when to admit it was time for a rest, after pushing herself to her absolute limits. This lady knew when to push for that next step and when to stop taking steps for a time. She knew when to tape up her feet and her legs and eat more bacon and get back on the trail. She also knew when to curl up in a blanket in the back of a van and close her eyes for a little while. She let herself cry, laugh, sing, shout, and be silent. There was always someone travelling with her, always supporters ready at the next rest stop. So I guess that's why I wanted

to write about this particular struggle of mine. Because in the sharing usually comes some relief for me, the burden seems lighter, the struggle seems easier to face. And hopefully I will gain some ground. Starting with that first step.

The colder temperatures definitely make it harder - but I have lots of warm clothing.

The barren white landscape outside doesn't excite me much - but there is always something to see.

The people I meet along the way might not be nice and friendly - but I've got many who love me already.

The distance I travel may not be as far as I hope - but it's only about one foot in front of the other.

And so I'll give it a shot today, even if the winter storm continues to rage outside. Even if I only step outside to shovel the front deck and grab the mail. Or maybe just take a few more steps down the street. Maybe around the corner to catch a glimpse of the frozen lake.

Maybe.

I'll start with one foot in front of the other, and see where the journey takes me :)


## February 22nd, 2017

### Dreams Can Come True

A few years ago Josh let a dream take root in his heart - to build a medical clinic in honour of our middle son - Caleb Joshua Freedom Sklar - who was stillborn in 2003. Some of you will remember Caleb well, some of you watched as my baby belly grew during the nine months I was pregnant with him, and some of you attended his funeral in a state of shock at the news of his passing. Others of you met him later on, in a story that Josh or I told about him, or maybe through blog posts or the book that was written about him. One thing I know is that his story has touched every single one of your hearts, and for that I am so grateful!

It is truly unique to learn to parent a child that has passed on from this world. We have found our ways to let his tiny life mean all that it can, ways our Caleb can touch this world with love and hope. This

medical clinic is one of those ways, and so we decided it was time to let the idea loose and see what God would bring. It has been the best way we can fathom to parent Caleb - to let him loose in the world in the ways he has touched our hearts, to dream, to love, to hope in his honour. We have seen him do amazing things as we seek to love others in tangible ways with the tangible love that was intended for him.

## Mid-August 2016

We started chasing the dream. We contacted an organization we know very well in Dominican Republic - **GoMAD.** We have watched this organization birth, grow, develop, change, and mature in many ways as they reach out to the people in the DR. When we contacted them to ask if they might have need of a medical clinic, and the amount of funds needed for a project of that size - here is what they answered...

*Anna & Josh -*

*Finally able to get a little time between team stuff to get back with you. First off, I am sorry for the loss you suffered. Doing something like this would be an awesome and lasting way to honor your son while helping many children.*

*Your timing could not be more perfect. Most of our work takes place in 4 communities. We now have children's medical clinics in 3 of those communities. We have been working with the ministry of health to get one into the 4th community, but that has not worked out. We just made the decision this past month that the community cannot wait any longer and we are just going to do it ourselves. So, this is why I said the short answer is...yes.*

*We have a building in the community that can be remodeled to serve as a clinic. The building is the community center and we use it for several different purposes right now.*

*One of the rooms is really large and could be remodeled to serve as a clinic...*

*I believe it will take right around $7000 CDN to remodel and outfit the clinic. We have some of the items we need, like beds we can use for examination, but will need to purchase most of the equipment. This would get everything done and have it ready to begin seeing patients.*

*Now there is also the ongoing expense and we would love to have some help raising this as it is really the tougher piece. It will run*

*$300/month for the doctor, $200/month for the nurse, an estimated $200/month for medicine and then of course the miscellaneous things that pop up. I could use your help in finding monthly sponsors in these areas.*

*I will say that this is a huge need in this community. It is very remote so the transportation cost alone keeps many people from taking their kids to the doctor.*

*Thank you for thinking of utilizing GoMAD's work as a way to honor your son. That you would entrust us with that means a lot.*

*Blessings,*

*Chantz Cutts*
*Executive Director*
***GoMAD***

We were so excited to get this news from Chantz and go ahead with learning about hosting an online fundraising campaign. We chose GoFundMe and had the campaign up and running within a couple of weeks.

## Mid-September 2016

It was wonderful to get this email from GoFundMe...

*Your fundraiser is live. You're ready to start getting the word out. Here's your campaign link: gofundme.com/calebmedicalclinic*

We watched in amazement as people grabbed hold of the idea for the medical clinic and donations started pouring in...

## October 1, 2016

GoFundMe sent us a message that about $2300 in funding had already come in, and we passed it along to Chantz.

## November 1, 2016

We received another email from GoFundMe that about $650 more had come in for donations for the clinic.

## December 1, 2016

And the most recent email from GoFundMe was so encouraging - about $3150 more had come in :)

And I know there is at least $400 more in donations waiting for us at our church.

**Do you know what that means?**

- **The $7000 goal is exceeded!**
- 34 donations of all sorts of amounts came in online - from people of all ages and places in the world
- 786 visitors checked out our online campaign page
- 160 shares on Facebook

**And here are a few encouraging comments from people who donated to the clinic**

- *So exciting to be part of Gods work*
- *Way to go, Caleb!*
- *We love your vision!*
- *May God bless your efforts*
- *So happy that Caleb is being commemorated in this special outreach. God bless!*
- *We love how your family dreams big. Your son will live on and do good through this clinic.*
- *What a great memorial!*

It has been such a blessing to watch as the clinic was funded and the dream spread to more than just our hearts :) Thank you is too small, but it's all I have :)

I will post updates as I receive them from Chantz and continue to share any news about the clinic.

For now, I will let you in on some news that I received from Chantz over the last few weeks...

**November 14, 2016**

*Anna -*

*We are having delays getting going on the construction. Major flooding going on here for the past two weeks. Rain just does not seem to want to stop. We have had two of our properties flood. Thousands and thousands of houses have flooded. That has kept us very tied up. We cannot even cross the bridge to get to Ascension at the moment.*

*I am hopeful that this week we will be able to get there and then get started on construction next week. I will keep you in the loop on how things are progressing.*

*Thanks,*

*Chantz*

**December 9, 2016**

*Thank you so much for your help in raising this money. The bridge and road just became passible yesterday to get to Ascension. We will begin with the remodel soon. I will keep you guys up to date with pictures when we start.*

*Thanks,*

*Chantz*

And so Chantz can move ahead with the clinic with full funding, and hopefully good weather!

There are ongoing costs of about $700/month USD to keep the clinic running, as Chantz mentioned in his first email to me about the clinic:

- *$300/month for the doctor*
- *$200/month for the nurse*
- *$200/month for medicine*

And so I hope to do some more fundraising to help with those costs.

For now, feel free to give on the GoFundMe campaign site as we end off 2016, and any time after. I'll pass along any funding that comes in to the ongoing costs of the clinic.

Blessings on you all!

**Thank you**


**GoMAD reports on January 24th**: SUPER EXCITED TO BE ABLE TO REPORT THAT CONSTRUCTION HAS BEGUN FOR THE CHILDREN'S MEDICAL CLINIC IN ASCENSION. WE LOOK FORWARD TO THE GRAND OPENING IN THE COMING WEEKS. WE WANT TO SAY A SPECIAL THANK YOU TO ANNA SKLAR FOR HEADING UP THE FUNDRAISING EFFORT TO MAKE THIS PROJECT POSSIBLE. THIS CLINIC WILL MAKE A DIFFERENCE IN THE LIVES OF THOUSANDS OF CHILDREN.

**GoMAD reports on January 31st:** MAKING PROGRESS ON THE CLINIC BUILD OUT FOR ASCENSION. NEXT WILL BE THE INSTALLATION OF DOORS, SOME ELECTRICAL WORK AND FINALLY PAINTING. THEN IT WILL BE TIME TO FURNISH IT AND OPEN IT UP TO SEE PATIENTS.

**GoMAD reports on February 22nd:** THE CLINIC IN ASCENSION IS UP AND RUNNING! STILL HAVE WORK TO DO ON FURNISHING IT PROPERLY, BUT PATIENTS ARE BEING SEEN AND THAT IS THE MAIN THING. THE PEOPLE IN THE VILLAGE ARE VERY EXCITED AND THANKFUL TO HAVE DR. KATZ AND NURSE ANA CARING FOR THEIR CHILDREN.


**May 13, 2017**

**Trying to Be Still**

Sometimes when you're trying to grab hold of the opportunities it's hard to live in the moments.

Sometimes stillness is elusive when it seems a million things are vying for your attention.

But I'll keep trying :)

There's God things coming for our family... good things, big changes, lots of unknowns, exciting adventures ahead.

We'll be moving to a place that's about 5 hours from where we've been raising our boys the past 13 years. But it's closer to family, near our old stomping grounds, and there's lots of opportunity there for all of us.

Josh will be taking a new job as a senior pastor.

Our boys will be navigating new schools and new neighbourhoods.

We'll all be saying goodbye to a place and a people that have poured into us for more than a decade. And we've poured into this place and these people too.

Some people are sure to visit us in our new place, and we'll continue to pour into one another's lives.

And there are new places and people coming - new places and people to pour into and allow them to pour into us.

Much transition.

It's been a whirlwind of finishing the last of the to-dos on our house, and cleaning/fixing our rental house so we can list them on the real estate market. And narrowing it down to the right neighbourhood in the place we're moving to.

But I see the light at the end of the tunnel.

We're rounding third and heading into the home stretch.

We've done our bit and we wait to see God do his bit.

It can be pretty fun to watch Him work out the details, can't it?

Like only He can.

And I can see more moments of stillness coming.

Thank God...

**May 25th, 2017**

**Free to Be ME ☺ An Introvert That Is…**

In case you didn't know... I'm an introvert.

I used to feel like it was something to hide, be ashamed of, like I'd

failed at interacting with society, inferior, etc. etc. etc.

Now I feel like shouting it from the rooftops, I'm so happy about it, about this description that so wonderfully encompasses... me.

I feel free.

Free to be me.

And it's awesome.

People have thrown that word at me over and over - it used to be shy, quiet, anti-social, nervous, anxious, afraid, weak even - and I never really took the time to completely understand it. I think I might have a lot of forgiving to do - of all the acquaintances, teachers, professors, leaders, speakers - all those who crossed my path and just had no clue.

That I didn't have to be like them to be a "normal" part of society.

That being me was, in fact, a good thing. And not something to be "fixed".

Ya - do you sense a little 'tude in my words? Maybe I do have something to work on :)

But it's not me - not the core of me, the essence of me - that can wholeheartedly stay.

Being an introvert, a perfectionist, a people-pleaser, a pastor's wife, and the oldest child of British parents is quite a recipe for potential angst, don't you think?

I'm sure we've all got our own ingredients to throw into whatever recipe we're trying to make ourselves into.

Mine? I have longed for a peaceful, fun, adventurous, meaningful, contributing, healthy life since I can remember. I treasure a couple of hours with a good book, a bike ride along the lake, a hike through the forest, a conversation with close friends or family, and a night at the movies.

And I LOVE watching my guys in their different activities. All 3 of them - from Josh preaching to Josiah and Elijah on their sports teams. And I love when sometimes I'm the only one that gets to see

their antics - like when we went for a walk in the forest just the four of us the other week. They got up to their usual playfulness, and I was the only spectator... what a treat! Once in a while I'll even join in with them... once in a while.

You know what? THAT'S OK!

I'm really coming to terms with it, no more trying to be someone else, because then the world would miss out on... me. Whatever it is that I can bring to the lives of my family and friends and whoever I cross paths with in my introverted way.

I guess I just wanted to encourage any of you fellow introverts out there... you're good. You're so good. You're ALL good. Deny it no longer. Believe nothing else.

You are free to be you.

Like I'm free to be me.

Maybe one day you'll tell me about it.

But probably not. You'll probably write me about it, if you tell me at all. And you know what? THAT'S OK!

Because I really, truly get it.


**June 6th, 2017**

**More On Introversion**

*When I speak I have no idea whose talking. When I write I hear my voice.*

315

I typed this out many years ago in an email to a *Mom's Moments* contributor. It's how I feel often. Don't get me wrong... I enjoy people, being around people, talking to people, doing activities with people... but when I put my fingers to the keyboard and start typing out words... that's when the magic happens for me.

I'll add another statement to the above gem...

*My keyboard is like my microphone, my stereo system, and my volume increase button.*

When I have something to share, when I hope to encourage others with an idea, or when I learn about something that excites me - this blog is where it goes first, sometimes after a few conversations with select individuals :)

Learning about introversion has been very exciting for me, very freeing, and I'm hoping will be very encouraging to readers who are introverts themselves or have loved ones who are introverts.

The next couple of blog posts will be about introversion...

I highly recommend the books The Awakened Introvert by Arnie Kozak and *Quiet: The Power of Introverts in a World That Can't Stop Talking.* I truly gained a lot of knowledge and encouragement about introversion from these books. *Quiet* is available in pdf form here.

And there's a wonderful blog I started following called *Introvert Spring.* Michaela is a very encouraging, gentle soul whose words are suited especially for introverts and those who have loved ones who are introverts. already shared a little about what it means to be an introvert so now I'd like to touch on what it might look like to be a suffering introvert, and how we might be adding to our own pain without even knowing it...

A couple of years ago I had a bout with anxiety & depression. This is so common in our world today, and there are many ways we can get to that point. For me it was a mixture of grieving, miscommunication with loved ones, pushing myself too hard and too fast out of my comfort zones, big lack of self-care, and a build-up of sleep deprivation. I was basically a ticking time bomb of confusion and emotion. Everything was on the surface, I'd forgotten how to tap into the inner strength of introversion, and I'd forgotten a lot of who I was underneath it all. My foundation had crumbled quite a bit and it was a long process of tearing down what I had built on shifty ground, finding the solid ground again, and rebuilding on the rocks in my life. I never lost my faith, it was nothing like that, there were just so many other noises in my life that I couldn't hear the still, small voice of the One who loved me most. I can't tell you how good it was to reconnect with Him, the first and firmest Rock of my foundation.

Going back further in my life, there was always this sense that something was wrong with me, that I was lacking in many ways, that I couldn't possibly hope to be like others in the world who were healthy, happy, strong, wise, contributing members of society. Recently I've come to realize that for most of my life I've been comparing myself constantly to people who are completely different from me - no wonder I was always coming up short.

My brother once wrote that we should only compare ourselves to Christ. He was so young when he wrote that. And so wise. He would sometimes post deep thoughts on the fridge for the rest of us to read, and I'm really glad he felt comfortable enough to share that side of himself, to let us into that part of his world. I'm really proud of my little bro.

I had a lot of negative self-talk going on in my head - it would consistently drown out any positive talk others were offering in my direction. The negative talk would slap the outstretched hand of the positive talk and not let it anywhere near me. This only added to the

anxiety and depression. I don't remember how it started - the turnaround from negative to positive self-talk, but I do remember one day just knowing I was pretty cool. In fact, I was awesome. I think it started when I heard the still, small voice. It rang true and it rang the loudest in my heart and soul and mind, and I liked it, and I wanted more of it. From then on, when positive talk was offered to me, I didn't immediately turn away from it - rather I looked it in the eye and opened myself up to the possibility that it might just be true. Then it was like a snowball - positive upon positive with me at the center - tumbling down the hill in unknown directions, smashing any obstacles in our way, actually having a jolly good time together - me and this new positive mindset.

And in social situations - I started understanding I wasn't ill-equipped but instead I was selective - about people, conversations, settings, time, etc. All these little quirks I'd been compiling into a negative mental list and beating myself up about were just normal for who I am, how I function in the world, indicators of how I could be at my best if only I'd see them in a positive light. I tended to shine in one-on-one conversations or small groups, I loved talking about the deeper issues, and my sense of humour was more subtle.

As I began to see myself in a more positive light, I also started learning how to care for my introverted self. I am learning not to berate myself for needing time alone, even from my husband and 2 sons whom I love more than I can say. And I'm learning to tell them my needs, and not cave when they protest because they want more from me. I know they want more because they love me. I also know that when there's no more to give there's no use in me trying to give - empty is empty. The best thing I can do is fill up so there's more to give - very practical, isn't it? The tricky part is finding a good balance in all the demands of a usually-noisy world so that there is usually some to give to the people in my life I want to give it to most.

So... if you're feeling tired, confused, stressed, or overwhelmed - please know you are not alone. Often you just need a good dose of time away from social obligations. If after a while you find this just isn't cutting it, you should see a health-care professional for advice.

In my own life, I had gotten so empty for a time that I needed some medical help, and it was a struggle to learn this was OK and not another way I was defective or weak. If it's a biological or genetic issue, help may continue for quite some time, and that's OK too.

Introversion is simply a personality tendency, and it can sometimes explain symptoms similar to depression - for me it was changes in appetite, sleep patterns, weight gain, fatigue, confusion, indecisiveness, memory difficulties, and feelings of low self-worth and value. Some of these things have been in my life since I can remember, but it was the sleep deprivation and increases in other symptoms that finally got to me. And there were a few causes working together to bring on my bout with anxiety and depression, it was not a single cause on its own.

Introversion is not an answer to major symptoms or symptoms beyond the ones mentioned here - in that case I would greatly encourage you in the most positive way to ask the advice of a professional. I know people that would not be in my life today had they not gone for the help they needed. Thank God for the help they received.

One last thing that can really bring unhappiness to an introvert is having a misalignment between your goals and your personality - not being true to who you are can cause great stress and frustration. I remember repeating a statement over and over in the time leading up to my "burnout" - *I don't know what I'm supposed to be doing. I don't know what my roles are at this point in my life. I don't know where my place is in this community.* I was so confused and always measuring myself up to what other people were doing and coming up short. I'd completely lost focus on who I was, what I wanted /liked to do, and how to go about living out my passions and dreams in my current situation. And when I tried an idea or tried fitting into a group and it failed, I was knocked down yet another notch, and felt even more like a failure. It was a pretty negative cycle to be stuck in.

Finally I tuned out everything that others wanted me to be, and everything I was supposed to be, and once again I listened for the still and small voice that spoke loudest into my life. He told me He loved me just as I was, that He made me just the way He wanted, and I had a lot to offer in my community circles. I was to remember that in this season of life, I would gain the most satisfaction and pleasure from simply finding my roles first in the smallest community that was my own home. I was needed, wanted, and invited into so much just by being a wife and mother. This was the first set of roles to solidify in my heart, everything else was extra at this point in my life. And soon enough, that would change, the seasons of life are always going to be shifting. But for now, it was so important to be present in the current season of family life.

And once that was solid, I could begin to dream and imagine what else I'd like to put into my life, where else I'd like to contribute. I went back to the beginning, remembered my hobbies and interests growing up, focused in on what I'd added through the years that I truly enjoyed, and began to see the colours on the canvas on my life. It was beautiful! Simple things like bicycling, sewing, watching my sons in their activities, baking, reading, listening to music, watching the trees in the wind, and going to the movies brought some colour. More complex things like international mission work, continuing education, simple living, global stewardship, local service ideas, and encouraging children to help others brought still more colour. Some parts of the canvas remain blank, and I look forward to seeing which colours will fill those spaces. Most likely in other seasons of life.

For today... I think that's all I've got to share... it's quite enough I think! :) I've given you lots of food for thought.

Enjoy your day - whether it be a welcome (or not so welcome ;) ) draining out in connecting with others, or charging up in solitude... which is the focus of the next Introvert post... coming soon :)

**June 8th, 2017**

**Just a Little More On Introversion...**

I was going to do another couple of posts on Introversion, but there is just so much I want to share with all you introverts and extroverts out there in hopes of understanding one another a little better. I decided to sum it up with a few graphics, some key points, and a heap of encouragement to dig a little deeper into this topic if it's of interest to you. It's worth it for sure :)

Let's get on with the show... SOLITUDE is key for introverts.

We simply need a break, need to be left alone. And sometimes it's our own thought whirlwinds we need a break from. Sometimes it's the noise of the world in general. Sometimes it's all the responsibilities that crowd out any semblance of peace and calm. Sometimes we need 5 minutes. Sometimes it's 5 hours or even 5 days (I've yet to take THAT long of a break - I think that would drive even me a little loopy). And because we're all at different

points on the introvert/extrovert scale, our time requirements and circumstances for solitude will all be different. So cool how none are the same, eh? No fitting into molds here. Not a chance.

Solitude doesn't necessarily mean a chair on the dock by the lake in the middle of nowhere. It can mean a 20-minute Netflix show. It can mean a few minutes with a good book. It can mean a glance out the window. A bike ride, a walk, a movie, a sewing project, a daydream, an idea, playing a few songs on a musical instrument, or listening to a few of your favourite songs. It's a break from what is draining you, a chance to reconnect with that inner side, a grounding moment.

Now, we can't stay locked away in our heads or in our homes or in our quiet places for too long. At some point we'll need to step back into the "noise" of our lives. I love some noise as long as I know there will also be quiet. Again, this can be mental noise or social noise, and mental quiet or social quiet.

When it's time to step out, remember you can be yourself. If extrovert qualities are needed for the occasion, you can pretend for a while even. I've picked up some small talk pointers and learned a lot about social interaction with crowds and people much "louder" than myself from being married to Josh for over 17. He's a pretty big extrovert, big personality, fills a room without saying a word, loves it when people are hanging on his every word, has a million stories to tell, can schmooze with the best of them, etc. It's actually one of the things I think is great about him, as long as I'm not expected to BE him. And that was HUGE for me to learn - I can be myself, can socialize with him in my own ways, leave much earlier than him, and it's all just fine. Really. I'm still good, he's still good.

We are just very different. And I like it that way, as long as we can accept each other for who we are - plain and simple. For the most part I am fascinated by Josh and all his extrovert ways. He's quite entertaining to say the least :)

And that about sums up the main concepts I wanted to share with you - there's SO MUCH more to learn about the topic if you're interested. There's a heap of information out there now - I guess the introverts have started to share more now that social media gives them the space they need between themselves and their audiences :)

## June 27th, 2017

### The Shore Is Nowhere In Sight

I watched this documentary on Netflix the other day...

*Losing Sight of Shore - "follows the extraordinary journey of four brave women known as the Coxless Crew that set out to row the Pacific Ocean from America to Australia unsupported. As they row over 8,000 miles during their nine months at sea, they face extreme mental and physical challenges they must overcome in order to go down in history. This is a story of perseverance, friendship, and the power of the human spirit. Everyone has a Pacific to cross."*

I'm not sure I'd use the word "courage" to describe our jump into the ocean of uprooting from our home of 13 & 1/2 years and moving to a city about 5 hours from the shore we've known for over a decade.

And I know our personal ocean is quite calm compared to others, and there is far less pain in our Pacific than others will experience in their own ocean crossings.

But here we are, smack dab in the middle of our ocean, riding the waves and facing the storms, and appreciating the calm days as best we can.

And on days like today, when the waves are relentless, I find it helps to write it all down and share it with you :)

Our shore disappeared from sight a few months ago. We had been staring at this particular ocean for a few months, wondering if it was time to set sail, to leave our shore of home, community, church, friends, and familiar sights and sounds. After much soul-searching and praying and chatting, we decided to step into the boat and start the journey to a new ministry, new schools, new focus, new community, new friends, and new every-days.

The ocean crossing has been so calm some days - with blue skies, whales breaching, birds soaring, and a view that extends far into the horizon. We can see so clearly on those days, we can almost see our destination across the water.

Then more waves, storm clouds roll in, rain pelts down heavy on us, the wind blows us this way and that, making it necessary to constantly correct course.

I am always reminded of my word for 2017...

**Still**

And the *Oceans* song that goes along with it.

And the quote *I can trust the waves for I know the One who made the ocean.*

We've been out on the ocean for a few months - embarking in our hearts before we removed ourselves physically from the safety of shore.

Our boat is slowly but surely taking us across the water, we are rowing as best we can, there have been breaks in the crossing along the way - moments of laughter, amused incredulity at our situation, utmost trust that God is, in fact, in control.

But there have been dark days, stormy days, and doldrum days.

Days when there's nothing else to do but sit on the water and wait.

Or days when the horizon disappears in the waves.

Or days when the clouds touch the water and I can't tell what's up from down.

Today the sky is gray, today I know there are waves coming. What I don't know is how big they will be, if they will be storm waves or fun waves, and how much they will toss our boat around as we ride them.

Like all the other days on the ocean so far, this one will end, and we will be that much further from shore, and that much closer to our destination.

The awaiting shore is still so unfamiliar to me, I can't even describe our new neighbourhood, or the schools the boys will attend, or the closest grocery store - because not even those things are solid ground to land on yet.

But I do know there are friends waiting, waving at us even across the expanse still to travel. There are family members scanning the horizon, keeping a close eye out for any sight of us.

And that helps in the crossing and the wave-riding, still far from shore, still unsure how many course-corrections there are yet to make, still hoping today will be calm waters, swift currents, blue skies and whale sightings.

I wish you well as you cross your Pacific, whatever it may be, whatever waves may come today - may you end today much farther ahead in your journey than where you began.


## July 19th, 2017

## Canada 150 East Coast Road Trip of 2017 ☺

"12 days, 5 provinces, 5 states, 4780 kilometers and 1 happy family."

That was my husband's Facebook post a couple of days ago. I like it. Sums it up well. Couldn't have said it better myself. But I'm going to share a little more with you about our time away... :)

I texted my mum and sister just about every day to give them an update on the trip, and I'm glad I did because I can look back and see what stood out for me each day. And it made me feel like they were sort of with me - I do love to share experiences with loved ones :)

One thing that I appreciated every day of our journey - the simplicity of the adventure. We weren't sure about being available for the trip with moving this summer and selling houses and still looking for a house to buy. In the end, we had to make a choice - to put family first. To step out of the chaos that is life, and sometimes the chaos is louder and busier and crazier than "usual", and make sure the priority list is still intact and say THIS is more important than all the rest. I wondered if it was irresponsible to go, then I realized that making memories with loved ones is never irresponsible, and it is, in fact, what matters most.

We chose an east coast road trip because I've wanted to do a road trip for years and seeing a chunk of Canada seemed very fitting for marking the year Canada turned 150. I thought, *Let's show the boys some of Canada - how big it is, how different the scenery can be, how varied the people and places of our country actually are within even a few hours of driving.*

There was hardly time to plan - I had mapped out a tentative route just in case we actually got in the car and did this thing. 12 days seemed good to space out a drive of this distance, and we could ferry across the Bay of Fundy and drive back through the U.S. Two days before we left we decided to just go for it. We looked up places to stay - camping some nights in provincial & national parks, staying in Air BnBs when they were available on such short notice, and cheap bookings at hotels or motels the rest of the nights. We grabbed a few needed supplies, cleaned the house in case there were showings while we were away, packed the car with room to spare, and jumped into the adventure on July 5th...

Day 1 - We drove to Ottawa but stayed just across the Quebec river in Gatineau. We found an Air BnB apartment downtown. I hopped out of the car and onto my bike just before we arrived and bicycled into Quebec :) This was after getting slightly lost on the insane bicycle routes in downtown Ottawa, but by the time I made it to the BnB the guys had already unpacked the car - so that was a bonus :) We walked around downtown and got some dinner.

Day 2 - We visited Parliament Hill, Rideau Canal, and the Canadian War Museum. All very important items on our to-do list for the trip (which was not a very long list). Parliament Hill because we were in our nation's capital, Rideau Canal because it's on the Unesco World Heritage List, and the museum gave a great overview of Canada's contributions in fighting for peace on a global scale. Heavy cost - both Josh and I had family members who served in the wars. For me it was my great-grandfather whose grave is found in a soldier's field in Germany. For Josh it was his grandfather who was just about to head out on his first mission as a belly-gunner when the war ended - thank God. After all the inspiring history lessons of the day we enjoyed the spectacular views as we drove into Mont Tremblant National Park. Then we had to set up for our first night of camping in the rain. Ugh. The weather broke and Josh cooked a one-pot dinner on our camp stove. We ate by lantern light.

Day 3 - We woke up to rain falling on the tents and dismal skies. Packed up early with everything still wet :( This day of travel started out with a couple of unexpected stops... first at a convent/monastery of sorts just off the road. Josh saw it and was completely drawn to it. There was an enormous statue of Jesus we could see from the road. Josh asked at the gate if we could look inside, they let us go into the chapel area after first giving us capes and a lace head-covering for me. It was all very ornate yet simple, you could feel the sacredness of the people and what they'd built - all dedicated to living an undistracted life of faith and service to their community. When we stopped in they were putting together boxes of food for locals - MANY boxes - and this is something they do every week - and they've done it for decades. All they have they built on site. They were highly creative and completely focused on their mission. It was overwhelming for me after a few minutes, and I headed back to the car to rejoin the boys as Josh chatted with the nuns. Only Josh right? :) Only Josh. The other unexpected stop was at an outlet mall where we found some great deals on a few necessary items for the family. Then we drove to Mont Ste. Anne to another Air BnB place - the only place we'd stop for 2 nights in a row - a beautiful condo nestled in the mountains. We couldn't believe the deals we got on some of these places on our trip - and this place was a GREAT deal. We bought groceries and settled in for a little while :)

Day 4 - We visited Montmorency Falls and rode the cable car to the top. Looked around a bit before heading into Old Quebec. We made it to a few historic spots before the rain hit, and then we still carried on for a little longer. Such a beautiful place, so unique, so quaint, so much history. We took a wrong turn as we were walking back to the car, and down an alleyway I saw *Au Petit Hotel.* I recognized it as the place my Grade 8 class stayed on our grad trip - WAY back in the day. A treat to be able to show the guys that little piece of MY history.

Day 5 - We left the comfort of the condo and started making our way to New Brunswick. We stopped at a mall that had a Ferris wheel, roller coaster, and huge arcade - we had some fun there before carrying on. 2nd night of camping on the trip - at De La Republique Provincial Park near Edmunston in New Brunswick. Such a peaceful place! The rain held off and we enjoyed a roasted hot dog and smores dinner over the camp fire. Along the way during our trip Josiah made a fun video of back-flipping as we entered each province - Elijah was his videographer.

Day 6 - We drove to Fredericton area and stayed at Riverside Inn. Another jackpot in terms of inexpensive lodging. Beautiful view of the big river, nice room, laundry only $1, and such friendly people! We spontaneously turned off the highway at one point to visit the Hartland Covered Bridge National Historic Site. Pretty cool :) We went to see the new Spider-Man movie that night at the local mall. By this point we were about half way through the trip, everyone was starting to get a little wiped and edgy, and I gave the choice of heading back home to Sudbury before we ventured out any further. I wasn't convinced that the sort of upcoming family time would be healthy in our current mental/emotional/physical states :) But the guys voted to keep going, and I voted to keep going, so I hoped for the best :) I'm so glad we made it through that day and stayed the course :)

Day 7 - We stopped at an outlet mall in Moncton on our way to PEI! I was so excited to be heading across the Confederation Bridge. I hoped PEI was everything I had built it up to be in my mind - and IT WAS! We camped at the Cavendish site of the National Park - right in the heart of Green Gables country :) We weren't sure about camping here - the winds were at about 70 knots (that's INSANE for those like me who have no idea of knots and such ;) ) It was almost impossible to set up the tent - it took all of us holding a corner and spiking it down wherever we could and then reinforcing it with strong rope and spiking some more. We weren't sure our tent would hold together through the night, but we just really wanted to try. So we did. At least there were no bugs ;) We were steps from the ocean, and the people were amazing. Friendliest bunch at the campsite. We chatted with everyone. No privacy but as long as I can step into the tent and block out the world for a few minutes, I'm good :) We all

slept so well despite the crazy wind, which died down overnight. Had my first Beaver Tail with fries for dinner since cooking over an open fire seemed a little ridiculous in that wind.

Day 8 - We hung around at the campsite just a little while longer. I ventured out for a long bike ride along the coast and into farmland - it was called the Homestead Trail and I LOVED it - the views were absolutely amazing. Biking into the wind at spots was exhausting but well worth it. When I got back to the campsite the guys had everything packed up and after a quick breakfast of fruit, PB & jam on buns, and hot chocolate - we were off to be tourists for a couple of hours. We visited Green Gables and it was crazy busy, but we still managed to get an idea of the place (for FREE with our Canada 150 Discovery Pass!) and it was really cool (at least I thought so ;) ) I read up on Lucy Maud Montgomery after that, and it turns out we had a lot in common actually - she was a minister's wife, a writer, she had 3 boys (the second being stillborn), and she suffered from bouts of anxiety/depression in her life. Her life really impacted me and I pondered a lot on her for the next couple of days... we can all learn so much from one another... But back to the trip - we drove on to Graves Island Provincial Park in Nova Scotia and camped for the night. No winds here, and no bugs again! This gem of a spot is just off the highway, on an island as promised, with ocean views surrounding it. So quiet, not many campsites, so glad one was available for us when we booked the trip! Peaceful night.

Day 9 - We lingered at the site a little while, I ventured out on another bike ride along the trail around the edges of the park, saw lots of fishing boats on the water. Packed up all our camping gear (that was our last night of camping) and headed out on the road again. We drove through the beautiful scenery of the Unesco World Heritage Site of Old Town Lunenburg (BIG fishing boats and colourful old houses). Then on to our Air BnB for the night - a big old farmhouse near Yarmouth. We sort of crashed here and enjoyed a celebratory dinner of ribs and cake - the sale of our rental house closed that day and we had gotten Josiah's final grades for school (and he did absolutely amazing :) ) Hard to settle in completely because we knew there was a very early morning coming so we could catch the ferry the next day. But here's a very cool thing, a God thing - there was a verse printed out and attached to the window frame across from my bed. Can you guess what the verse was? My verse for the year - *Be still and know that I am God.* Yep, can't even begin to try to make that a coincidence. I was SO THANKFUL for the reminder.

Day 10 - We woke up early and made it in plenty of time for the CAT ferry across the Bay of Fundy to Portland, Maine. None of us have sea legs, so it turns out :( But we made it through the 5.5-hour crossing. We slept, watched the on-board movies, played games, walked around the ship (ugh - I get seasick just thinking about it!) Just before leaving port on the Canadian side there were so many sea lions and herons to see - it was amazing! After the ferry we waited for an hour just off the ship to get through customs. Then we drove for 3 hours to our hotel in the Hartford, Connecticut area. We had a hard time finding a place to eat dinner (we were all not feeling quite well and were sick of fast food) but we settled on Wendy's near the hotel. As we checked into the hotel we knew there might be issues because management had JUST changed and the hotel was in rough shape. It was a Travelodge, so we thought it would be fine, but it wasn't. Nothing worked as promised except our beds. I won't go into it all too much, but we did ask for a refund on our stay, and they didn't hesitate to give it to us. Folks, it really was THAT bad. So it was quite a day, but we seemed to make it through OK, and I was happy to realize we'd come to a point in the trip that it didn't really matter what was going on around us, our family could stay tight and keep going through a lot. And that is SO GOOD to know as we move into a season of so much change ahead.

Day 11 - We were happy to pack up from the hotel and drive out once again. At this point the trip was mostly about heading back home and taking in what we could along the way. We had been trying to find a place for Josiah to do a little cliff-jumping and hadn't had any luck with the places we tried. But we tried again this day - heading to a State park that boasted a good spot. And legal too! Just as we walked down the trail to the river to jump, we noticed a crew putting up *No Swimming* signs. Apparently someone had actually died and another had gotten injured recently. Oh my. We drove through some beautiful scenery of mountains and rivers, stopped at an outlet mall (good places for food courts and stretching your legs a little) and continued on to Utica, New York. We had found a deal on a motel there. It was not what we expected, but it was nice enough and clean, so we stayed. Did some laundry, hit the grocery story, and we settled in for the night.

Day 12 - We drove to the BIG outlet mall in Buffalo - and met my sister there! She had just been at Darien Lake with her family, and we just happened to be at the same mall, on the same day, at the same time - SO COOL! It was a quick visit but I got hugs from my niece and nephew, so it was all good :) Then crossed the border back into Canada and stayed at a motel in Niagara Falls. Greatest deal we got yet, and a nice place with an outdoor pool we enjoyed :) The guys headed down to the falls that night for a Ferris wheel ride and some ice cream. I stayed behind - I think I needed to regroup because we were heading home the next day. Needed to wrap my head around the trip ending - it had been so amazing, so much more than I expected, and I didn't want it to end, but I was OK with it ending because we'd accomplished everything AND MORE that I'd hoped for. Such a successful trip. I was so glad we actually did it. Actually got in the car and just started driving and waited to see what the road brought us. Amazing.

Day 13 - (I just now realized it was actually 13 days!) We headed home! One last stop at Grundy Provincial Park for Josiah to FINALLY get to some cliff jumping - funny how we drove all that way and the only good option was less than an hour from home :) Grundy seemed like a nice place, the weather was beautiful for jumping into the water, Josiah gave us a good show (our family plus

some others who were camping there), and Josh managed to overcome his fear and jump off the highest cliff (they call it Kong). We rolled back into Sudbury just before dinnertime. Unpacked the car. Grabbed our last fast-food dinner. Got reacquainted with our house and all that is happening in our "real" lives. Lots to do. Back to it.

**SO GLAD we'll always have the memories of the Canada 150 East Coast Road Trip of 2017.**

**September 16th, 2017**

**Back to Writing...**

My fingers have been itching to get back to typing.

My thoughts have been organizing into blog posts and book chapters and family resource titles.

The words have been piling up, spilling over, and I'm starting to lose too many of them in the waiting.

Waiting to share them.

With you.

It's been almost 2 months since our Canada 150 East Coast Road Trip of 2017 :).

I can try and begin to tell you what's happened since then...

- We've sold two houses in Northern Ontario and bought ourselves a house in Southern Ontario - there are long stories behind each of those transactions... maybe I'll tell you about those another day...

- Josh travelled south alone and started a new role as senior pastor on August 1st - me and the boys were still living in the north, trying to sell the second house

- The house finally sold and we travelled south to pick a new house all together - fantastic!

- The boys were amazing as we decluttered even further, packed what we wanted to keep, sold or donated what we wanted to let go of, and emptied out our home of 13 years

- We enjoyed a week at family camp - Josh joined us for 3 days before heading out to load our belongings into a U-Haul and drive them south

- Our oldest took his G1 driving test and passed!

- We said goodbye to friends and places in the north - joined Josh in southern Ontario August 27th

- Our oldest started a pre-lifeguarding Bronze Cross crash course the same day we got the keys for our new house!

- We got the keys for our new house on August 28th, unloaded the U-Haul onto the main floor only, tore out definite allergy-causing carpets on upper and lower floors of house

- We painted and started cleaning and tried to find a few belongings in boxes on August 29th

- New carpet and linoleum installed August 30th, lots of boxes moved to different floors of the house, it begins to slightly look like it might possibly be a home in the near future

- More unpacking, lots more unpacking, more cleaning, and the beginnings of settling in

- Boys start at new schools Sept 5th with all the clothes, backpacks, and school supplies previously located in the unpacking!

- Pictures go on walls, our mattress is delivered, rooms are almost clear of boxes Sept 8th

- First BBQ and visit from family Sept 9th - who all live within 0.5 - 1.5 hours of driving now - YAY!

- More settling in during the week, finalizing Sudbury house sale details, oldest lands a seasonal job at local farm, youngest tries out for school sports team
- Sudbury house sale closes Sept 15th
- Josh's brother visits from the U.S. for the weekend, oldest takes a weekend 1st Aid course for further lifeguard prep
- Tomorrow (Sept 16th) a special induction service for Josh at church - to welcome him officially into his new position as senior pastor

And there's been LOTS more happening in the details - but I think that's good for now :)

I just needed to get to typing today - I have this rare treat of a couple of hours where nothing is pressing, nothing is planned, and it was a total surprise.

Feels good just to put my fingers on the keyboard and see this familiar WordPress screen in front of me as I type.

You'll be hearing from me again soon - there's ideas running rampant in my head and my heart.

Some are more of the same you're used to hearing from me, some maybe a little different than you're used to.

Keeping things simple, focused, intentional, productive, positive, and forward-moving.

Back soon :)


**November 18th, 2017**

**No Longer**

They've been singing this song in Church…

***No Longer Slaves***

You know how one line will just grab you sometimes?

Then another and another?

And the song grows in you, the message heard loud and clear.

But it started with such a gentle whisper.

God loves to speak in whispers - like with Elijah on the mountain.

And the whisper becomes louder inside of you than any earthquake or strong wind or fire could have been from the outside.

*Elijah was afraid and ran for his life - 1 Kings 19:3*

He'd just defeated 450 false prophets and lifted a severe drought from the land.

God used Elijah in mighty ways, then Elijah's life was threatened by the queen, and Elijah just crashed.

Physically, emotionally, spiritually - his confidence was shattered and he saw only death as an option.

He asked God to take his life.

But God wanted to renew his life.

Doesn't he always?

There's always another side of things - that we cannot see - hidden from us - and we have a choice to trust or fear.

Fight or flight.

This choice that comes with fear, worry, anxiety.

When I was younger it was easier to choose flight. I was always changing my mind, trying new things, seeking new experiences, running, running, running.

But for the past almost two decades I have been a wife and a mother. Not so easy to physically choose flight. But I often chose flight mentally.

That really messes with living in the moments.

So the last few years it's been a different choice...

Now it seems I usually choose to fight - with myself, with God, with my circumstances - I am my own worst enemy at times.

All I can see is fear - disguised as concern, or indecision, or perfectionism.

When I was younger it was terrible nightmares. Then the past few years it's been insomnia. Always messing with my rest, my peace, my feelings of safety.

This verse helps so much... I claim it as a promise over and over....

*In peace I will lie down and sleep, for you alone, Lord, make me dwell in safety. - Psalm 4:8*

And the last few days it's been this song...

And the lines repeating over and over...

*I'm no longer a slave to fear. I am a child of God. You split the sea so I could walk right through it. You drowned my fears in perfect love. You rescued me so I could stand and sing... I am a child of God.*

Over and over...

This promise contained in a few simple words.

*No longer... I am...* telling me I am truly free of what was and truly free to grab hold of what is.

*You split the sea... You drowned my fears... You rescued me...* telling me it's all Him - He will use His power to care for His child - that's me :)

*So I could stand and sing...* telling me I can face what comes. He simply wants my love in return, my worship, me sharing God stories with whoever will listen, so they can know the same precious truths, and experience the same freedom in their own lives.

*You unravel me with a melody. You surround me with a song.*

So true.

I am unraveled.

In a very good way.

Can't wait to see how He puts me back together.

How He puts my family back together.

After the biggest transition we've ever faced.

But I don't want to choose flight.

Or fight.

I just want to listen.

To His whispers of love and freedom and hope and new life.

May they get louder and louder as time goes on.

Louder than any earthquake or strong wind or fire.

And may they spread farther than I'll ever know.

# 2018

## January 2nd, 2018

## Word for 2018

Still stuck on this verse...

Last year my word was **Still**.

And time after time I would remember to be still in the midst of the big move and new roles and letting go of familiarity.

At the end of 2017 this verse was still on repeat in my heart and my mind.

Looks like I'm not done with it yet.

My word for 2018 is a continuation of dwelling, meditating, soaking in this verse to the core, the marrow, the depths of me.

Because there's one part I struggle with daily, one part I'd love to put to rest in a big way as I move into a new year.

## Know

Knowing I'm a child of God, knowing I'm actually free of the worries, fears, anxieties that often weigh down, knowing I'm where God wants me to be & doing what He wants me to do.

I'd love to be so sure about all this.

To live with confidence in who He is, who I am, what direction to take.

To hear His voice alone, to listen for the applause of my Audience of One, and be able to tell all others to *Ssshhh, quiet*.

I'll be asking Him a lot of questions as the year plays out, and I'll be listening for His answers.

Tough to do sometimes, isn't it?

**Know** that it's His voice you're hearing, His direction you're following, His applause you're hearing.

Like Elijah on the mountain, listening for God's voice, it came in a whisper - so close, so personal, so clear.

That's what I'll be listening for as I seek to grow in **Know**-ing in 2018.

## February 21st, 2018

### An Honest Answer

I never quite know what to do with this blog.

It was never my intent to start blogging when I sat down at my ancient computer 11 &1/2 years ago and typed out some encouragement to share with a few moms I knew.

I love looking back at my first newsletter sometimes :) I **mailed** it out to a few friends and **handed it out** to a few more. A few months before that I had started inviting moms into my home once a week, then moved the gathering over to the church when the extensive home renos started.

I'm not sure what I was hoping for back in the fall of 2006. The original vision was *Connect, Encourage, Support.* I think that's still where I'm at, all these years later, simply wanting to connect with others myself and also connect others together, encourage hearts with words & ideas as God grants them to me, and offer support in figuring out this whole life/faith/wife/mother journey.

Back in 2006 a friend suggested a blog instead of a newsletter, or to add to the newsletter. I honestly didn't even know what a blog was at first. I had a huge learning curve ahead of me :) This blog became an extension of the monthly newsletter and a greater opportunity to share life. All the writing for the newsletter and blog gave me confidence to start putting together the books I'd always wanted to write. Rejection letters from publishers pushed me to learn how to self-publish. And a publishing budget of $0 pushed me to learn about book cover design.

And here we are :)

I've tried it all in this blog - recipes, DIY, finances, writing about my boys, writing about my hubby, writing about faith, writing about simple living, writing about enjoying the moments of life, sharing book projects and personal goals and deep thoughts.

In this year of **Know** I wonder about this blog.

What will I share as I listen for the whispers?

How can I connect with you, encourage you, and support you in the moments of your days?

The honest truth, the honest answer is this...

All I **Know** how to do is share my own journey and hope it speaks to yours somehow.

That first newsletter 11 &1/2 years ago started as a whisper in my heart. I feel like it got very loud very quickly. Eventually I had to let go to find some peace again. Most of the books started as whispers. The loudness came when I tried to make it my all. I learned the hard way, over and over for the past decade, that writing can only happen in my life if it lives in balance with everything else God has granted me to do.

This is great for me to **Know.**

I could easily hole up for months on end and just write and write and write. But that luxury is not mine to live. And so I focus on the luxurious life I do live. The blessed life.

We can all find the luxury and blessings in our lives if we simply look.

And listen.

I think that's what I'll be sharing here in the coming weeks/months.

Again, always, back to the simple things.

And writing about them for you.

And me.

I'm blessed by writing.

I hope you are blessed by reading.


**February 26th, 2018**

**Beginning to Know**

Every year around Christmas time I scan through the clearance books on CBD.com and pick out a stack for myself. I used to justify it as stocking stuffers from Josh, but he would just buy me a slew of other things for my stocking, so I suppose the truth is it's my Christmas/birthday present to myself :)

The first book I read through was *Taming the To-Do List - How to Choose Your Best Work Every Day* by Glynnis Whitwer.

It's a good one, and seemed to speak right at my Word for 2018 - **Know.**

Life was still feeling pretty hectic after the move, we still seemed to be reeling from it, and as I looked to the months ahead I had no idea what I could realistically fit into my days on top of just the basics. And I wasn't OK with that. I wanted more, do more, see more, connect more - to the people and places of our new city. Yet whenever I tried to plan and book and arrange life to meet the goal of **more** something would come up - something normal like illness or household repair or car accident or bad weather. And I felt like I was being held back from all the things I'd looked forward to before the move.

Then I remembered – *Living in the Moments.*

It always comes back to this for me.

And there were such encouraging words in the book I was reading...

*If you've ever been in that crazy-busy place, you know the most urgent issues, the ones that fill your day, aren't always the most important ones. And if you've become chronically chaotic, you might not even know what your priorities are anymore.*

Chronically chaotic - yes, I get this. Whatever is loudest, whoever is loudest - they scream for attention and usually end up getting it. Because it becomes very hard to hear anything else.

*That's because the most important needs in our life tend to be the quiet ones... When our schedules are overloaded, we push the hushed, undemanding needs to the bottom of our lists. The ones that don't shout for attention are the ones we plan on addressing tomorrow. Or the next day, when things settle down. However, when we tend toward overload, tomorrow is just as busy...*

What are the quiet, most important needs? What are the things that keep hanging on at the bottom of the list, grabbing for dear life, hoping they'll get noticed tomorrow, or the next day, or the next?

*The dreams of my heart speak in a whisper, not a roar. Especially when I press them down over and over.*

What am I pushing down? What are the dreams of my heart? Will I still recognize them as mine if I try to look?

*My reality may include cluttered and chaotic circumstances, but it also includes the Spirit of God and the mind of Christ. The natural mind hears the shouts of the urgent. The mind of Christ allows me to hear the whisper of God in the midst of it all.*

So I ask God. I listen for the whispers. **Know**ing He's going to help me hear them.

I think it often calls for a little solitude. And this can be found anywhere, even in the middle of a busy crowd, if you realize solitude happens within. Taking a moment, the possibility in the moment, listening for God's whispers even as you're talking with others or completing a task. Some of my best talks with God happen when I'm cleaning around the house. It's been this way for years.

There's been 2 months so far of listening for the whispers in 2018. And for me it always comes back to the same things, same dreams, same hopes...

- Make a little money
- Give a little back
- Develop as a person
- All the while enjoying my family and nature

Breaking that down...

I've come to realize I like to contribute to the household finances. For me this means saving lots of money whenever I can on whatever I can. Unless it adds to the chaos - then I try to let it go and pay what's needed to keep things simple. It also means managing our rental property and publishing books and family resources to sell on *Amazon* and *Etsy*.

I love to give back - whether it's with time or prayer or finances. Through the years it's looked like volunteering at school, church, and summer camps, inviting tons of people of all ages and stages into our home, fundraising for different organizations, local and global mission trips, and praying for others as needed. It has also looked like writing encouraging letters, giving someone a hug or a few minutes of conversation, or even just smiling at the kindred quiet spirit in the corner of the room. It's whatever I have to give that year, month, week, day, minute. It's often very different. The trick is not to beat myself up when there's less to give, when I'm already emptied out, when all I can hear are the shouts instead of the whispers.

Develop as a person means reading through the Bible in a year, finally finishing my Bachelors degree and now looking ahead to a Masters degree :) It means growing in friendships. It means being open to new experiences, places, and people. It means moving your family a few hours away and trusting God with it all ;) It means *Just... Keep... Going* when the move affects your family in ways you hadn't predicted. It means continuing to trust even on the hard days. It means going to counselling. It means reading helpful books. It means writing it all out here on this blog :)

And that brings me to - *enjoying my family and nature*. Yes please :) For me this looks like walks, hikes, bike rides, looking out the window, etc. It means that making dinner is actually important and it's OK if I focus on healthy meals for my family. It means family get-togethers and outings and vacations are actually a priority. And it's good to be available and fully present for random conversations and unplanned adventures. The challenge comes for me in prioritizing the things that are solely for my enjoyment. When continuing to enjoy my family means I need a break for a little while. Or when no one else wants to venture into nature with me or stop for a few minutes to look out the window (what I really mean is just slowing down for a few minutes and looking around at whatever there is to experience). That's when it gets tricky.

Where does all this take me? Now that I've listened at least a little and heard at least a few whispers of the heart... what now? Where to start? Because even the simple things can seem a tad overwhelming on the hard days. And **Know**ing can fly out the window sometimes.

Back to the book...

*Sometimes I talk myself out of starting a project because I only have a short block of time...*

*When setting a plan for the day or week, add a few small tasks to your list. Then when a little window of time opens up, you can quickly check one more item off your list.*

*Valuing minutes, not just hours, helps us become wise time managers. I often think of the Parable of the Talents...*

*Did the servant not value his one talent? Did he think it insignificant compared to what the other servants received? The Lord values what seems meager to others. Every effort we make, every small step we take, if it is done with a right heart, pleases God.*

*Zechariah 4:10 says, "Do not despise these small beginnings, for the Lord rejoices to see the work begin" (NLT).*

*Perhaps the wisest thing we can do is to learn to value our minutes. The greatest accomplishment on earth started with someone working for just sixty seconds.*

Love that.

And that's where I'll begin.

By **Know**ing that my hopes and dreams are important to God. That He sees my efforts. That He's pleased even with one talent if I use it to His glory. Making dinner is a talent. Household finances is a talent. Keeping my body healthy by exercising is a talent. Encouraging others is a talent. Being there for my family is a talent.

The shouts of the world have caused me to compare myself to others many times over - those with lives much busier and what seems much more peaceful than mine. Lives full of accomplishments I'll never attain, gifts and abilities I'll never have, and luxuries I'll never own.

The whispers of my heart - the gentle and personal and convicting and intimate voice of God that speaks right into my soul - says *I love you just the way you are. I love the way you've grown. I love how you will still grow. One talent at a time, one day at a time, one whisper at a time. Together.*

Such quiet confidence in that.

Feels great to begin to **Know.**


### March 12<sup>th</sup>, 2018

**Slow**

I'm heading into the slow season.

The books and resources I've had the joy of publishing cycle through seasons of interest and sales.

The *Lunchbox LOL* series takes the spotlight in the summer for back-to-school, *Jesse Tree* for Advent, *Bible in a Year* for Christmas/New Year, and now *Jesus Tree* for Lent.

There's about 3 months of the year that are super-quiet in terms of answering questions, tracking sales, and reviewing feedback.

The slow season.

I love to take this time to reflect on the creating/publishing year behind me and look ahead to the year in front of me.

And try to be realistic about where I'm at and what I CAN add in the coming months.

Because sometimes it feels like there's a million ideas swirling around in my head and my heart.

I try to listen for the familiar sounds of the ideas that have been swirling for more than one season. Some have been around for more than a decade of seasons. Still waiting for their time, not yet knowing if they will ever have a time to shine.

As each new slow season enters into my life it gets much easier to recognize it for what it is. To **Know** its purpose.

I used to rush ahead to the next thing, and the next, and the next. Always more. Chaos. Never taking a break.

Breaks are healthy. If used wisely they make you more productive, more focused, more confident in moving ahead once the break is over.

Rest.

So important.

I listen for the whispers of God's wisdom as I enter the slow season of 2018.

I wait to **Know** about a 6-year, part-time, online Masters program that I CAN actually see fitting into my life. The application is in and now I just hope for a positive response.

My family still needs much care, availability, and flexibility as we head into finishing up the first school year after major transition. Still hard, but better. Still unfamiliar but becoming normal. Still treading so lightly in some areas, but each step becoming more sure.

I think it will get easier once the warm weather returns. I think it will get easier once a whole school year is behind us. I think it will get easier once we've added a few more months of good memories in our new space. I think it will get easier once the actual one-year milestone comes around in late August. Still a ways to go. Getting there.

In the meantime, what do I see in the slow season? Not a lot of new, actually. I see some revisions after a couple of years of feedback on certain resources. I see enjoying what's been accomplished.

Beyond that I see a focus on some necessary home projects in our new space (which I'd love to blog about :) )

I see discovering more of our new city and surrounding areas.

I see visiting friends and family.

I see meeting new people.

I see things becoming more familiar and more normal.

Looking forward to the slow season. Hoping it brings more peace and more certainty and an increasing sense of **Know**ing to listen for God's voice in my every-days.

**April 2ⁿᵈ, 2018**

**11 Years of Blogging**

I've been blogging since 2007.

That's a good 11 years worth of sharing thoughts, ideas, and resources online.

There have been times when I've known exactly what I'm doing with this blog, but for the most part it's been an enigma. It's almost always been a way of connecting more with those who appreciated whatever resource I was publishing at the time. The blog has taken on different shapes through the years of resources - newsletters, women's articles, books, family resources.

I think I finally see a connection, a familiar thread that runs through the tapestry of this 11-year-old blog.

For the most part, I'm attempting to pour into family life.

At first I was sharing glimpses into my family's life, and hoping to encourage other families (mainly through moms). As the boys grew older and no longer wanted me sharing so much about them online, the focus of the blog turned more towards practical issues. Things like saving money and DIY projects. And I started putting some of the family resource ideas into hard copy in hopes of encouraging families that way - ideas like *Advent* and *Lent* resources and *Lunchbox Notes* and *Bible in a Year*.

As I was putting together all those resources for family fun and growing in faith together, I started to see another familiar thread in the tapestry of all the writing and creating I so enjoy.

My inspiration... I began to realize who my inspiration was... I was inspired to create and publish resources for the next generation. Simple resources that will hopefully never quite go out of style :)

Personally, these resources that have blossomed and bloomed in me the last few years were filling gaps in what was available (or not available) as I was trying to raise my boys. And they worked. And it was fun. And easy to use.

And I've had an idea...

347

I think over the next little while I want to package this 11-year-old blog up into a compilation-style book that holds most of what I've written so far. Newsletters, articles, devotionals, etc. For my own bookshelf as well as anyone else who might want to add it to their bookshelf.

We'll see how it goes! :)


**April 12<sup>th</sup>, 2018**

### Guess I Had A lot to Say

I went through and compiled all the blog posts that I think might make up a good blog-to-book publication.

650 pages and 155,000 words later, it became clear to me that I guess I had a lot to say in my 11 years of blogging :)

Looks like I'll draft up a book just for me - a chronicle of the blogging years that I can read through at my heart's content.

Then I'll draft up a book that others might enjoy. Something much smaller.

I also hope to revise my *Discovering Hope* book since it's been 5 years since I first published it as a book, and I've written a few more things about our Caleb and all his tiny life has meant in this world.

And the *Lunchbox LOL* Series could use a few tweaks, now that people have given it reviews and shared ways to improve the format of those books. I'd like to get the tweaks done before the next back-to-school season starts.

For now I'll keep working on wrapping up this blog into a book. It might take a little while, but I'm excited to see it finished.

I'll let you know how it's going...

:)

## May 13th, 2018

### Blog to Book for Mother's Day

It's been a great way to spend this Mother's Day morning.

In lieu of spending the morning at church with some really nice people, and the afternoon at the zoo with my mum and sister (and niece, nephew, Dad and brother!), it was back to bed for me.

Take a nasty cough that's going around, add some aches and pains from that, throw in a less-than-stellar night's sleep, and don't forget the ongoing health issues that require tests (ugh) - and you've got a recipe for a morning in bed. Maybe I'll load up on Advil and venture out this afternoon. Maybe :)

But I've had a lovely morning, nonetheless.

It felt like I spent it with my family as I read over the almost-done blog post-to-book project I've been working on.

I realized this morning, as it is my youngest son's 13th birthday today also, that the childhood years are officially over in our household, and the blog is, I hope, a wonderful journal of those precious years of raising my sons - this far at least :)

And Happy Mother's Day to all those ladies out there who care for children - be it physically, spiritually, or emotionally - we all need one another to accomplish the fantastic feat of raising up the next generations.


## September 12th, 2018

### Wow... What a Year...

We've hit the one-year milestone in our new home in Southern Ontario.

It felt great to watch as the marker approached, knowing it had taken its toll to get there, hoping life beyond the marker would just be... better.

I'm not going to go into all the dark details of the past year - I've decided that doesn't do anybody any good. Not for now.

I will skim the surface details, emotions detached for now, so that I can move beyond the marker and tell you about what's coming...

There was major transition, letting go of "familiar" and "normal", mental health issues, personal health issues, SO MUCH uncertainty, tension and strain and pulling away, my grandfather's passing, my dad's heart attack...

And that's just the surface. Just skimming across the top of it all, not looking down into the depths of it all, just the facts.

Because you can only look back for so long before you can't see ahead. You can only look down for so long before you can't see up.

Sometimes the choice to look ahead and up is Herculean in effort. Especially if you've had your head turned in those directions for far too long.

So here we are... one entire year has come and gone... and the boys are back in their new-to-them schools, and I'm back to running our new-to-me household, and Josh is back at his new-to-him ministry.

We had an absolutely amazing summer of fun and friends and travel and exploring around home and just making really good memories. Two summer's worth of memories packed into one (because last summer was a bit of a mess). Going with the flow and seeing where the days led and being very intentional about living in the moments.

It was worth the effort to position our faces forward, and up. To look ahead as much as possible, only looking back to see the good that was, making sure to take the good with us instead of trying to live in it beyond its time.

We went back "home", back north, for a couple of weeks this summer. We saw some of our favourite faces, and visited some of our favourite places, and remembered the years past, and gathered it all up to bring with us, and gave it a place in our new "home".

You see, I've really come to understand "home is where the heart is".

And sometimes if you really put your heart into something or someone or some place, it's hard to let go. And you need to be able to grieve after you finally find yourself able to release it. And then it

350

might still take a while before you let your heart loose in what comes next.

Huge doses of patience and flexibility and understanding have been required this past year. Anything goes... and let's try this... and just - keep - going... and living in moments that feel like they should never exist... doubting, confusion, even bitterness... then hoping, believing, trusting there will be good from it all.

And here we are... deep breath... we made it through the first year! Yahoo!

Because I've heard it before and lived it myself - once you pass that first-year milestone it often changes everything.

Suddenly we are doing things for the SECOND time since moving here, and so it feels more familiar, more like tradition, more reliable, more stable. More like "home".

Being at camp gave me much-needed quiet time to edit the blog-to-book and it's just about ready. Really!

And editing the book, reading all those blog posts through the years, allowed me to see a common theme. I mention Elijah on the mountain quite a few times, like I just love that story of Elijah hearing God in the whispers. He kept looking for God in the loudness of life, like the wind and fire and earthquakes, but instead found him in the intimate quietness of a whisper.

At the camps I worked at growing up (and on into adult years too!) they gave each leader a camp name - something that focused in on something about their personality, etc. My camp name was Wispa - it's a British chocolate bar - and it fit with my British heritage, my love of all things chocolate, and my quiet nature. Now I can also see this theme of whispers in another area of life, even in my camp name, going back to when I was a teenager.

And I proceed through the start of another year here in our new-to-us places and faces and routines, and I add in a couple of things now that we're a bit more settled (finally starting my Masters degree online and also a part-time job from home!) I trust that on the loud days of life, and especially when those days turn into loud seasons instead, I'll **Know** to listen for the whispers. I'll **Know** we're safe in God's hands no matter what comes. I'll **Know** we are loved.

Oh, and I'll let you know as soon as the blog-to-book is finally finished :)

## ABOUT THE AUTHOR

Anna has been writing ever since she can remember. It is the best way she can make sense of this life. She's tried it all – poems, short stories, children's stories, articles, essays, newsletters, blog posts, and books. Anna loves to make easy-to-use resources for the family that encourage a simple life and a chance to truly live in the moments of each day.

She has a Bachelor in Liberal Arts (with a minor in International Studies) & a college diploma in Environmental Protection.

Anna loves to volunteer at church, in the public schools, and at the local children's summer camps.

She has been married to a minister/church-planter/rugby professor since 1999. She is raising two wonderfully spirited, funny, kind, intelligent, and handsome sons.

Anna lives in Ontario, Canada. She loves to read, write, weave, quilt, bake, walk, and bicycle.

# OTHER RESOURCES BY ANNA

***Bible in a Year Series Published Annually Starting in 2017***
*(Available in paperback on Amazon)*
*-Bible reading plans change slightly each year to line up with Lent & Advent-*
**Bible in a Year Reading Companion -** With Daily Suggested Reading, Scripture Summary, Author Reflection, and Space for Your Notes
**Bible in a Year Blank Journal -** With 365 Suggested Readings and Space for Your Daily Reflections

***The Jesus Tree Series***
*(Available in paperback on Amazon or digital download on Etsy)*
**48 Family Devotions for Lent** *(also available on Kindle)*
**48 Colouring Pages with Stories for Lent**
**48 Ornaments with Family Devotions & Illustrations to Colour for Lent**

***The Jesse Tree Series***
*(Available in paperback on Amazon or digital download on Etsy)*
**28 Family Devotions for Advent** *(also available on Kindle)*
**28 Colouring Pages with Stories for Advent**
**28 Ornaments with Family Devotions & Illustrations to Colour for Advent**

***Lunchbox LOL Series***
*(Available in paperback on Amazon or digital download on Etsy)*
**200 Jokes for the Lunchbox**
**200 Fun Facts & Trivia for the Lunchbox**
**200 Riddles for the Lunchbox**
**200 Holiday Jokes**

**Living in the Moments**—Enjoying the Moments of Life, Faith, Marriage, and Motherhood—11 Years of Blogging by Anna Sklar
*(Available on Amazon & Kindle)*

**The Princess of Dreams -** a children's story *(Available on Amazon & Kindle)*

**Thy Word**—A Journal of Reading Through the Bible in a Year *(Available on Amazon & Kindle)*

**Discovering Hope**—Sharing the Journey of Healing After Miscarriage, Stillbirth or Infant Loss *(Available on Amazon & Kindle)*

## MORE FROM ANNA
Blog—*Living in the Moments* - annasklar.ca
Etsy Shop—*SklarInk*—etsy.com/ca/shop/SklarInk

Made in the USA
Lexington, KY
03 October 2018